Crime and Criminology

AN INTRODUCTION

Third Edition

Rob White & Fiona Haines

OXFORD
UNIVERSITY PRESS

OXFORD
UNIVERSITY PRESS

253 Normanby Road, South Melbourne, Victoria 3205, Australia

Oxford University Press is a department of the University of Oxford.
It furthers the University's objective of excellence in research,
scholarship, and education by publishing worldwide in

Oxford New York

Auckland Bangkok Buenos Aires Cape Town Chennai
Dar es Salaam Delhi Hong Kong Istanbul Karachi Kolkata
Kuala Lumpur Madrid Melbourne Mexico City Mumbai Nairobi
São Paulo Shanghai Taipei Tokyo Toronto

OXFORD is a trade mark of Oxford University Press in the UK and
in certain other countries

National Library of Australia
Cataloguing-in-Publication data:

White, R. D. (Robert Douglas), 1956–.
Crime and criminology.

3rd ed.
Bibliography.
Includes index.
For tertiary students.
ISBN 019 551732 6.

1. Crime—Textbooks. 2. Criminology—Textbooks.
I. Haines, Fiona. II. Title.

364

Typeset by Cannon Typesetting
Printed through Bookpac Production Services, Singapore

Contents

List of Charts

Preface

It is with great pleasure that we present the third edition of *Crime and Criminology*. As each year passes, it is clear that change is fundamental to what is happening in contemporary global society and that this, too, needs to be reflected in a book of this nature. Furthermore, we are aware that the relevance of any particular theory or perspective will vary according to current developments in both the world of academia and in the world outside of the academy. In the light of this, we have modified the text once again, in ways that attempt to make new analytical connections, summarise present trends in criminological theory, and be of general interest to the reader. Specifically, in this edition we have added important new discussions of peacemaking criminology, restorative justice, cultural criminology, and environmental or green criminology. Simultaneously, we have tried to keep the size of the book manageable through judicious pruning and moderate revision of the latest text. In future editions, we hope to develop both our explanations and the critiques of some of the newer perspectives, including some of those discussed here for the first time. We believe that we have provided a comprehensive, yet concise, introduction to the major theories and perspectives in criminology. We hope that you find the book of use and interest as you explore the wide variety of explanations for many different types of crime and social harm.

Acknowledgments

We are grateful to many people for their assistance in the development and further revision of this book. Our special thanks go to Steve James and Santina Perrone, who, as fellow lecturers in the introductory criminology subject at various points in time, helped to mould and shape the ways in which the material was actually developed for teaching purposes. We are also grateful to the many tutors and students over the years who, each in their own way, have assisted us in refining and simplifying the core ideas of the field. Thanks are also due to the academic and general staff in the Department of Criminology at the University of Melbourne for their ongoing encouragement for projects of this nature, and to support staff at the University of Tasmania for their assistance. Finally, we are grateful once again to all the people at Oxford University Press for their constant enthusiasm and genuine interest in the book.

CHAPTER 1

The Study of Crime

This book is about the causes of crime. More specifically, it describes the diverse and at times competing perspectives within criminology, and their attempts to explain why certain types of people engage in certain types of behaviour that have been identified as being criminal in nature.

The aim of this chapter is to introduce the reader to the study of crime, and in so doing to explore a series of issues relating to the definition and measurement of crime. A major part of the chapter describes the criteria that serve to differentiate the many perspectives on crime. In particular, we will explore the different levels of analysis used to explain crime, and the different political perspectives that impinge on a criminological analysis. Thus, one purpose of this chapter is to provide a sense of how we can distinguish between different theoretical perspectives by looking at similarities and differences in broad approach.

CRIMINOLOGY AS A FIELD OF STUDY

Before we discuss the nature of crime, it is useful first to say a few words about criminology as a field of study. As we shall see, criminology, like crime, is not a monolith; it contains varied and competing perspectives. This variety of perspectives should be considered in light of the social context of the production of intellectual knowledge.

For instance, the production of knowledge is itself a social and material process. When any kind of knowledge is produced, we must ask who has control over this process—not only the production of knowledge itself, but also the ownership and use of the results of research and scholarship. In a similar vein, specific types of 'knowledge' or 'truth' are not always recognised or visible in the public domain. This can happen for a variety of reasons—because there is no market for it, because of publishing rivalries, or because the 'knowledge' is not deemed to conform to particular academic standards or mainstream political agendas.

Knowledge also has distinctive international dimensions. For example, in the field of criminology each country may have its own unique social concerns, intellectual milieux, political traditions, historical development, and, hence, its own theoretical emphases and biases. In the UK, for instance, debates over policing and antisocial behaviour have been prominent in recent years, whereas in the USA major concerns have been expressed over ghetto neighbourhoods, unemployment, and the social prospects of the huge numbers of offenders re-entering the community after serving time in prison. In Canada debates have centred on changes to drug law enforcement, while media treatment of criminal justice issues in Australia has featured extensive moral panics over so called ethnic youth gangs.

Cutting across all of these debates in each of the regions, however, have been a series of general issues relating to the nature of crime and the social control of crime. Invariably, analysis of specific issues has employed abstract concepts that are designed to explain why particular phenomena should be dealt with in any particular way. Major themes of this book are: to explore the nature of the more generalised statements regarding crime; to examine the broad social and historical context within which certain theories and concepts have emerged; and to demonstrate the application of these theoretical understandings to selected issues and criminal justice reform.

While 'theory' informs everything that criminologists do, not every criminologist is a theorist. So what should criminologists actually do, and why is theory relevant to their practice? To answer this, we need to appreciate the dual nature of much contemporary criminology. On the one hand, many people adopt what could be called a vocational or professional approach to criminology. In this view, the role of criminology is tied to improving the immediate practices of the criminal justice system. This approach seeks to study, analyse, and research alternative theories in order to institute reform of some kind. Generally, it is directed at making some aspect of the criminal justice system 'better' at some level—a programme, an institution, or a strategy. Often it is linked to attempts to solve a 'social problem' or an administrative difficulty within the existing system.

On the other hand, there is a strand of criminology in which the emphasis is on a critical or analytical approach. Unlike the previous approach, this tends not to be a nuts-and-bolts view of the criminal justice system, particularly in respect to making minor changes within the existing institutional frameworks of criminal justice. Rather, it is suggested that one must stand back from policy decisions and ask bigger questions, such as 'What if … ?' This approach delves into the deeper philosophical issues of the day; for example, why do we continue to have and use institutions such as prisons when they demonstrably do not work to prevent offending or reoffending? The approach here is not to suggest improvements to the existing penal system, but to question whether it is valid or viable to begin with. Indeed, an informed opinion might simply advocate the abolition of such institutions in their present shape and form.

It is essential to note, however, that often there are strong links between these two approaches. The variability in criminological perspectives in general is due in part to the nature of the relationship between the practical vocational orientation (with a focus on what can be done here and how to improve the system) and its critical counterpart (with a focus on why things ought to be done in one way or another). We must also be aware of the uncertainties of knowledge. For instance, whatever area of criminology one may concentrate on, there are almost always unintended consequences that emerge from the knowledge we acquire and the reforms we put forward. Knowledge is a guide to the future—it does not fix the future on one single pathway.

Generally speaking, criminology focuses on three main areas:
- the sociology of law, which examines social aspects and the institutions of the law
- theories of crime causation, sometimes referred to as criminogenesis
- the study of social responses to crime, which examines in more depth the formal institutions of criminal justice such as the police, courts, and corrections.

As pointed out earlier, the main theme of this book is the theories that relate to the causes of crime. As will be seen, however, the other domains of criminology often overlap and are inseparable parts of any review of causal theories.

DEFINING CRIME

What is crime? There is no straightforward answer to this question, as there are constantly changing ideas, perceptions, and conceptions regarding what constitutes criminal behaviour. To a certain extent, both crime and criminology are uncertain in the sense that one's definition of crime is dependent upon one's particular interests and particular world view. This becomes clearer when we discuss the various definitions put forward for crime.

There are competing views of crime. Crime is always socially defined. This, of course, can lead to debate: for example, should crime always be defined by law? Could or should it instead be based upon moral and social conceptions, such as social harm? To illustrate the difficulties surrounding different definitions of crime, we might consider the film *Schindler's List*. In the movie (and in real life) Schindler broke Nazi law in order to assist Jewish people. But was he then a criminal? Who defines the law? What about cases today where people may actively break the law in the name of social justice? There are unjust systems in the world, and it may well be the case that many legal definitions are built on highly contentious and unjust or unfair propositions.

Legal and sociological definitions of crime

There are many diverse conceptions of crime, each of which reflects a different scientific and ideological viewpoint. Hagan (1987), for example, identifies seven different approaches to the definition of crime, ranging from a 'legal-consensus' definition to a 'human rights' definition. For present purposes, we can summarise broad differences in definition in the following way:

- A **formal legal** definition says that a crime is whatever the state identifies as a crime; that is, if something is written into the criminal law, and is subject to state sanction in the form of a specific penalty, then that activity is a crime.
- A **social harm** conception of crime says that crime involves both criminal offences (e.g., assault) and civil offences (e.g., negligence), in that each type of action or inaction brings with it some type of harm. Each should therefore attract some sort of penalty.

- A **cross-cultural universal norm** argument states that crime, in essence, does not vary across different cultures. Thus, murder is murder regardless of the society, and we can postulate conduct norms that cut across diverse cultural backgrounds.
- A **labelling** approach to the definition of crime argues that crime only really exists when there has been a social response to a particular activity that labels that activity as criminal. If there is no label, there is in effect no crime.
- A **human rights** approach says that crime occurs whenever a human right has been violated, regardless of the legality or otherwise of the action. Such a conception also expands the definition of crime to include oppressive practices such as racism, sexism, and class-based exploitation.
- A **human diversity** approach defines crime in terms of the manner in which deviance represents a normal response to oppressive or unequal circumstances. A major focus here is on power relations, and the attempts by dominant groups to restrict human diversity of experience, language, and culture.

Our intention here is not to explain fully each type of definition of crime, nor to evaluate the explanatory or practical usefulness of each definition (instead, see Hagan 1987; Nettler 1984). Rather, we wish to alert the reader to the fact that there are important differences in how people conceive of crime.

Further to this, the variation in definition often has real consequences upon how different types of behaviour are dealt with at a practical level. For example, we might consider the issue of violence:

> In the home, parents hit children; on the playing field, sportsmen assault each other; at work, industrial 'accidents' occur; in our community, dangerous chemicals are dumped; our governments turn a blind eye to the practices of some police officers; and our governments are responsible for the mass violence of war.
>
> *Alder (1991: 61)*

How violence is perceived and responded to by criminal justice institutions depends very much upon a range of political and social factors. Crime is not inherent in an activity: it is defined under particular material circumstances and in relation to specific social processes.

Historical constructions of crime

While criminologists may argue about the definition of crime, ultimately it is the legal definition of crime that determines how we as a society respond to certain acts deemed to be wrongful. But, we might ask, who actually makes the laws, and why are they made? Whose interests are reflected in those laws and how are they enforced? In line with the broad theme of the variability of definitions of crime, it is also useful to acknowledge that legal definitions of crime themselves change over time. The law itself is thus socially produced and is not static. As it changes, so too does the definition of crime. In this sense we can say that morality itself is variable, at least insofar as it is reflected in the laws of a country.

What is legally defined as crime varies according to social and historical contexts. This is shown in the following examples.

- As of 1530 in England there existed the crime of being a vagabond, which in effect meant that a person was unemployed and idle. Any person so identified could be branded a criminal—figuratively and literally (through burning of the gristle of the right ear with a hot iron). Vagabonds over the age of eighteen could be hanged if they did not obtain suitable employment for two years. Revived in 1743, the Vagrancy Acts expanded the types of persons liable for prosecution to include a wide variety of homeless and poor people (see Chambliss 1975a). This crime no longer exists, although one could be tempted to draw similarities with the negative status accorded to the young unemployed today.

- In the seventeenth century, the crime of witchcraft was the commonest of all crimes in Europe. Crime here was constructed in terms of religion and referred to conduct allegedly against (the Christian) God. By and large, such laws pertaining to witchcraft targeted women, particularly those displaying eccentric and secretive tendencies, as a means of controlling them and their knowledge (see Inverarity et al. 1983). Such laws of course are not common in the criminal law today. However, in some jurisdictions crimes related to witchcraft are still on the statute books, such as reading of tarot cards. Similarly, some of the public concern about heavy-metal or Gothic 'shock rock' (e.g., Marilyn Manson) music appears to have vestiges of the moral and religious panics over witchcraft that swept Europe several hundred years ago.

- Property and theft are historically and culturally specific concepts. In many traditional Australian Aboriginal and other indigenous communal societies, everything is shared. There is no concept of theft (which is premised on the notion of ownership of personal property), because in these cultures property is communal. Concepts of land ownership likewise differ from mainstream legal conceptions. Some members of indigenous communities hold the belief that they do not really own the land, so it cannot be taken away from them. To put it differently, land is not a possession, it is something that you have a relationship with. Crime in traditional indigenous communities is associated with the abuse of sacred knowledge, custom, spirituality, witchcraft, and ritual—it is not centred upon property as is most Western law (see Bottomley et al. 1991).

Crime is thus an offence of the time. In European history it was for a while intimately linked to moral prescriptions, as defined by religious bodies. One reason for this was that in the 1400s to 1600s, the Church was the body that had access to the tools of justice administration. This was because literacy tended to be the preserve of the clergy, who therefore were in a position to construct the laws. Later on, it was the preserve of the state to determine laws. Accordingly, crime became defined as a transgression against the state, not against God. Even today, however, there are vestiges of conflict between the secular and non-secular law, as indicated in legal action taken over the ordination of women in some Christian denominations.

Popular media images of crime

The media have a significant influence on the general portrayal of crime in society. The images that permeate popular consciousness of crime are mainly generated by, and reflected in, the electronic and print media. Obviously the media have a tremendous impact in terms of how crime is generally defined in society (see Sarre 1994; Grabosky & Wilson 1989; Ericson et al. 1991).

According to the media, in both fictional and factual types of programmes and reportage, crime tends to be defined primarily as 'street crime'. Such crime is thus associated with personal terror and fear, and violence is seen as central. Crime is sensationalised, with important implications for the fear of crime among certain sections of the population. This fear is heightened by the way in which crime is seen to be random in nature, with anyone and everyone a possible target for victimisation.

As well, there is often the idea that crime is related to morality, and specifically to the decline of that morality. What is 'wrong' is plain for all to see. Furthermore, the 'criminal' is distinctive and identifiably different from everyone else in society. Overall, the idea is that there is a continuing 'law-and-order' problem in society, and that things are constantly getting worse. Against this tide of disorder and lawlessness, the police and other crime-fighters are generally portrayed as 'superheroes', who are infallible and who use violence legitimately in order to counter the violence of the streets.

The media are important not only in shaping our definitions of crime and crime control, but in producing legal changes and reinforcing particular types of policing strategies. For example, the 'moral panics' (see Cohen 1973) generated by the media on problems such as 'youth gangs' may lead to changes in the law (e.g., introduction of youth curfews) and the adoption of certain police methods (e.g., increasing the use of 'name checks' in particular locales). It has been demonstrated that the interests of the police and the media are entwined; they have a symbiotic relationship in that the media rely upon the police for much of their information, and the police use the media to portray certain images relating to their work.

The media thus convey a sensationalised image of crime, and a protective view of police and policing practices—and they make unusual events usual events in our lives. As Grabosky and Wilson (1989: 11) comment: 'The most common types of crime according to official statistics, crimes against property, receive relatively little media attention. By contrast, crimes of violence, which are very uncommon in actuarial terms, are accorded much greater coverage.'

Similarly, there is a skewed focus on 'street crime' and bizarre events. Meanwhile, the destruction of the environment, domestic violence, white-collar crimes, and occupational health and safety crimes tend not to receive the same kind of coverage or treatment by the mainstream media outlets.

With regard to crime control, the usual implication is that once a crime has been brought to the attention of the authorities, investigation will generally lead to detection and capture of the offender. This is a far cry from the reality of much police work, and in specific cases of serious street crime a significant proportion of cases do not get to the prosecution stage. In fictional accounts of crime fighting, the police are usually endowed with special qualities (e.g., big guns, martial arts abilities), and violence is central and always justified because of the nature of the 'criminals' at hand. The nature of actual policing is once again misconstrued, and the mundane aspects—interviewing, looking over file material, research, traffic regulation, and so on—are generally absent. Another facet of fictional accounts is that the police are not accountable to anyone; they can even step outside the bounds of the law, because we all know they are on 'our' side. Thus, the police are always honest and incorruptible, even though evidence in real life, such as the Fitzgerald inquiry into police in Queensland (Fitzgerald 1989), reveals widespread and systematic corruption.

It is important therefore to separate the images and realities of crime in society. The media shape our perceptions of crime, and in the process they define crime in particular ways. One aspect of this process is that the media often portray crime in terms of distinct **crime waves**. This refers to the way in which increased reporting of particular types of crime (usually street crimes such as assault, rape, or homicide) increases the public awareness of this crime. Significantly, there need not have been an actual increase in the crime for a crime wave to occur. The increase exists only in public perception.

Nevertheless, 'crime waves' can and do have real consequences regardless of factual basis. For example, extensive media coverage of child abuse may lead to changes in the law, such as the introduction of mandatory reporting of suspected incidents. Or the fear generated by press coverage of assaults on elderly people may lead to calls for more police, tougher sentences, greater police power, and so on. Given the close relationship between the police and the media, major questions can be asked as to who benefits from the selective reporting of specific crimes, especially around government budget time.

MEASURING CRIME

Given the limitations and problems of relying upon media definitions and treatments of crime, it is reasonable to accept that any statement made about crime should be tested by referring to the 'facts' about crime. This usually means that we need to confirm particular crime trends and consider official data on criminal activity. However, even here there are difficulties with how crime is defined. For what we 'measure' depends upon how we define crime and how we see the criminalisation process.

In fact, criminologists are not united in their approach to crime and crime statistics (see Nettler 1984; Jupp 1989). For present purposes, we can identify three broad strands within criminology that deal with measurement issues:

- The **realist approach** adopts the view that crime exists 'out there' in society and that the 'dark figure' of crime needs to be uncovered and recorded. There are limitations to the gathering of official statistics (such as reliance solely on police records of reported offences), and the role of criminology is to supplement official statistics (those generated by the police, courts, and prison authorities) through a range of informal or alternative measures. The emphasis is on the **problem of omission**—to uncover the true or real extent of crime by methods such as victim surveys, self-report surveys, test situations, hidden cameras, and so on.

- The **institutionalist approach** adopts the view that crime is a 'social process', and it rejects the notion that we can unproblematically gain a sense of the real extent of crime by improving our measuring devices and techniques. This approach instead concentrates on the manner in which official institutions of crime control actually process suspects and thus define certain individuals and certain types of behaviour as being 'criminal'. The emphasis is on the **problem of bias**—to show how some people and events are designated by the criminal justice system as being criminal, while others are not.

- The **critical realist** approach argues that crime measurement can be characterised as having elements of both 'social process' and a grounded 'reality'. The task of measurement from this perspective is to uncover the processes whereby the crimes against the most vulnerable and least powerful sections of the population have been ignored or underrepresented. The emphasis is on the **problem of victimisation**—to demonstrate empirically how certain groups are especially vulnerable to crime and to the fear of crime, and conceptually to criticise the agencies of crime control for their lack of action in protecting these groups.

Thus, there are debates within criminology over how and what to measure, and these ultimately reflect basic divisions within the field regarding the very definition of crime itself. As the preceding discussions make clear, the study of crime is fraught with a wide range of competing viewpoints and perspectives. It is useful, then, to develop an analytical framework that can make sense of these differences and the basis for different points of view on crime and crime control.

CRIMINOLOGICAL PERSPECTIVES

The style of questions you ask necessarily determines the answers you receive. As we have indicated, there are competing definitions of crime: these produce competing answers or explanations of the causes of crime, and these in turn produce different kinds of responses to crime. Criminologists vary in how they approach the study of crime.

Criminological theory can be presented in abstract fashion as being made up of a series of separate perspectives or approaches. Each approach or paradigm attempts to understand a particular phenomenon by asking certain types of questions, using certain concepts, and constructing a particular framework of analysis and explanation. In practice, it is rare to find government departments or academic criminologists who rely solely or exclusively on any one particular criminological framework or approach. Often a wide range of ideas and concepts are combined in different ways in the course of developing policy or in the study of a specific empirical problem.

For the sake of presentation, it is nevertheless useful to present **ideal types** of the various theoretical strands within criminology. The use of ideal types provides us with a means by which we can clarify main ideas and identify important differences between the broad approaches adopted in the field. An ideal type does not exist in the real world. Rather, the intention behind the construction of an ideal type is to abstract from concrete situations the key elements or components of a particular theory or social institution, and to exaggerate these elements if need be, in order to highlight the general tendency or themes of the particular perspective (see Freund 1969). An ideal type is an analytical tool, not a moral statement of what ought to be. It refers to a process of identifying different aspects of social phenomena and combining them into a 'typical' model or example. For instance, an ideal type of bureaucracy would include such things as impartial and impersonal merit and promotion structures, the following of prescribed rules and regulations, a hierarchical chain of command, and so on. We know, however, that people who work in bureaucracies are not always promoted on the basis of their qualifications, and nor is decision-making always rational. But by constructing an exaggerated 'typical' model of a bureaucracy we are able to compare the actual structure of different organisations and how they actually work in the real world.

If we are to construct ideal types in relation to criminological theory, then it is useful first to identify the central focus of theory, and in particular the level of analysis and explanation at which the theory is pitched. There are three broad levels of criminological explanation: the individual, the situational, and the structural. Different theories within criminology tend to locate their main explanation for criminal behaviour or criminality at one of these levels. Occasionally, a theory may attempt to combine all three levels in order to provide a more sophisticated and comprehensive picture of crime and criminality.

Levels of analysis

- **Individual**—The main focus is on the personal or individual characteristics of the offender or victim. Study may consider, for example, the influence of appearance, dress, and public image on the nature of crime causation or victimisation (e.g., tattoos or earrings as indicators of a 'criminal' attitude in men). This level of analysis tends to look to psychological or biological factors that are said to have an important role in determining why certain individuals engage in criminal activity. The key concern is to explain crime or deviant behaviour in terms of the choices or characteristics of the individual person.
- **Situational**—The main site of analysis is the immediate circumstances, or situation, within which criminal activity or deviant behaviour occurs. Attention is directed to the specific factors that may contribute to an event occurring, such as how the participants define the situation, how different people are labelled by others in the criminal justice system, the opportunities available for the commission of certain types of offences, and so on. Key concerns are the nature of the interaction between different players within the system, the

effect of local environmental factors on the nature of this interaction, and the influence of group behaviour and influences on social activity.

- **Social structural**—This approach tends to look at crime in terms of the broad social relationships and the major social institutions of the society as a whole. The analysis makes reference to the relationship between classes, sexes, different ethnic and 'racial' groups, the employed and unemployed, and various other social divisions in society. It also can involve investigation of the operation of specific institutions—such as education, the family, work, and the legal system—in the construction of and social responses to crime and deviant behaviour.

The level of analysis one chooses has major consequences for how crime is viewed, the nature of the offender, and how the criminal justice system should be organised. For example, a biological positivist approach looks at characteristics of the individual offender (e.g., genetic make-up) and sees crime as revolving around, and stemming from, the specific personal attributes of the individual. A situational perspective might consider the interaction between police and young people on the street, and argue that 'crime' is defined in the process of specific types of inter-actions, behaviours, and attitudes. From a structural perspective, the issue might be seen in terms of the relationship between poverty and crime; that is, the elements of social life that underpin particular courses of action. The individualist, the situational, and the structural approaches would all advocate quite different policies because of their particular perspective. The vantage point from which one examines crime—a focus on personal characteristics through to societal institutions—thus shapes the ways in which one thinks about and acts upon criminal justice matters.

The different levels of analysis apparent in criminology are also partly a reflection of the diverse disciplines that have contributed to the study of crime over a number of years. Researchers, scholars, and writers in areas such as biological science, psychology, philosophy, law, sociology, forensic medicine, political economy, education, history, and cultural studies have all contributed to the multidisciplinary nature of criminol-ogy. Each discipline brings to bear its own concepts, debates, and methods when examining a criminological issue or problem. This means that within criminology there is a natural diversity of viewpoints, as different writers and researchers 'see' the world through very different analytical spectacles. Such differences are also reflected in the adoption of a wide range of different techniques and methodologies in the study of crime. These include historical records, use of surveys, participant observation, interviews, evaluation of official statistics, study of policy documents, and discourse analysis.

Most theories of crime tend to congeal into one of these analytical categories; that is, most lean on one of these particular areas, advancing different theories relating to the causes of crime. For example, the classical theory focuses on choice—the offender chooses to offend or not offend; the response is punishment. This approach focuses on the criminal act. The biological positivist looks at the offender's personal characteristics, and focuses on treatment. Some researchers attempt to integrate all three levels of analysis into their approach. The questions one asks will obviously vary according to the approach or combination of approaches one adopts, as will the consequences.

Political orientations

Differences in broad levels of analysis, and in specific discipline-related perspectives, can also be linked to some extent to differences in the political framework of the writer. The political orientation of a writer partially can be gleaned by trying to understand their overall picture of society. For example, consider the following representations of society (see Brown 1979):

- **The geometric circle**—implies society is harmonious, and people share the same values of community and equality. The concept of crime is that perpetrators are deviant, or outside the circle, and thus they need to be either pulled back into the circle or kept outside the circle's confines.
- **The triangle**—Society is viewed as a hierarchy, since some people are situated at the top, possessing the wealth and power, and the majority are situated at the bottom. This vision of society implies conflict and inequality. The concept of crime is that it occurs in the context of struggles and hierarchies of control and power. Situated within this perspective are both meritocratic and critical views. A meritocratic view of the triangle argues that within the existing structure anyone who plays by the rules of the game is capable of rising to the top of the hierarchy, and that success is a question of ability and

hard work. The laws are seen to exist as a means of sustaining the rules of the triangle. A critical view of the triangle translates inequality into injustice. The laws are seen to be unequally applied; it is argued that people on the bottom of the triangle are overrepresented in the criminal justice system, and this representation is questioned.

- **The rectangle or square**—Society consists of a variety of inter-related rectangles representing different interconnecting institutions, such as the family, work, and school. Crime is studied in relation to how these institutions impact upon, and reflect upon, crime. The concern here is not with values, as in the circle, but with the smooth running of the interconnected institutions. The issue is one of administrative efficiency and application of the right kinds of techniques to fix the particular social problem.

- **Non-geometric forms such as stick figures**—Here the focus is on individuals, as opposed to society as a whole, and the emphasis is on examining individual creativity and the way individuals construct their realities. The idea is that reality is socially constructed, and that how people act and react in relation to each other has a major impact in terms of defining behaviour and individuals as being deviant, normal, or whatever. How people think about themselves and each other is a significant factor in how they subsequently behave in their interactions with others.

The manner in which we view society influences the way in which we view crime. The various competing perspectives within criminology reflect different points of view regarding the nature of society. We can identify three major paradigms (conceptual frameworks for understanding social phenomena) in criminology. These paradigms inevitably incorporate specific kinds of value judgement. The motivation, conceptual development, methodological tools, and social values associated with a specific approach are usually intertwined with one of three broad political perspectives: conservative, liberal, or radical.

- **Conservative**—A conservative perspective on society tends to be supportive of the legitimacy of the status quo; that is, it generally accepts the way things are, the traditional ways of doing things, and traditional social relationships. Conservatives believe dissenters should be made to conform to the status quo. They believe that there is a 'core value system' to which everyone in society should conform. The function of the main institutions is to preserve the dominant system of order for the good of society generally. The values and institutions of society should apply equally to all people regardless of social background or historical developments.

- **Liberal**—A liberal perspective on society accepts the limits of the status quo, but encourages limited changes in societal institutions. This approach tends to avoid questions relating to the whole structure of society. Instead it emphasises the need for action on particular limited 'social problems'. Specific problems such as sexism, racism, poverty, and so on can be resolved without fundamental changes to the economic or social structure. Rather, policies and programmes can be developed that will serve to reform existing institutions and day-to-day interactions. Problems tend to be studied in terms of their impact on specific individuals (e.g., 'the poor' as the focus of research) and the disadvantage suffered by these individuals or groups.

- **Radical**—The radical perspective on society wishes to undermine the legitimacy of the status quo. Like the conservative perspective, it looks at society as whole, but it sees 'social conflict' as the central concern. Society is seen to be divided on the basis of class, gender, ethnicity, 'race', and so on. (The use of the term 'race' implies that it is a social rather than a scientific construct, and distinguishes it from any biological connotation the word otherwise may have.) The key issue is who holds the power and resources in any particular community. The focus of the radical perspective is fundamental change to the existing social order. Specific issues, such as poverty, are explained in relational terms (e.g., the relationship between the rich and poor), and the solution is seen to involve dealing with the structural imbalances and inequalities that lead to the problem (of poverty) in the first place.

If we acknowledge the centrality of politics in criminological analysis, then we must accept that there is no such thing as value-free criminology. Values of the right (conservative), left (radical), and centre (liberal) are embedded in the criminological enterprise. The political orientation of the particular approach has major implications for how crime is defined. For example, chart 1.1 presents a radical view of how crime can be defined. As opposed to more conservative perspectives, this approach emphasises both the crimes of the powerful and the crimes of the less powerful. Each particular theory of the causes of crime is generally linked in some way to these broad political perspectives, and thus each sees crime as informed by certain values and philosophical principles.

CHART 1.1   A Radical Definition of Crime

Crimes of the Powerful	
Typical crimes	**Examples**
Economic	Breaches of corporate law, environmental degradation, inadequate industrial health and safety provisions, pollution, violation of labour laws, fraud
State	Police brutality, government corruption, bribery, violation of civil rights, misuse of public funds
Crimes of the Less Powerful	
Typical crimes	**Examples**
Economic	Street crime, workplace theft, low-level fraud, breach of welfare regulations, prostitution
Socio-cultural	Vandalism, assault, rape, murder, resistance via strikes and demonstrations, public order offences, workplace sabotage

Source: adapted from Cunneen & White 1995.

A further aspect relating to the politics of criminological theory is that the dominant paradigm or approach that is adopted by governments and represented in criminological circles (professional journals, conferences) varies over time. That is, there are competing general perspectives within criminology, but in different periods particular perspectives will be ascendant over others. For example, the conservative perspectives (within which lie a number of related theories, usually associated with classical and positivist views, and which centre on punishment and control strategies) held considerable sway at the level of policy formulation and action in the 1950s. By the late 1960s, the liberal perspective (centring on labelling and efforts at rehabilitation) informed much of the reform activity related to the criminal justice system. By the mid 1980s there had been a swing back to the right, which persisted into the 1990s, with strident calls for the adoption of tougher measures to deal with issues of 'law and order'. Simultaneous with the conservative push at the level of policy were both liberal and radical critiques of the effectiveness and fairness of such measures. By the late 1990s and early 2000s, the crime debate incorporated conservative elements stressing offender responsibility and strong state action against anti–social and illegal behaviour, and, as well, liberal perspectives that spoke of the need for restorative justice as a key philosophical principle in responding to crime and criminality. Criminological theory is thus always related in some way to specific historical contexts, specific material conditions, and specific political struggles.

The objectives and methods of analysis used in criminology reflect certain underlying ideas and concerns of the writer. In reading criminological material, then, it is important to examine the assumptions of the writers—the key concepts they use, and the methods or arguments used to support their theory—to identify their conceptions of society and of human nature, and the kinds of reforms or institutions that they ultimately support. It is also important to identify the silences in a particular theory or tradition; that is, what questions are not being asked, and why not? Finally, it is crucial to consider the social relevance of the theory or perspective. What does it tell us about our society, and the direction that our society is or ought to be heading? Fundamentally, the study of crime involves the values and opinions of the criminologist, and this, too, is part of what the student of crime must be aware of if they are to develop an informed view of the issues.

CONCLUSION

The objectives and methods of criminology reflect and are affected by a wide range of ideas and concerns. This chapter has provided an overview of how the study of crime is built upon a variety of different definitions, how it involves recognition of historical and cross-cultural processes, and that it must acknowledge the impact of popular media images on perceptions of crime. The chapter has also indicated the approaches within criminology to measure crime, and the analytically and politically diverse nature of the criminological enterprise.

The main purpose of this book as a whole is to explore how criminology explains the 'causes' of crime. Our concern is not to discuss general social theory as such, although the influence of specific social theorists, implicitly if not explicitly, permeates many of the discussions. For example, the ideas of Foucault (1980) are particularly evident in certain strands of feminist criminology and critical criminology. In a similar vein, we do not deal with the application of general social theory to specific institutional processes as in the case of Foucault (1977) on prisons or Cohen (1985) on community corrections. Indeed, the book is not designed to explain issues relating to the 'responses' of society to criminal behaviour and activity, except in a very general sense and only when directly related to the theories that are discussed. Such questions are considered in greater detail elsewhere, as in the case of Garland (1990) on punishment, Howe (1994) on penality, and White and Perrone (1997) on criminal justice institutions generally.

In providing a broad overview of the major frameworks of analysis within criminology we have structured each chapter in the following way: Introduction; Social Context; Basic Concepts; Historical Development; Contemporary Examples; Critique; Conclusion. By organising the material in such a fashion, we hope to offer the reader a useful guide to the background, development, and core ideas of each theoretical strand in a way that also makes comparison between the diverse theories relatively easy.

It is our belief that good criminology is that which is self-consciously reflective of the theoretical and political basis of its understandings and analysis. How we view crime, how we define what is harmful or serious, and how we study criminal activity—all have major ramifications for how we propose to deal with crime at the level of policy, institution, and strategy. It is our hope that this book will assist the reader in situating the social, theoretical, and practical implications of whatever perspective they may draw upon in trying to come to grips with crime and criminology today.

FURTHER READING

Einstadter, W. & Henry, S. (1995) *Criminological Theory: An Analysis of Its Underlying Assumptions*, Harcourt Brace, New York.

Jupp, V. (1989) *Methods of Criminological Research*, Routledge, London.

Muncie, J., McLaughlin, E. & Langan, M. (eds) (1996) *Criminological Perspectives: A Reader*, Sage, London.

Nettler, G. (1984) *Explaining Crime*, McGraw-Hill, New York.

Taylor, I., Walton, P. & Young, J. (1973) *The New Criminology*, Routledge and Kegan Paul, London.

CHAPTER 2

Classical Theory

INTRODUCTION

This chapter provides an outline and review of the classical theory in criminology. It describes the historical context within which classicism emerged, and the basic principles and concepts of the classical model. The contribution of this model to present criminal justice issues and institutions is discussed, along with the strengths and limitations of the perspective.

The foundations of the contemporary criminal justice and legal systems were laid down in the eighteenth century. This was the period when the basic principles and practices of classical theory were developed and institutionalised for the first time in Europe. The emergence of classical thought constituted a radical challenge to the institutional and class relations underpinning the system of justice at that time, and resulted in a departure from previous methods of criminal justice adjudication.

SOCIAL CONTEXT

The specific contours of legal change associated with the classical perspective in criminology varied greatly depending upon the national context. For example, in England, the seventeenth century was the epoch of greatest importance in the history of political and legal theory. It was a time when the power of the monarch was directly challenged in a number of ways. One outcome of the conflicts over power, authority, and the role of law embodied in this struggle was the development of a body of principles about the supremacy of law, the fundamental rights of human beings, equality before the law, and the democratic basis of political authority (Kelly 1992). Major political and legal changes were to occur at different times and in different ways in the other European centres such as France, Germany, Spain, and Italy. These changes were heavily influenced by the eighteenth-century intellectual movement, the Enlightenment, which looked to rebuild social structures on the basis of purely rational principles. Assertion of the rule of law, and of the importance of thinking about society and the state in terms of a social contract, were eventually to prevail. As part of the reform processes taking place across Europe, the basis of criminal law and the nature of punishment were called into question.

The development of classical conceptions of law and the criminal justice system was grounded in the transition from feudalism to capitalism. Major social, economic, and political changes were occurring throughout Europe that were revolutionising the institutions of power and social relationships generally. The 'revolutions' were at two levels: economic and political. In production, economies based primarily on agriculture moved to become commercial market economies and then industrial economies; and in the political sphere, the rule of the landed aristocracy was challenged by the emerging bourgeoisie or capitalist class. Thus, over a period of several centuries to the eighteenth century, there occurred a transition from one mode of production, feudalism, to another dominant mode of production, capitalism.

Under **feudalism**, land, wealth, and power were concentrated in the hands of a small group of people—the landed aristocracy—which maintained its rule through a combination of repression (e.g., putting down peasant rebellions) and appeal to tradition and custom (e.g., the idea of a preordained social order with kings and queens at the top). Ideologically, law was maintained by appeal to such notions as the 'divine right of monarchs', which said that monarchs ruled by God-given right. Since law-making was a matter of birthright and religious conviction, the aristocracy was for a time able to rule with absolute power. Disobedience or challenge to that order was repressed. Basic social patterns, in particular the relationship between serf and lord, were cast as 'natural' and permanent social arrangements.

In the feudal era, there was an absence of formal legal status as such. Rights were not acknowledged as being common to all. Rather, any rights that did exist were linked to individual station and class. For example, peasants and (most) women were accorded few formal rights, while members of the aristocracy and the upper levels of the Christian church had special rights associated with their position in society. One's social rank thus determined the nature and extent of the rights one was able to claim or exercise.

The administration of justice tended to be haphazard, localised, irregular and unsystematic (see Hall & McLennan 1986). Just as rights and laws were moulded around the specific interests of powerful individuals, so, too, the 'justice' system reflected the personal ties or connections of the powerful (e.g., derived from patronage, familiarity, or business associations) and the personal whim of the local ruling class. Men (women were generally not decision-makers, unless part of royalty) held judicial office as an extension of their wealth and rank in society. Furthermore, there was a proliferation of different types of courts, including local manorial courts, ecclesiastical (religious) courts, and the King's or Queen's courts.

Justice was personalised. That is, decisions regarding whether particular acts were deemed to be criminal or not, and the responses to criminal acts, were essentially a matter of the personal opinion or whim of the presiding judge. Decisions were unpredictable. Persons holding legal office could display mercy if they so desired, but this in itself reflected the absolute power they held in their hands to make decisions. There were few institutional checks or balances on this power. The legal system was highly localised, and revolved around the existing power relationships of the landed gentry and church officials.

The penalties for crime were also highly individualised and varied greatly. Torture and death were not uncommon penalties for even minor offences. The brutal nature of the punishment also reflected the fact that the long-term holding of prisoners in particular sites (e.g., prisons) was not used as a general form of sanction. It also reflected the arbitrary use of draconian or extreme measures when the first priority of the day was maintenance of order and orthodoxy, rather than justice and reform.

The exercise of power was, however, circumscribed by certain customs and traditions that, ultimately, served to legitimise the existing social structure (see Fine 1984). For instance, while the serf or peasant was bound to do extra work or provide an amount of their produce for the lord, the lord was in turn obligated to protect his vassals from outside threat or harm, and to ensure that certain social responsibilities were maintained (e.g., in time of famine to provide a share of social goods to the poor).

The rise of the state, initially linked to the extension of monarchical power, saw the legal and criminal justice systems start to change. Over time, if we take the English case, the monarchs were able to fuse local traditions and customs into a general form of law administration—and hence the development of a 'common law' system of justice. In other European centres such as France, extensive centralised laws were established (e.g., the Code Napoléon) that were to provide a national structure for the legal system. Each system of law served to entrench and consolidate the power of the monarch over that of local landowners (e.g., barons), so that the monarch was then able to rule much more absolutely than had previously been the case.

The next stage of legal development was linked to the formation of the capitalist class, beginning with the age of **mercantile capitalism** (i.e., merchant trading in the context of nation–states). The absolute power of the monarch constituted a fetter on the activities and aspirations of this new class. For example, the ability of monarchs to grant monopoly trading rights to selected companies (e.g., Hudson's Bay Company in North America) was seen to be unfair, restricting the trading activities of the mercantile capitalists. Furthermore, given that the law was still essentially reflective of personal whim and establishment prerogatives (since decision-making at both national and local levels resided in the hands of the landed aristocracy), a political revolution was necessary to change basic relations of power.

This manifested itself in the form of a series of armed struggles and revolutions, including the French Revolution and the American Revolution. The power of the monarchy was circumscribed or replaced by new institutions (e.g., parliaments), and the aristocracy was pushed to the side as the only or major ruling force in society. For economic reasons (i.e., long-term planning purposes) as well as political reasons (i.e., holding of decision-making power), a new form of law and criminal justice system evolved. A central feature of this system was that it was bureaucratic in nature (rather than personalised), and it provided a more systematic and impersonal method of judicial administration.

The concept of **individual rights**, as opposed to customary and traditional bonds, was central to the political, economic, and social project of the bourgeoisie. The new class, the capitalists, called for the universalisation of rights (at least to those who had wealth and property) against a regime based solely upon hereditary privilege. Accompanying the demand for recognition of the 'rights of man' was an insistence that the state no longer simply rule on behalf of a monarch, or the aristocracy. Rather, the role of the state was now to preserve the **rule of law**. In this system the state apparatus acts as a distinct public authority to guarantee 'equality under the law' in relation to freedom, rights, and obligations. In this conception of law, not only were all equal in the eyes of the law, but the law-makers themselves were likewise bound by the laws they devised.

The claim for universal and equal rights was relevant to the political domain and, as well, to the law and courts. The idea was that all social attributes such as class, rank, and social background should be ignored once a person entered the court. People should not be subject to arbitrary judgement and a justice system based upon different rights for different classes of people. Once in court, participants are transformed into 'abstract legal subjects' who, regardless of background, should be treated equally (O'Malley 1983).

Economically, the demand for individual rights was important in a number of ways (Fine 1984). First, it helped to bolster the idea that 'private property' was a right that did not have to be seen in relation to customary or traditional obligations. For example, ownership of land had been linked to certain social obligations for those living on the land; it was now asserted that the use of property was something that was absolutely and exclusively a matter for the owner to decide. An owner could decide to plant cash crops for the market, rather than subsistence crops for the peasant residents. Any obligations to help the poor, or find work for the peasant who had been dispossessed of land, were effectively transferred from private hands to the state.

Second, the notion of rights was used to justify a breaking of bonds between peasants and the landed aristocracy. No longer tied by tradition or custom to the land, peasants were allowed the legal right to freely sell their labour. Coupled with the new legal basis of private property, which soon led to the closing of land to the peasant class, the position of individuals as 'free labourers' served to swell the cities as urbanisation gathered pace. This provided the capitalist class with a huge reservoir of labour from which to choose, and with which production could be magnified in ways hitherto not seen in the history of humankind. The 'freeing' of people from the land was, in fact, crucial to the later development of full-scale industrialisation.

The classical approach in law and criminology was thus born of momentous changes occurring across the political, legal, social, and economic domains. At the core of these changes was the relationship between individual rights, the state, and equality. The rights of human beings, it was felt, should be protected against arbitrary uses of power. Likewise, a rational system of production and exchange (i.e., the capitalist market) demanded a legal system that was predictable, systematic, and regular. Such a system, involving competition between producers, should also ensure that the power of the state be limited, particularly in regard to issues surrounding private property and personal accumulation of wealth.

BASIC CONCEPTS

Classical theory is premised upon the notion of individual rights, the human capacity to reason, and the rule of law (see chart 2.1). The theory assumes a particular view of human nature, and of the relationship between individuals and the state.

CHART 2.1   Classical Theory

Definition of crime	*Legal* ▪ violation of law ▪ rights and social contract
Focus of analysis	*The criminal act* ▪ specific offence ▪ the criminal law
Cause of crime	*Rationality* ▪ individual choice ▪ irrational decisions
Nature of offender	*Voluntaristic* ▪ free-will, self-interest, and equal capacity to reason
Response to crime	*Punishment* ▪ proportionate to the crime ▪ fixed or determinate
Crime prevention	*Deterrence* ▪ pleasure–pain principle ▪ reform of the legal system to make it more accessible
Operation of criminal justice system	*Legal–philosophical approach* ▪ basic principles

In the classical view, human beings are seen as being essentially self-seeking and self-interested individuals. What we do with our personal talents, skills, and energy is a matter of individual initiative and choice; that is, the classical theory has a **voluntaristic** view of human nature that emphasises free will and individual choice. We are thereby seen as ultimately responsible for choosing what to do with our time and energy, and for the consequences that may arise from our actions.

Rather than analysing the customary or other links between people, the theory emphasises the status of human beings as **rights–holders**. Individuals are deemed to have an equal capacity to reason and to act in accordance with what is rational from the point of view of their own self-interests. Institutionally, each individual is to be granted equal rights under the law. The fundamental objective of the law is to protect individual rights, and to allow the free exercise of choice among individuals as far as this is possible without leading to social harm.

In order to guarantee both individual rights and some semblance of order, classical theory considers the role of the state to be central. Specifically, the theory rests upon the notion of a **social contract** between individual rights–holders and the state. In this model, there is an implied consensus or agreement: that individuals in society give up certain rights to the state in return for the protection of their rights and the security of their person and property from other individuals, and from the state itself. If human beings are seen as essentially self-interested and self-seeking, then there needs to be some kind of mechanism that will, in effect, protect us from the self-interested behaviour and actions of others. Hence, the role of the state is to regulate human interaction, and to be a site where rights in general can be protected by not allowing their infringement in specific instances.

The legal manifestation of the social contract is expressed in the phrase 'the rule of law'. The rule of law means that everyone is to be treated equally, without fear or favour, in the eyes of the law. Further, even the law-makers are bound by the law set down for the general populace. Thus, the first principle of the justice system is equal protection of rights. A crucial assumption here is that the social contract will protect each individual against the excesses and corruption of institutions and other individuals by treating all people the same way. For this to occur in practice, it is necessary to have a criminal justice and judicial system that is systematic, predictable, and regular.

The law is seen to be intrinsically good, and to reflect the reasoned beliefs and values of the law-makers. The theory assumes a consensus in society regarding what is considered 'good' and what is 'bad', and this is reflected in the specific criminal laws. Crime is defined in the first instance as simply a **violation of the law**. Adherence to the law in general, and to specific laws in particular, is seen to be an essential component of the social contract that protects individual rights generally.

In this framework, criminality is seen as primarily a matter of making the wrong choice, by violating the law. Put simply, individuals are to be held **responsible** for their actions. Since each person is seen to have equal capacity to reason, and given that every effort is made to make citizens familiar with the law, and with its punishments, crime is in essence a matter of free choice. The source of criminality thus lies within the rational, reasoning individual. Crime is the result of individuals either making a calculated decision to do wrong (by weighing up the potential rewards and negative consequences) or engaging in what might be seen as irrational behaviour (by not using their reason adequately or properly).

The social contract is maintained in practice through the use of punishment. The purpose of **punishment** is to deter individuals from violating laws, which in effect means an interference with the person or property rights of another. Deterrence should be directed both at the individual (specific deterrence) and at members of society at large (general deterrence) through the use of a wide range of sanctions or penalties appropriate to the offences committed. Punishment was based on the **pleasure–pain principle**, in which the pain of the sentence would outweigh any pleasure to be gained from committing the crime.

The response of the criminal justice system is focused primarily on the **criminal act**. The rule of law demands that each violation of the law be treated in the same way—that is, like cases should be treated alike. To put it differently, the emphasis is on equality in legal proceedings (everyone is equal in the eyes of the law) and equality in punishment of offenders (similar crimes are punished in the same way).

The uniformity of the law is guaranteed by set penalties for particular offences. The punishment is thus meant to fit the crime. For the sake of equality, penalties should be fixed prior to sentencing, and be administered in accordance with the actual offence that has been committed. Punishment, therefore, is to consist of **determinate sentences**, which clearly link specific offences with specific penalties, and which are applicable to anyone who has committed the offence in question.

HISTORICAL DEVELOPMENT

The two leading figures in the development of classical criminology were Cesare Beccaria and Jeremy Bentham (see Taylor et al. 1973). The work of Beccaria provided a profound critique of the existing systems of law and criminal justice. He opposed the arbitrary nature of judicial decision-making that was characteristic of the courts of his day, and he was critical of the unduly harsh and barbaric forms of punishment, which included extensive use of the death penalty and the routine use of torture.

According to Beccaria, the basis for all social action should be the utilitarian concept of the greatest happiness for the greater number in society. Translated into the criminal justice sphere, this meant that crime should be considered an injury to society as a whole (and not explained in terms of 'sin' or dealt with solely on the basis of 'privilege'). The purpose of punishment is not simply social revenge or retribution, but to ensure the greatest overall good for everyone. This means that punishment should be oriented towards deterring individuals and others from committing crime, rather than wreaking vengeance.

It was felt that prevention of crime was more important than the punishment itself. To this end it was important to make sure that everyone knew the laws. Human beings were seen as essentially rational. For punishment to work in a deterrent sense, it needed to be rationally applied (rather than be seen as draconian or unfair). It also needed to be applied in a systematic manner; one that was not subject to the individual whim (including personal granting of mercy) of the judiciary. Further, the deterrent effect of punishment would only be attainable if there was a certainty of punishment, which in turn could be provided only by the establishment of a professionalised police and judicial system.

Ethically, the utilitarian principle demands that the punishment should fit the crime. Hence, the use of torture and the death penalty was condemned insofar as these represented gross violations of individual rights and were disproportionate to the offences actually committed by offenders. Alternatively, incarceration was viewed as a form of punishment that would be particularly effective given the goals of punishment in the classical framework. As Beccaria (1767: 43) put it:

The end of punishment, therefore, is no other, than to prevent the criminal from doing further injury to society, and to prevent others from committing the like offence. Such punishments, therefore, and such a mode of inflicting them, ought to be chosen, as will make the strongest and most lasting impression on the minds of others, with the least torment to the body of the criminal.

Such an approach necessarily was founded upon a heightened importance attached to formal law, which should set out clearly the range of penalties pertaining to particular kinds of infringements. Judicial discretion should be limited to the area of deciding the 'facts' of the case; it should not extend to selection of penalty once guilt had been ascertained.

The classical view was further developed in the writings of Bentham. Likewise, seeing human beings and society within a framework of utilitarianism, Bentham argued that all behaviour is reducible to that of seeking pleasure and avoiding pain. Criminal behaviour, in particular, was also seen as reflecting this universal tendency or generalised pleasure–pain principle (see Gottfredson & Hirschi 1990).

Given that human beings were seen as having free will, and having equal capacity to reason, the central question for criminal justice revolved around how to make crime painful and how to reduce the rewards for criminal behaviour. The criminal law reflects a social contract between individuals and the state, a contract that is based upon a rational exchange of rights and obligations. Enforcement of the criminal law should be based on making adherence the most rational thing to do, in the light of the fact that violation would almost certainly mean the experience of negative sanctions. In a nutshell, punishment should offer more pain than the transgression of the law is worth.

To commit or not commit a crime was thus seen as a matter of free choice. Self-interest dictated, however, that if punishment outweighed the potential gain, then crime itself would be the result of either irrational or bad choices. Those who did commit a crime should be punished because the responsibility for doing so in the first place ultimately rests in their own hands.

Although cogent in abstract principle, classical thinking met considerable challenges when put into practice. These came from three directions. The first challenge was to make such general principles serve the interests of justice and equality when faced with a specific defendant in court. Some defendants clearly did not conform to the abstract concept of being rational and equal. Questions could be raised about the rationality of children and people with mental illness, for example. To cope with the reality of life in court, reforms took place (sometimes known as the 'neoclassical' reforms). These developed rules to cope with extenuating circumstances where individuals could be deemed not to be totally responsible for their actions.

The second challenge came from the growing bureaucratisation of the state. As capitalism grew, so did the need for a coordinating bureaucracy to ensure the smooth running of commerce. The state fulfilled such a role. The courts, as part of the state, had to fulfil the bureaucratic criterion of efficiency as much as those of justice and fairness. Where the criteria of efficiency and justice were incompatible, conflict resulted. Changes to the state that result from the demands of bureaucracy have been labelled 'corporatisation', where procedures are put in place to increase efficiency, rather than to emphasise qualities such as justice.

The third challenge to classicism came from vested interests. Those in positions of power viewed classicism as a challenge to their entrenched authority, which they wielded through considerable discretion in application of the law in practice. Codification of legal principles therefore threatened the autonomy of the aristocracy, who naturally resisted such changes. The system that resulted, particularly in the UK and Australia, represents a hybrid of classical and pre-classical models.

CONTEMPORARY EXAMPLES

The classical perspective is reflected in many aspects of the contemporary criminal justice system, despite the three challenges outlined above. Classical thinking is evident in legal doctrine that emphasises conscious intent or choice (e.g., the notion of *mens rea* or the guilty mind) in both sentencing principles (e.g., the idea of culpability or responsibility) and the structure of punishment (e.g., gradation of penalties according to seriousness of offence).

Philosophically, the classical view sees its modern counterpart in the supporters of a 'just deserts' approach to sentencing. In this perspective, four basic principles are proposed (see Pettit & Braithwaite 1993):

1 No one other than a person found to be guilty of a crime must be punished for it.
2 Anyone found to be guilty of a crime must be punished for that crime.
3 Punishment must not be more than of a degree commensurate with, or proportional to, the nature or gravity of the offence and culpability of the criminal.
4 Punishment must not be less than of a degree commensurate with, or proportional to, the nature or gravity of the offence and culpability of the criminal.

Such principles clearly rest on a classical foundation. They encapsulate notions of free will and rationality, as well as proportionality and equality. As we have said, these notions form part of the 'just deserts' understanding of criminal behaviour, and seek to focus on the offence not the offender; to deter the offender from reoffending according to the pleasure–pain principle; and to ensure that justice is served by equal punishment for the same crime. 'Just deserts' philosophy eschews individual discretion and rehabilitation as aims of the justice system. Justice must be done (i.e., proportional punishment must be meted out) and must be seen to be done (i.e., there should be no exceptions).

The 'just deserts' model has formed the basis for much sentencing reform within Australia. The focus of these reforms has been to rationalise the sentencing structure by specifying more clearly the appropriate penalty for the offence. In reality this has been seen to reduce the discretion of the judiciary by controlling penalties more closely in legislation, dictating length of sentence (or more accurately period of incarceration), and removing or reducing parole and other periods of non-incarceration. However, it should be noted that maximum penalties may also have been reduced, so the actual term served more closely reflects the original sentence handed down by the judiciary, and the sentence provided for in legislation. The aim is not necessarily to increase penalties (although this may in fact be what happens); rather, the aim is for the penalty to be reflective of the offence and to be administered without favouring one individual over another.

Such sentencing reforms revisit many of the debates that surround application of classical principles. In particular, debates concern the fairness of a system that has curtailed considerations of extenuating circumstances of the offender and reduced judicial discretion to a large degree. Those who argue for the need to rehabilitate the offender are particularly troubled by the change in legislation, with rehabilitation being irrelevant to both classical and 'just deserts' thinking.

It is perhaps misleading, however, to focus on sentencing as the primary concern of classical theory. Classical theorists were equally concerned with codifying and simplifying the law so that it was easily understood by the majority of people. Both these aims have had limited success. For example, codification—the passing of legislation that states exactly what constitutes an offence—has not occurred in all states in Australia. Victoria, New South Wales, and South Australia do not have criminal codes. This means that a number of offences, such as manslaughter, are not clearly defined in law but rely on common law judgements.

Simplification of law to make it open and accessible has faced similar obstacles to codification. Although there have been some attempts to simplify law, and make it accessible to all, many aspects of law remain obscure and impenetrable to the majority. Furthermore, legal expenses often prove prohibitive to all but the wealthy when it comes to pursuing justice through law. To some extent, though, there have been advances in making the law accessible to the general populace. The provision of legal aid, the Community Legal Centre movement, and the provision of small claims courts and tribunals throughout Australia can be seen to have at least some origin in these concerns of the classical perspective.

CRITIQUE

The limitations of classical theory have been signalled throughout the chapter. Here they will be summarised for clarity. Concerns with classical theory can be broken down into two groups; namely, problems with fairness in the case of individuals, and neglect of inequalities in the broader social structure (see Young 1981; Taylor et al. 1973).

The problem of fairness in individual cases formed an early critique of classical theory and led to the first wave of neoclassical reforms. Despite such reforms, the problem still remains where a system focuses on the offence and not the offender, coupled with principles of equality and fairness when responding to such criminal behaviour. People are not endowed with equal capacity to reason (e.g., children and people with intellectual disability or mental illness). The decision to offend may or may not be the result of an irrational choice, and the theory gives no insight into how to deal with cases where offending results from an incapacity of reason.

The second critique follows from the first and is concerned with the classical concept of rationality. If offending results from a temporary irrationality, how is it that the distribution of crime (as measured by official statistics) is not spread equally through the social structure? Such measures place the bulk of offending among those with low incomes. The findings suggest that for some people offending may be entirely rational in a manner that is not amenable to the deterrence resulting from punishment. In a world of deep social inequalities, universal equality cannot be realised by treating everyone equally before the law. Rational choice may lead some to offend precisely because of social inequalities. Equality before the law masks this reality.

On a broader level, it has long been recognised that there are clear differences between formal law (that which is written) and substantive law (that which happens in practice). The way law was written tended to assist some individuals who understood the law and knew how to exploit it, while disadvantaging others who did not have the same access to lawyers nor understand the way law works in practice. It is a common complaint that a powerful individual or organisation appears able to avoid the 'spirit' of the law, while complying with the 'letter' of the law.

The legal process is itself influenced by the broader social inequalities. Some people are more equal than others, and this in turn affects the legal process. The wealthy have access to legal advice that in turn affects how they are dealt with by the justice system. Furthermore, punishments may be proportional to crime, but will be experienced in markedly different ways—the rich may retain income and wealth, while the poor lose out on income and future work opportunities.

Despite these problems, classical theory had a real and positive effect on the justice system. It did promote a more open, systematic system of justice when compared to the previous system based on the arbitrary whim of the aristocracy. Classical principles argue for the rights of an individual within the system, and place limits on judicial discretion. Finally, the theory espouses a humanitarian approach to punishment when compared to the barbaric practices of the previous era. For example, classical theorists such as Beccaria argued against capital punishment, which was very much a radical proposition for the era.

CONCLUSION

Classical theory was developed at a time of great social change, namely the transition from feudalism to capitalism. Just as that transition challenged the pre-eminence of the aristocracy in economic matters, so classicism challenged the discretion of the aristocracy in matters of crime and justice. Classical theory sought to promote the rights of individuals as equal and rational. According to this perspective, people are inherently self-seeking and endowed with free will. This free will, coupled with a rational system of laws that deters individuals from offending, will ensure few have the motivation to offend. Under this system punishment will be meted out without reference to whom the offender is, in a manner that ensures the pain of punishment outweighs the gain from the offence.

Classical thinking had a profound effect on the justice system, and can be seen particularly clearly in debates in the 1980s and 1990s concerning 'just deserts' principles in sentencing. However, the focus on the offence rather than the offender has problems where individuals lack the capacity for reason, or where offending can be seen to reflect the wider inequalities in society. Classical theory can have the effect of masking the reality of these broader inequalities in the social structure, and in this way entrench such equalities through a pretence of equal access to justice through the legal system.

No system has ever reflected the total demands of the classical system. In Australia, the justice system can be seen as only a partial reflection of the classical model, while retaining large areas of pre-classical processes and procedures, such as case law, in which the law is made not by the parliament but by the judiciary. Even where classical principles hold in practice, there have been continuing neoclassical revisions (i.e., acknowledgement of individual differences).

The classical thinkers initiated a period of lasting debate and controversy over how we should understand crime and criminal behaviour. Although ostensibly focused on the offence and not the offender, the very process of raising issues concerning law and offending inexorably leads to closer scrutiny of the reasons for offending. It is the reasons for offending that form the basis of the theories in the next chapter, namely the positivist perspective.

FURTHER READING

Beccaria, C. (1767) *An Essay on Crimes and Punishment*, J. Almon, London.

Fine, B. (1984) *Democracy and the Rule of Law: Liberal Ideals and Marxist Critiques*, Pluto, London.

Gottfredson, M. & Hirschi, T. (1990) *A General Theory of Crime*, Stanford University Press, Stanford.

Kelly, J. (1992) *A Short History of Western Legal Theory*, Clarendon Press, Oxford.

Taylor, I., Walton, P. & Young, J. (1973) *The New Criminology*, Routledge and Kegan Paul, London.

Young, J. (1981) 'Thinking Seriously About Crime: Some Models of Criminology', in M. Fitzgerald, G. McLennon & J. Pawson (eds) *Crime and Society: Readings in History and Theory*, Routledge and Kegan Paul and the Open University, London.

CHAPTER 3

Biological and Psychological Positivism

INTRODUCTION

This chapter discusses positivism as a central theoretical and methodological approach in the history and contemporary practice of criminology. As will be seen, the development of positivistic perspectives constituted a major break with the classical tradition that saw crime as primarily a matter of individual choice. For the positivists, crime is explained by reference to forces and factors outside the decision-making ability of the individual. Thus, the classical and the positivist viewpoints are often seen as being directly counterposed.

The rise of positivism represents a shift from what was seen as armchair theorising or philosophising to a more rigorous, hands-on, scientific enterprise. The chapter explores the origins of the 'science' of criminology, and discusses two major approaches within positivism: the biological and the psychological. Central to each of these perspectives is the idea that crime can best be explained by examining individual differences between people, and by demonstrating how these differences are, in turn, linked to certain biological and/or psychological factors that predispose certain people towards criminal behaviour.

SOCIAL CONTEXT

Positivism as a perspective is associated with a very different view of society and human nature from that expressed in classical criminological theory. It emerged in the nineteenth century, a period of further consolidation of capitalism and the capitalist mode of production in Europe. This was a period that witnessed major technological developments and the entrenchment of mass production (rather than agricultural production or merchant trading) as the dominant form of production and source of profit.

The nineteenth century saw the further concentration of peasants and villagers into large cities, the creation and expansion of the factory system, the introduction of new production technologies and sources of energy (such as the steam engine), and expanded communication and transport networks (e.g., extensive railroad and highway construction). Changes in basic production techniques and relations, and the flow of 'free labour' into employment in the industrial sphere, saw the emergence of a new social class—the working class or proletariat.

The rise of the proletariat as a distinct and growing class was accompanied by major industrial, social, and political conflict and upheaval. The previous centuries had been marked by periodic struggles between the aristocracy and the peasantry (in the form of peasant rebellions), and between the established ruling class (the landed gentry) and the bourgeoisie (capitalists). Now the dominant class, the capitalist class, was faced with opposition from the working class over the conditions and nature of work, and in some cases over the very ownership and control of production in society.

Life was hard for the members of the working class: child labour was not unusual, and a thin line separated those who worked for a living from those who were condemned to the poorhouse. Living conditions and working conditions were harsh, dirty, and crowded. Meanwhile, the capitalists as a class were amassing huge fortunes and adopting opulent lifestyles. The contrast in circumstances and opportunities was stark.

Not surprisingly, the nineteenth century was also a time when the working class began to organise itself industrially, politically, and, in some cases, militarily. Although banned by law, workers began to combine into industrial organisations, the trade unions. Simultaneously, the material conditions experienced by the working class meant that there was greater analysis of, and sympathetic hearing for, the idea of forging a new type of 'classless' society. This was reflected in the proliferation of alternative working-class publications, pamphlets, and daily press, and in the formation of socialist, anarchist, and labour political organisations and parties. Over the course of the century a number of compromises were made by the ruling capitalist class. These included, for example, the legal recognition of industrial unions, and the extension of the vote to male members of the working class.

The nineteenth century in Europe was also a time of new thinking about the nature of human beings, and of society generally. The European powers had been involved in carving up the world's resources for several centuries—from Latin America to Africa, the Indian sub-continent to Asia, the Europeans had been extracting resources and exploiting the labour of indigenous people since the 'voyages of discovery' in the fifteenth century. This was justified initially by the simple expedient that 'might makes right'. However, the justification became more sophisticated with the advent of theories of social and biological evolution.

In particular, the great leaps forward in technology and industrial development, combined with reliance on and appreciation of the importance of 'science', meant that the European nations asserted their pre-eminence in the global economic and political structure on the basis of a presumed national and biological superiority. Science and technology ensured the expansion of European influence and power into all corners of the globe. Domination was seen as a natural outcome of the fruits of a European 'civilisation' founded upon innovation, invention, and technological superiority.

Simultaneously, the work of natural scientists such as Charles Darwin, and especially his general theory of evolution (based upon notions of natural selection and competition), were (mis)appropriated to justify and explain the dominance of the white European over the rest of the world's populace. Colonialism and imperialism were seen as a consequence of the natural biological superiority of the white European. White supremacy was thus justified and intertwined with notions of a racist biological determinism, one in which white Europeans were at the top of human hierarchy.

The visible presence of class conflict and social misery in Europe, the rise of scientific interest and industrial innovation, and the idea of evolution and stages in human development were all to influence the establishment of positivism as an approach to human affairs. Positivism was founded upon the belief that society ('civilisation') is progressing ever forward, and that the social scientist can study society, provide a more accurate understanding of how society works, and ultimately provide a rational means of overcoming existing social problems and ills by using scientific methods.

Social scientists were interested in promoting a positive view of the social order, and in providing positive interventions in social life to make things better. This required systematic study of existing social problems, and the development of a wide range of techniques and strategies to deal with issues relating to schooling, poverty, and family life.

Institutionally, the development of positivism was closely associated with the rise of the **professions** during the nineteenth century. The passing of legislation in Britain that banned the use of child labour in factories, for example, was accompanied by the introduction of compulsory schooling and expanded welfare concern over the plight of the children of the poor. Under the rubric of positive reform, a wide variety of 'experts'—medical doctors, psychiatrists, health workers, teachers, criminal justice officials, and social workers—began to devise 'scientific' ways to raise children better, to professionalise parenting, to deal with personal troubles and individual deficiencies, to deal with young offenders, and, generally, to engineer wide-scale social reform.

Liberal reform rested upon the idea of progress, humanitarianism, and the active construction of a more caring and supportive society. The main tool of investigation used by professionals and reformers in fostering particular forms of social change was the scientific method. Indeed, the persuasive power of the professionals relied upon the notion that their judgements and strategies were derived from science. That is, people no longer relied upon appeals to God, revelation, faith, or opinion to devise appropriate institutional responses to social problems; rather, social change was to be managed rationally by use of the scientific criteria of logic and empirical study.

The intrinsic appeal of such an approach is understandable, especially since science and technology played a crucial role in industrial capitalism, and a high level of bureaucratisation and specialisation were a necessary part of an advanced industrial economy. The model of the natural sciences had worked well for capitalist production techniques and manufacturing processes. Now it could be put to use in the social arena as well.

The adoption of concepts and methods from the natural sciences was manifest in several overlapping ideas about the nature of society. For instance, borrowing from the biological sciences, positivist social scientists often viewed society as a type of organism. It was made up of different

components, which worked together in order to ensure the proper func-
tioning of the system as a whole. If any one of these components was or
became 'dysfunctional', then correction was required to restore the social
equilibrium. This could apply to specific institutions (e.g., school, family,
work) and to particular individuals or groups in society (e.g., the poor,
sole parents, the unemployed). Social scientists had the tasks of identifying the nature and source of dysfunctions, and attempting to devise
programmes and strategies to alleviate them.

The positivist method in doing so was guided by certain assumptions
regarding the applicability of natural science methods to the study of
society. Three premises in particular underpinned the scientific approach
as conceived by the positivists (see Taylor et al. 1973):

- Social scientists are seen to be neutral observers of the world, and their
  work is 'value-free'. This is because the world was seen to be 'out
  there', as an external reality, and the role of the scientist is merely to
  record the 'facts'.
- The key method of the positivist is to classify and quantify human
  experience and behaviours through a range of objective tests. This
  means developing various ways to measure human activity.
- As with the natural world, the social world is seen to obey general
  laws of operation. The task of the positivist is to uncover the causal
  determinants of human behaviour (i.e., to identify 'cause' and 'effect'
  relationships), and thus both to predict and to modify future behaviour
  outcomes.

The development of positivism was thus related to efforts to adopt
natural science methods and concepts in the study of society. This meant
accepting certain ideas about the human experience, and attempting to
quantify and classify this experience in the expectation that expert
intervention could forestall or rectify particular kinds of social problems.

BASIC CONCEPTS

Positivism is based on the idea of a scientific understanding of crime and
criminality (see chart 3.1). It assumes that there is a distinction between
the 'normal' and the 'deviant', and attempts to study the specific factors
that give rise to deviant or criminal behaviour.

One of the hallmarks of the positivist approach is the notion that
behaviour is **determined**; that is, the activity and behaviour of individuals

are primarily shaped by factors and forces outside the immediate control of the individual. Behaviour is a reflection of certain influences on the person, whether biological, psychological, or social in nature.

It is believed that offenders vary: **individual differences** exist between offenders, and these in turn can be measured and classified in some way. Rather than seeing people in terms of equal capacities, or equal rights, the positivist view emphasises difference, which reflects varying conditions affecting each person.

The focus of analysis therefore is on the nature and characteristics of the offender, rather than on the criminal act. Offenders can be scientifically studied, and the factors leading to their criminality can be diagnosed, classified, and ultimately treated or dealt with in some way. It is the job of the 'expert' to identify the specific conditions leading to criminality in any particular case.

CHART 3.1   Positivist Approaches

Definition of crime	*Natural* ■ violation of social consensus ■ extends beyond a legal definition ■ deviant behaviour with respect to social norms
Focus of analysis	*The offender* ■ characteristics of offender
Cause of crime	*Pathology* ■ individual deficiency ■ not a matter of individual choice
Nature of offender	*Determined and/or predisposed to certain types of behaviour* ■ biological and social conditioning and individual differences
Response to crime	*Treatment* ■ diagnosis on individual basis ■ indeterminate to fit offender
Crime prevention	*Diagnosis and classification* ■ early intervention
Operation of criminal justice system	*'Scientific' approach* ■ measurement and evaluation ■ essentially neutral

In addition to identifying the specific attributes of offenders, the positivist also sees crime and deviance as something that likewise can be studied in a scientific manner. In other words, the incidence of such behaviour is not assumed to reside only in official violations of the law. This is because the social or **moral consensus** in society (which can be described and measured independently of the law) can be violated without necessarily being detected or processed formally in the criminal justice system.

Furthermore, given that deviancy is seen to lie within the (abnormal) individual, and is not always reflected in who actually ends up in court or in the hands of the police, the extent of deviant behaviour is an open-ended empirical question. As such, it requires research into the **natural crime** that hitherto has been undetected, but that nevertheless is occurring in society. It is necessary, then, to measure the **dark figure** of unrecorded crime and deviant behaviour, through the use of techniques such as large-scale questionnaires, interviews, and various other measures.

A central proposition of positivism is that a moral consensus exists in relation to what constitutes deviant and normal behaviour. Given this, positivists generally see behavioural problems in terms of **individual pathology** or deficiency. Those who do not conform are seen as having personal difficulties related to biological, psychological, or social factors. The task of the expert is to identify these factors and to correct or fix the deficiency.

Rather than being oriented towards punishment, the positivist approach is directed towards the **treatment** of offenders. Offending behaviour is analysed in terms of factors or forces beyond the conscious control of the individual. To respond to crime therefore means to deal with the reasons that caused the offending behaviour to occur in the first place.

Since each individual offender is different from all others, treatment must be individualised. This translates at an institutional level into arguments in favour of **indeterminate sentences**; that is, the length of time in custody should not depend solely on the nature of the criminal act committed, but must take into account the diagnosis and classification of the offender (e.g., severe or not severe problem, dangerous or not dangerous), and the type of treatment appropriate to the specific individual.

HISTORICAL DEVELOPMENT

The origins of positivist perspectives in criminology lie in two inter-related developments in the latter part of the nineteenth century. One strand of scientific research attempted to provide biological explanations for criminal behaviour; the other focused on psychological factors associated with criminality.

Biological positivism

Biological positivism was first popularised through the work of Lombroso (1911; see also Taylor et al. 1973). Borrowing heavily from evolutionary theories, Lombroso attempted to distinguish different types of human individuals, and to classify them on the basis of racial and biological difference. In a form of 'criminal anthropology', the argument here was that a general theory of crime can be developed on the basis of measurable physical differences between the criminal and the non-criminal. Specifically, Lombroso wanted to establish a link between criminality, and the assumption that individuals exhibit particular traits that roughly correspond to the various stages of human evolution.

For Lombroso, the criminal was born, not made. The idea of a 'born criminal' reflected the notion that crime is the result of something essential to the nature of the individual criminal. In the early formulations of this view, discussion focused on the concept of the 'atavistic criminal'; that is, a person who was biologically inferior in that they represented a reversion to an earlier human evolutionary period. To put it in crude terms, the atavistic criminal was, developmentally, closer to an ape than contemporary human beings. Such a person could be identified through a series of physical stigmata, including abnormal dentition (protruding teeth), asymmetric face, large ears, supernumerary fingers and toes, eye defects, and even tattoos.

Lombroso later modified his views somewhat, although the element of biological determinism remained. For example, he developed a typology of criminals that divided the population into the 'epileptic criminal', the 'insane criminal', the 'occasional criminal', and so on. In explaining female delinquency and criminality, the argument was put forward that, due to the essential nature of the female sex (which was seen as passive), the female offender in fact was biologically more like a man than a woman.

The emphasis on biological factors in explanations of crime was reflected in a number of subsequent studies. Indeed, the search for a single physiological cause of criminality has persisted to this day. Certainly the 'science' of phrenology was popular in criminology for a number of years around the beginning of the twentieth century. This doctrine assumes that the shape and size of the skull correspond to the functions and ability of the brain. A study undertaken in 1912 at the University of Melbourne provides an illustration of this kind of research (Brown & Hogg 1992). The study was conducted on 355 male inmates of Pentridge prison. The skulls of the prisoners were examined and estimates of the cubic capacity of their brains were made in an attempt to correlate the size of skull to intelligence. It was concluded that cattle stealers had the lowest brain capacity, and that forgers and embezzlers had the highest.

Attempts to measure intelligence, and to argue that criminals were innately less intelligent than the general population, were also popular. In 1913, for example, Charles Goring published the results of his work, which involved examining some 3000 convicts. He concluded that people with criminal tendencies were endowed with less intelligence and were of a smaller stature than other people. To measure intelligence, he simply talked to people and decided for himself whether or not they were intelligent.

Another type of study is that which looks to physiology or body structure as a key determinant of criminal behaviour. In the 1940s William Sheldon (1940) proposed a theory based on body build (somatotype). He wished to establish a link between different body types and criminality. According to Sheldon, human body types can be classed into three broad categories: endomorphic (soft and round), mesomorphic (muscular and strong), and ectomorphic (thin and fragile). Each body type was associated with a particular temperament: endomorphic (relaxed, sociable, and fond of eating), mesomorphic (energetic, courageous, and assertive) and ectomorphic (brainy, artistic, and introverted). It was further argued that mesomorphs were most likely to become criminals. In other words, there was a positive correlation between body type and criminal activity.

As a final example of biological explanation, we turn to research that examined genetic factors (see Taylor et al. 1973). According to the XYY chromosome theory, criminality is related to a deviant genetic make-up. The normal female chromosomal complement is XX; the normal male composition is XY. However, an XYY combination was also discovered. It was held that those who had this kind of chromosomal complement were far more predisposed to criminal activity, due to their 'abnormal' height and mental structures. Fundamentally, a central problem nevertheless remained—that is, how genetic differences actually translate into behavioural traits.

Biological explanations of the kind considered above tend to be fairly pessimistic about positive actions to prevent or deal with crime. This is because crime is seen to be the result of something **essential to the nature of the individual**. Thus, we are born with certain biological attributes that we cannot change, but that may lock some of us into a life of crime and antisocial behaviour.

Psychological positivism

Psychological positivism had different historical origins and a different orientation towards the offender and criminal activity. In this instance, crime was seen as the result of externally caused biological problems (e.g., war injury) or internal psychological factors (e.g., mental illness) that were treatable. The criminal was made, not born. And the task of the criminal justice system was to understand the underlying causes of criminality, and to find the appropriate treatment strategy.

This strand of positivism emerged in England from within the criminal justice institutions themselves (see Garland 1988). Doctors and psychiatrists who worked within the medico-legal framework, and who spent most of their working life with inmates, became ever more sophisticated in their classification and diagnosis of offenders. As practitioners within the criminal justice establishment, they had daily contact with a wide variety of 'subjects'. They discovered that there were major differences between individual offenders and, furthermore, that there was a whole range of offenders who did not seem entirely responsible for their actions.

Given their medical background, it is not surprising that these practitioners saw the issue as one of pathology. If offenders were deemed to be 'sick' in some way, then the obvious solution to crime was to find some way to 'cure' them. Thus, an offender might exhibit the conditions of criminality, but these conditions could be dealt with. This could be accomplished by scientific diagnosis, classification of the condition or illness, and devising the appropriate treatment to fit the condition of each offender.

Such ideas and reasoning were reinforced by the experiences of medical practitioners in treating soldiers who returned from the battle fronts of World War I. Many of these men were shell-shocked and physically disabled. They presented a number of pathological tendencies, ranging from varying forms of mental illness through to antisocial behaviour. Deviancy in this case was clearly related to trauma of some kind. The problem was not with the innate characteristics of the individual, but with the consequences and impact of the trauma on the individual.

Broadly speaking, psychological theories tended to centre attention on the processes of the mind in explanations of criminal behaviour (see Feldman 1993). They included several kinds of perspectives:

- Some made reference to psychoanalytic theory, such as analysis of the conscious and unconscious, and how basic emotional and developmental processes affect behaviour.
- Some focused on personality traits, such as studies of aggression and passivity, and the psychological structure of personality as these related to behaviour.
- Some dealt with psychiatric issues from the point of view of childhood experiences, such as analysis that saw deprivation of universal needs during childhood as leading to the formation of certain personality patterns in later life.

CONTEMPORARY EXAMPLES

Two major strands can be found in contemporary examples of biological and psychological positivism. First is the field that can be seen as a contemporary variant of early psychiatric interest in criminality, a field now encompassing both forensic psychiatry and forensic psychology. Leading theorists in this field are most often also practising forensic psychologists or psychiatrists. Second are theories that have, to a greater or lesser degree, taken a more academic turn. As suggested in the previous section, there is a wide range of such theories, all of which focus on the characteristics of offenders, but arguably the two most prominent examples are 'control theory' and 'bio-social' explanations, which, as the name suggests, link biological and psychological factors in explaining criminal behaviour.

The predominant concern of forensic psychologists and forensic psychiatrists is in the provision of services to the criminal justice system. Alongside this practical role they have developed a range of theories, not only to assist rehabilitation but also to interpret culpability of the offender to the court, as well as predict possible reoffending. This knowledge is required within different aspects of the criminal justice system. In the courts the role of forensic psychologists or psychiatrists is to provide pre-sentence reports and act as expert witnesses. In the corrections area their role is to manage and treat offenders, as well as provide expert advice concerning parole decisions. Perhaps forensic psychology's most contentious application is in police investigations. Here practitioners undertake 'criminal profiling', which, it is claimed, can pinpoint the personality profile of an 'at large' offender as part of the investigation process, or in another variant identify the likely area where the offender lives.

Control theory can be seen as an extension of psychodynamic theories that emanated from Freud. Psychodynamic theories have a common link in that a central concern is how individuals learn self-control. As with Freud, the underlying assumption of these theories is that, left to our own devices and desires, humans are necessarily impulsive and antisocial. We only become social by repressing basic desires. According to Hirschi (1969) and later Gottfredson and Hirschi (1990), the basic question criminologists need to answer is not 'Why do some people offend?' but 'Why do most people not offend?' To put it simply, these theorists argue that individuals learn not to offend through developing self-control. By extension, those who do offend lack self-control. Gottfredson and Hirschi see self-control as a single psychological construct or personal attribute. This single construct is made up of several elements, namely:

- impulsivity, or an inability to defer gratification
- lack of perseverance
- preference for risky behaviour
- preference for physical, as opposed to mental, activity
- self-centredness
- low threshold for frustration.

Gottfredson and Hirschi argue that child-rearing is critical to the development of self-control, a focus that draws inspiration from the early work of Glueck and Glueck (1960). Poor child-rearing practices, such as lack of supervision (particularly by the mother) and poor attachment to the father, lead to low self-control and higher rates of criminal offending. The theory also asserts that opportunity for offending is important, but only when combined with low social control. Adequately socialised individuals would not succumb to criminal opportunity. It is interesting to note that they see their theory applies as much to white-collar crime as to street offending, since a manager who embezzles company funds has the same problem of low self-control as does a teen-ager caught shoplifting.

Psychological approaches also include those that focus on 'personality types' (see Farrington 1996a), and that present typologies of abnormalities in the psychological structure of individuals (for example 'over aggressive', 'highly strung'). Such approaches often see the formation of particular personality types as linked to certain biological predispositions as well as developmental experiences.

The best known of the **bio–social explanations** is that provided by Eysenck (1984). He argued that behaviour could be explained by a combination of psychological and environmental influences. Human beings are not totally determined by their biology, but nor are they unaffected by their social circumstances. Behaviour, and in particular criminal behaviour, can be explained in terms of two key variables:

- **The differential ability to be conditioned**—This referred to the way in which genetic inheritance can affect one's ability to be conditioned. That is, the sensitivity of the autonomic nervous system that you have genetically inherited will determine whether you are an extrovert or introvert, and this in turn influences how well you are able to be conditioned in society.
- **The differential quality of conditioning**—This referred to the effectiveness and efficiency of the family in using appropriate conditioning techniques. That is, the content and method of child-rearing will have an impact upon the child's subsequent behaviour.

The argument, then, is that biological potentials (such as the ability to be conditioned or socialised) are set through inheritance. These interact with environmental potentials (shaped by parenting practices), and together these factors determine the overall propensity of individuals to commit crime.

Today, the connection between biological and social environmental influences is seen in very sophisticated terms. It is a case of 'nature' plus 'nurture', rather than one or the other as the sole—or even dominant—factor in producing certain types of behaviour. It is generally argued that human beings have a 'conditional free will', and individuals can choose within a set, yet to some degree changeable, range of possibilities (Fishbein 1990). Human behaviour thus contains a biological and a social element (see, for example, Moffitt 1996).

Present-day positivists define and identify criminality in a manner geared to establishing those people who are 'at risk' of certain behaviour. There is no longer a one-to-one link between crime and behaviour; rather, certain groups are seen to be more predisposed to crime than others because of biological and social environmental factors. Individuals are not born criminal, but are exposed to baseline biological and psychological processes that shape their personality in childhood. Once the child is introduced to the school, the personality manifests itself in certain types of behaviour. The social influences encountered in the school environment may then further contribute to antisocial behaviour, depending upon initial personality formation.

Contemporary positivists see a dynamic relationship between biological factors (inherited predisposition) and environmental factors (external inputs that modify behaviour). Nevertheless, within this more open and less deterministic framework there has been a resurgence of interest in explanations for crime that are heavily weighted towards the biological. Recent research, for example, has examined the contributions of various factors to criminal behaviour (see Fishbein 1990):

- **Genetic contributions**—These studies have examined the effect of inheritance on criminal behaviour. Particular traits such as intellectual defects or aggression are seen as genetically given, and as being closely associated with criminal behaviour. Comparisons of identical and non-identical twins, and adoption studies to compare biological and non-biological siblings, are means by which one can test the influence of genetic inheritance.
- **Biochemical contributions**—These studies look at the impact of biochemical differences on human behavioural patterns. Hormonal activity, metabolic processes, and the influence of toxins (such as lead poisoning) are examined in terms of various behaviours such as aggression, and the overall propensity to commit crime. Another strand of research examines psychophysiological variables such as heart rate, blood pressure, brain waves, arousal, and attention levels. It is suggested here that different physiological processes have implications for neurotransmission and psychological impairment.

- **Psychopharmacological inducements**—A third area of research examines inducements such as cocaine, alcohol, amphetamines, and so on, and their effects on human behaviour, especially criminal behaviour.

In a number of these areas it is now possible to conceive of some kind of biological 'corrective' being developed to prevent criminal behaviour from occurring. This could take the form of simply removing the source of the problem (e.g., eliminating lead from one's living environment, or banning alcohol sales), or in the case of more complex responses, regulating the biochemical and physiological operations of the body through appropriate treatment measures (e.g., drugs designed to restore hormonal equilibrium or ensure a regular heart rate).

Whether it is efforts to re-jig the biological balance (e.g., through drug therapy) or to restore a psychological norm or balance (e.g., through parenting classes), a key emphasis in positivist approaches is that of self-control. In other words, efforts will be made to reinforce external and internal regulatory measures so that individuals will conform to the conventional norms of behaviour.

CRITIQUE

Within the positivist aegis then, there exists a plethora of explanations concerning what factors predispose individuals to commit crime. However, virtually all such explanations are concerned with 'street crime', predominantly violent crime or juvenile delinquency of one type or another. The reasons behind white-collar crime and state crime are generally left untouched by positivist criminology (however, see Gottfredson & Hirschi 1990 for an exception to this).

Furthermore, much positivistic research has taken subjects from incarcerated populations, or those adjudicated as criminal by the law. This poses a problem of the conflict of definitions: the reasoning is that because criminality is the result of psychological or biological abnormality, someone who is adjudicated as criminal by the judicial process must be psychologically or biologically abnormal (Empey 1982). Thus, all incarcerated populations are, by definition, either psychologically or biologically deficient. This problem results from what is known as **circular reasoning** where A (criminality) is supposed to be caused by

B (impairment), and all those in prison are tested as impaired, and are by definition criminal. Hence impairment is assumed to cause criminality. This conclusion is false for a number of reasons; among them:

- It is not clear whether criminality causes impairment, or impairment causes criminality (problem of the direction of causality).
- It is not clear if the imprisonment was the cause of impairment (confounding variable).
- It is not clear whether those in the general population who have the same impairment also offend (i.e. are the two factors simply correlated, or is there a causal connection?).

All explanations of this type thus face considerable challenges in proving the causal connection between biological and psychological factors and criminal behaviour. These challenges concern defining what exactly is being measured (the specifics of a psychological malfunction or chemical imbalance, for example), and designing and undertaking rigorous studies where extraneous variables are excluded. That is, the study must really measure what it says it measures, and there must be no other plausible explanations for what the study found.

While the problem of circular reasoning outlined above can be eradicated through appropriate use of control groups and application of scientific method, the possibility of undertaking such experiments has considerable ethical implications and they remain rare. Those that are done face considerable difficulty in matching the variables (such as age, educational attainment, or employment status) of the control group with the experimental group. Unless these factors are carefully matched, the claims of the study can be severely compromised.

Many studies that purported to find biological or psychological reasons for offending have been discredited because of the inability to control all variables (Feldman 1993). A good example of this problem is the purported connection between violence and the genetically controlled abnormal metabolism of neurotransmitters that was reported in *New Scientist* (26 February 1994). Further research revealed that compounding environmental factors could not be ruled out, and the strength of the relationship between genetics and criminality was greatly downplayed (*New Scientist*, 25 February 1995).

Much critique of positivist theory revolves around the blurred distinction between sickness and criminality. Largely undiscussed are the underlying assumptions behind definitions of criminality or, more specifically, deviation from norms. If criminal behaviour is likened to a sickness, it must, like sickness, be undesirable and in need of eradication. There is an assumed consensus within positivism concerning what constitutes criminality and deviation from norms, without adequate discussion concerning whose norms are used as the benchmark for deviation.

The analogy with sickness brings further problems. There is a tendency within positivism to reduce the reasons for criminal behaviour to a single cause, either biological or psychological. It assumes that adult behaviour and personality are totally determined and reducible to single overarching factors (e.g., childhood experiences). This assumption ignores, or fails to acknowledge, that life is a process of continual development, renewal, change, and transformation.

This reductionism to a single cause can lead to both racist and sexist conclusions. Where offending is linked to biology, the logical extension of the line of reasoning can lead to attempts to correlate certain people (e.g., Aboriginal people, poor people) with certain 'biologically determined' traits (e.g., intelligence as measured by IQ) and so to criminal offending. Without adequate discussion of the assumptions underlying positivism, the search for the causes of criminal behaviour leads inexorably to racist and unwarranted conclusions (see, especially, Gould 1981).

Once a cause of offending has been isolated, further problems arise. The question of diagnosis, classification, and treatment of offenders becomes important. How is treatment to be administered and on what criteria? Treatment may, for example, require biological 'corrections' (e.g., chemical castration) that raise considerable implications in terms of human rights and human dignity. Even where treatment seems to be relatively benign, such as enhancing parenting skills, there still may be gross assumptions concerning what constitutes adequate parenting. Because of the intrusive nature of treatment suggested by positivist theories, both the theories themselves and the suggested treatments require close scrutiny.

With identification of a biological or psychological cause of crime, positivism suggests that early detection of criminal potential is entirely possible if not desirable. This means intrusive intervention in people's lives may take place long before any crime is committed. Such intervention may be extreme, such as sterilisation, or relatively benign, such as pre-school activities in disadvantaged areas. The intrusiveness of the technique must be weighed against the positive outcomes, with each closely analysed. Do pre-school programmes or pre-natal care really affect behaviour in adolescence and beyond? While there is some evidence that this is the case, should they be conceived of as part of a crime-reduction strategy with the stigma that entails, or are they simply a normal part of society's responsibility to its citizens? Some intrusions such as sterilisation of course should be disallowed on ethical grounds alone. Alternatively, a focus on the characteristics of an individual also may provide a ready excuse to cut government services; that is, to reduce the level of general state intervention. If violence within schools, for example, can be pin-pointed to certain individuals, governments may decide that general programmes to help disadvantaged schools are no longer necessary since the problem has been isolated to individuals and 'dealt with'.

Positivism, with its focus on the scientific method, leads to the pro-duction of knowledge that by its nature is inaccessible to the general community. Common-sense understandings of ordinary people are seen as unscientific, and therefore not valid. This reduces the accountability of such professionals, and leaves little avenue for democratic participation in policy that results from positivist research. Specialised knowledge tends to entrench power in the hands of medical or paramedical professionals and other experts.

As we have seen, it is the forensic psychiatrists and psychologists who are most likely to perform this role of the expert. Judges are uniquely sensitive to the concerns of the community regarding the possibility of releasing someone who is a danger to the public at large, and so will draw on this expertise. However, there remain major problems in predicting which person will, and which person will not, pose danger to the com-munity in the future.

The inability to predict dangerousness was dramatically illustrated in New York in the 1970s. A man by the name of Johnnie Baxtrom had been kept in prison after his release date because doctors argued he was dangerous and in need of psychiatric care. All psychiatric hospitals were full, so he remained in prison. Baxtrom challenged the constitutionality of his incarceration beyond the end of his sentence for assault. He won his case, and as a result 967 similarly incarcerated patients were released, all of whom were considered criminally insane (that is, they were considered a danger to the community). A team of researchers, led by Henry Steadman, followed up each of these people after four years in order to ascertain how many had reoffended. Only 2.7 per cent of the original 967 had behaved dangerously and were either in a correctional facility or a hospital for the criminally insane (Steadman 1973). Studies such as this pose tough questions to those who incarcerate individuals deemed to be a danger to the community beyond the term warranted by their criminal offence.

Certainly there have been improvements in the prediction of dangerousness. Forensic psychologists now estimate that they are right in their predictions of dangerousness in about 50 per cent of cases (Litwack & Schlesinger 1999). Nonetheless, significant problems remain. The first is that this percentage still remains the same as chance; that is, in one out of two cases the forensic expert will be wrong. The second is that forensic psychologists will readily agree that they are ascertaining the level of risk a particular offender poses to the community, which is separate from a prediction of actual violent behaviour occurring. This is because the context of violence is an important precursor to a violent crime occurring and it is these contextual factors that are impossible to predict. No one can tell if an aggressive person will wake up in a bad mood exactly at the same time a number of unrelated events occur (such as a chance meeting with an old enemy, losing their job, or having a car accident), events that tip them over into violent behaviour. Finally, such assessments can only be made when the person is found and assessed. In many cases what criminal authorities want is to know the dangerousness of an individual who remains at large—hence the attraction of criminal profiling. This is an entirely separate problem to that of a risk assessment on a person brought to a forensic psychologist or psychiatrist. There remains considerable debate as to the efficacy of criminal profiling. The problem of 'false positives'—bringing under suspicion people who are innocent simply because they match certain personality traits or live in a certain area—remains a major concern.

These criticisms aside, the impact of positivism has been beneficial. It did signal a shift away from hard-line classical thinking concerning individual responsibility. People can act for reasons that are outside their own control, and such factors may mitigate their responsibility for their criminal behaviour. Further, punishment must fail if it does not take account of factors that are beyond the control of an individual's free will.

CONCLUSION

Positivism emerged within a specific historical context that promoted the virtues of scientific reasoning over the philosophical approach championed by the classical thinkers. It was assumed that discoveries about the natural world, and natural laws, would find a counterpart within human behaviour, both individual and social. The emphasis of positivism is on the scientist as neutral observer with the task of uncovering natural laws that regulate human behaviour, including criminal offending. Specific methods, such as experimentation and survey design, are seen to be able to reveal specific causes of criminal behaviour within the individual, causes that are either biologically or psychologically determined. Once discovered, reduction of offending is seen as possible through treatment programmes aimed at ameliorating or eliminating causal agents. Sentencing should therefore be aimed at rehabilitation rather than deterrence. Further extension of investigation into individuals who are 'at risk' of offending may be seen as preferable, since offences may be prevented before they even occur.

Criticisms of positivism centre on the characterisation of criminal offending as akin to a sickness. While criminal behaviour may well be defined as deviation from society's norms, such norms are determined socially, not biologically. Further, society's norms may in fact be the norms of the dominant majority, which marginalise the norms of other social groups within society. In this way positivist research may entrench the current social order by accepting dominant understandings of 'normal' and 'deviant'. Further, positivism has a tendency to reduce the complexities of human behaviour to single identifiable causes, and to prescribe treatments that are intrusive, and in some cases unethical.

Recent writing within positivism has tended to move away from overarching generalisations concerning human behaviour (Moffitt 1996). Fishbein (1990) serves as a good example of a theorist who seeks to establish the place of biological and psychological factors among others as the reasons behind criminal offending. She accepts, for example, the very real place of sociological factors behind offending. It is to these factors that we now turn.

FURTHER READING

Eysenck, H. (1984) 'Crime and Personality', in D. Muller, D. Blackmann & A. Chapmann (eds) *Psychology and Law*, John Wiley and Sons, New York.

Feldman, P. (1993) *The Psychology of Crime*, Cambridge University Press, Cambridge.

Fishbein, D. (1990) 'Biological Perspectives in Criminology', *Criminology*, 28(1): 27–72.

Garland, D. (1988) 'British Criminology before 1935', *British Journal of Criminology*, 28(2): 1–16.

Lombroso, C. (1911) *Crime: Its Causes and Remedies*, Little, Brown, Boston.

Moffitt, T. (1996) 'The Neuropsychology of Conduct Disorder', in P. Cordella & L. Siegel (eds) *Readings in Contemporary Criminological Theory*, Northeastern University Press, Boston.

CHAPTER 4

Strain Theory

INTRODUCTION

This chapter provides an overview of various types of strain theory, and includes a discussion of subcultures and the ways in which deviant or criminal behaviour is learned in interaction with others. Rather than focusing on factors relating to the individual, these types of theories are sociological in nature. That is, they point to aspects of social structure and social learning that contribute to the creation of criminal behaviour and attitudes.

While sharing many of the philosophical and political features of biological and psychological positivism, sociological approaches such as strain theory view crime as manifestations of social pathology, rather than individual pathology. For example, tension or strains are seen to be generated by society itself; they do not reside within the individual (as in the case, for example, of a person feeling strained or pressured by circumstance). The chapter discusses the two main wings of strain theory—those that place emphasis on 'opportunity structures', and those that speak about the learning of particular norms, values, and subcultural attributes.

SOCIAL CONTEXT

The social context in which strain theory emerged and developed can be divided into three key periods. The first period was from the middle of the nineteenth century to the beginning of the twentieth, which saw the rise of sociology as an academic discipline. As with comparable social sciences (such as psychology), it was felt that one could apply the approaches and concepts of the natural sciences to the study of society. In particular, society itself could be studied as if it were external to the observer. As with positivism in general, most sociology presumed that there existed a consensus of values and norms across society. As such, it was supportive of the status quo. The role of the social scientist was to intervene in shaping the direction of social development by providing positive solutions to identified social problems.

The sociological method adopted at this time was one that constructed broad categorisations of different types of societies (e.g., pre-industrial, industrial), and that attempted to show how the structure of a society moulds and shapes individual behaviour. Criminal behaviour, in particular, was seen as a manifestation of a social pathology—the outcome of something wrong in the structures and values of the society generally. Thus, if we are to respond adequately to the incidence of crime, we must go beyond measures that see it as being simply the result of individual malaise. Some type of institutional reform would be necessary if the problem were particularly acute.

The second key period in the development of strain theory was the early 1920s through to World War II. The industrial revolution had fostered the development of the professions (including sociology) and was linked to the idea of expert or technical solutions to problems such as poverty and crime. By the early decades of the twentieth century, the conceptual tools of sociology were being turned to examine problems with a specifically modern character.

In 1917 the Russian Revolution occurred, with long and lasting impact on developments in the West. A series of class struggles and armed conflict occurred throughout Europe in the early 1920s, and the example of a successful workers' revolution was creating alarm in ruling circles in the advanced capitalist countries. Within Russia itself, many people were displaced from their former positions and residences, and later, under the rule of Stalin, a series of purges was carried out that cost millions of lives.

Meanwhile, two further developments were accelerating the tendency towards crisis and war in Europe. On the one hand, one legacy of World War I was a German nation that had suffered impoverishment and deep loss of dignity as a result of the actions of the victors. As in Spain in the 1930s, and later in Italy, there also arose a strong fascist movement in Germany by the early 1930s. Simultaneously, from 1929 the Great Depression was having a devastating impact on workers and farmers in Europe, North America, and elsewhere.

The developments in Europe and the newly constructed Soviet Union, combined with the dramatic changes in economic fortunes, were to lead to mass movements of people. Events such as the counter-revolutionary war in Russia, the purge of selected classes and social groups across different political systems (e.g., attacks on Jews in Nazi Germany, forced collectivisation of farmers in Russia), and the diffi-culties of economic survival under rampant inflation and high levels of unemployment created large numbers of war, political, and economic refugees in Europe. This led to wide-scale migration to countries such as the USA and Canada, as well as Australia and New Zealand.

A crucial question emerged within the ranks of those who were studying crime as a social phenomenon: How did the successive waves of immigration impact upon crime rates? Furthermore, the issues of unemployment and poverty were put on the agenda in a more systematic and theoretically informed manner by sociologists. These issues were particularly of interest to researchers in the USA. While such people were unlikely to suggest a Russian-style revolution as an appropriate or desirable response to the depression in the heartland of world capitalism, clear links were now being drawn between unemployment and crime. The economic position of the individual in society was now seen as an important factor in the commission of crime.

The third period of note with respect to the development of strain theory was the post-war period of the late 1940s and into the 1950s. By this time, many of the advanced capitalist countries had entered a long boom period of economic growth. People in these countries were generally optimistic about the future, living standards were rising steadily, and capitalism was indeed appearing, for many, to be the 'best of all possible worlds'. The problem, however, was how to explain persistent crime rates even in the face of apparently good general economic and social conditions. The answer, here, was to examine more closely the dis-tribution of opportunities in society, and also the ways in which people interact with and learn from each other. As with the general orientation of strain theory, the intellectual task was to formulate concepts that would best express the social nature of crime.

BASIC CONCEPTS

The starting point for strain theory is the notion that crime is essentially a social phenomenon (see chart 4.1). It is based upon a sociological understanding of individual and group behaviour—one that sees specific activity such as crime as somehow being related to and shaped by wider social processes and structures.

CHART 4.1   Strain Theory

Definition of crime	■ natural ■ violation of consensus
Focus of analysis	■ structure of opportunities ■ nature of social learning ■ youth subcultures
Cause of crime	■ social strain, viz opportunity structure ■ learned behaviour
Nature of offender	■ determined (by) social pathology
Response to crime	■ provide an opportunity to reduce strain, resocialise offender
Crime prevention	■ expanding opportunity and fostering healthy peer-group activity
Operation of criminal justice system	■ essentially neutral ■ individual rehabilitation combined with social programmes

Rather than looking at aspects of personal psychology or individual biological traits, strain theory argues that crime is socially induced. Thus, a 'criminal' or 'deviant' is a product of a specific kind of social order. In essence, the activities and values of the offender are **determined** by wider societal forces and factors, and they have few conscious choices regarding their available social options.

Crime tends to be defined in conventional terms. However, rather than viewing it as solely the behaviour that formally violates the legal code (as evidenced by court conviction records), this approach sees crime and deviancy in wider terms. In particular, crime is seen as any **violation of the general consensus** of values and norms in society. Furthermore, given this definition, and given the high levels of activity that go undetected by the formal criminal justice system, it is important to measure **natural crime** by alternative means, such as victim surveys and self-report studies.

The basic proposition of strain theory is that crime is due to social disjuncture or social processes that represent a **social strain** within a society. The strains or sources of tensions are social, not individual in nature. That is, the cause of crime is located in social structures and/or value systems that in some way are socially pathological. It is this wider **social pathology** that best explains crime as a social problem.

The main focus of analysis in strain theory is on strains associated with 'structural opportunities' and 'cultural processes'. The cause of crime is often seen to lie in inadequate or inappropriate means or **opportunities** to achieve certain goals relative to other people in society. Hence this aspect or type of strain theory is sometimes referred to as 'opportunity theory'. It is argued that restricted or blocked opportunities can lead some people to pursue alternative means, including criminal avenues, to gain desired social goods.

A second broad approach examines how, through various social circumstances, people associate with others who share their **cultural understandings** regarding acceptable and unacceptable behaviour. The emphasis in this kind of approach is on how criminal behaviour is learned in social situations. Analysis is undertaken of particular subcultures and how norms and values are transmitted from one person to another. This type of analysis is sometimes called 'social learning theory' or 'subcultural theory'.

The response to crime according to strain theories is to **enhance opportunities** in order to reduce social strain. This can take the form of educational programmes, employment projects, and leisure and recreation outlets for particularly 'disadvantaged' individuals and groups. A related crime-reduction strategy is to **resocialise** the offender into conventional goals and means. This may involve removing them from their previous associates in order to minimise the learning and/or affirmation of deviant norms and values. Overall, the stress is to combine **individual rehabilitation** with a series of social programmes.

From the point of view of crime prevention, strain theory leans towards measures that **expand educational, employment, and social opportunities**, and that **foster healthy peer-group activity**. The focus is on developing strategies and policies that involve some degree of institutional reform, rather than solely changing or modifying the individual in some way. Since deviance or criminality is related to problems faced by groups of individuals in disadvantaged situations, the solution to crime must be to remedy the disadvantage as far as possible.

HISTORICAL DEVELOPMENT

Contemporary strain theories have their origins in the emergence of sociology as an academic discipline and a recognised field of intellectual endeavour. One of the central figures in this process was French sociologist Emile Durkheim, who was writing around the beginning of the twentieth century. His work was of great importance in that he consistently presented analysis of society, and of social problems, in a manner that demonstrated the close relationship between social structure (the organisation of society) and the norms and values of society (social and cultural life).

Durkheim's analysis was premised upon the notion that there are 'social facts' that can be studied and used to describe social phenomena (see Lukes 1973). These social facts are seen to be independent of the wishes or actions of individual people. While external to the individual, nevertheless a certain phenomenon has a marked impact upon their behaviour. Thus, for example, one can quantify such social facts as the distribution of population in a certain area or district, or one can ascertain the prevailing norms, rules, regulations, religious beliefs, and legal codes of a society. In either case, these kinds of phenomena represent social facts, which can be measured and which exist as independent entities in their own right.

It order to analyse a particular social phenomenon, it is necessary to acknowledge that different societies give rise to different structures, different beliefs and sentiments, and thus different behavioural patterns. In his famous study of suicide, for instance, Durkheim (1979) demonstrated empirically that suicide rates vary according to whether or not a country is predominantly Catholic or predominantly Protestant in its religious orientation. The point here is that suicide could not be explained simply or solely in terms of individualistic choices or psychological factors. It is a social phenomenon.

More generally, Durkheim employed two basic conceptual tools in analysis of society (Lukes 1973). On the one hand, it was argued that society is structured around a particular kind of 'division of labour', with specific types of work tasks and roles. A distinction is made between mechanical solidarity and organic solidarity as indications of the division of labour. The first describes pre-industrial types of society in which individuals tend to share the same skills, work tasks, customs, beliefs, and religion. The second describes an industrial society, which is far more heterogenous in terms of wealth, ethnicity, religions, and beliefs, and which has a high level of work specialisation.

On the other hand, each society was said to be characterised by a particular form of collective conscience (or consciousness). This referred to a set of beliefs and sentiments common to a whole society, which forms a determinate system. In a nutshell, what we collectively think is greater than any one individual, and the collective conscience has the feature of shaping and regulating our behaviour as an independent, powerful external force. In a society characterised by mechanical solidarity, the emphasis tends to be on rigid conformity and cultural homogeneity. Alternatively, the organic solidarity of industrial society is one in which people are linked though law and interdependence, rather than similarity of life experience.

In applying these concepts to the specific area of criminology, Durkheim was able to argue that the nature of the society in which one lives will determine the manner in which deviants will be dealt with (see Inverarity et al. 1983). A society with mechanical solidarity tends to generate repressive justice, which reaffirms the common beliefs and values by distancing the deviant from the wider collectivity. Conversely, a society with organic solidarity tends to generate restitutive sanctions, which aim to restore the social disruption by reintegrating the deviant back into the network of interdependencies.

Fundamentally, the organisation of society, as shaped by its division of labour and its collective conscience, determines the nature of crime and the regulation of criminal behaviour. Within differently organised societies, there exists a certain amount of crime since, Durkheim argued, crime is a normal and integral part of any society. Durkheim said that where you have an unhealthy division of labour (e.g., based upon force rather than choice) or an unhealthy regulation of the collective conscience (e.g., norms not well established), there is greater likelihood of widespread crime, and the level of crime will be greater. There is another aspect of Durkheim's view that is not picked up by strain theory, but is related to the idea of the collective conscience. This is that by defining a behaviour or person as criminal, people are reassuring themselves about their own society. In a very real sense, society defines itself by what it is not—and it is this that is defined as criminal.

A normal, healthy division of labour occurs where occupational relationships are in accordance with individuals' aptitudes. In such a situation, two potential types of deviant can be identified: the biological deviant (who is impossible to predict or prevent), and the functional rebel (who acts as a constructive force for limited social change). Where there is an unhealthy or pathological division of labour, there will be conflict between the individual and the social. That is, it will be difficult to regulate the behaviour of individuals in a society under such circumstances.

Societies vary in their ability to impose social regulation, and this is due in part to the nature of the division of labour. The collective conscience may not be developed sufficiently, or may be skewed in some way, and this can affect behaviour as well. The general condition of society (not the individual) may be one where norms and values are in flux or even partially destroyed. We may thus have a situation in which shared beliefs and values have broken down, and where moral guides to and constraints on behaviour have weakened.

Applying these ideas to the specific area of crime and deviancy, it is argued that a healthy society is characterised by a collective conscience that regulates behaviour smoothly. An unhealthy society is one in which values are not well established, or where they work against the aims of integration and regulation (see Taylor et al. 1973).

According to Durkheim, individual desires are unlimited; it is the society that gives direction and a limit to desire. Durkheim drew a distinction between 'egoism' and 'anomie', both of which revolve around social norms. **Egoism** refers to the desires of the 'pre-social self', desires that society must shape and limit. Dysfunctional societies can be characterised by an overemphasis on egoism, where value is placed on the unrestricted pursuit of individual desires. Here, the norms of society itself can produce deviant behaviour. The concept of **anomie** refers to a lack of social regulation in which the unrestricted appetites of the individual conscience are no longer held in check: we have a state of normlessness in which society fails to impose norms that inhibit such behaviour. This would describe, for example, a society or community at breaking point, where rapid change has destroyed many of the values and norms.

Societies experiencing either kind of normative problem would be expected to have abnormal levels of crime.

The importance of Durkheim as a founding thinker within the strain theory tradition is that he established that crime is essentially a social phenomenon; it is inextricably related to the nature of society itself. And criminality is thus a product of a specific kind of social order.

Moreover, it was Durkheim who emphasised that crime is due to social disjuncture or social strains in a society. These are linked to both the division of labour (later seen in terms of opportunity structures) and the collective conscience (later seen in terms of cultural norms and learned behaviours).

Crime and opportunity

These themes were picked up by later theorists in several different ways. In the 1920s and 1930s, for example, Shaw and McKay (1942) explained crime in terms of social disorganisation theory. The main focus of their work was on the links between a particular kind of urban environment, and the nature and extent of crime associated with this. More specifically, the researchers were interested in undertaking a form of 'social ecology' that examined crime in terms of the changing composition and settlement patterns of the city.

Based in Chicago, Shaw and McKay were writing at a time of great change. The political turmoil and economic hardship experienced by many people in Europe translated at a practical level into mass migration to other parts of the world and, in particular, to the USA. Shaw and McKay were interested in the way in which the successive waves of immigration were linked to the incidence of crime in American cities. Accordingly, they studied the settlement patterns of migrants, noting the movement first into the spatial grid of the inner-city neighbourhoods and then into outer-city areas.

The process of settling into a new country was accompanied by high levels of chaos and tension, and whole communities were characterised as being in a constant state of change, flux, and social disorganisation. Shaw and McKay examined documents relating to the life histories of juvenile offenders in these areas. They found that crime tended to be associated with particular neighbourhoods, and that it flowed from the cyclical process of social change involving shifts in basic social organisation, towards disorganisation and reorganisation. They argued that delinquency can be viewed as part of the natural process of migrant settlement, because customary social controls that normally produce conformist behaviour are disrupted in such circumstances.

To put it differently, Shaw and McKay believed that behaviour is regulated via customary social norms and values. In a situation of high social disorganisation, characteristic of concentrated immigrant settle-ments in the inner city, young people are not subject to the same kinds of controls that customarily produced conforming behaviour in their country of origin. Furthermore, young people in these circumstances will also tend to associate with like-minded individuals who are sharing the same kind of transitional experiences. Since the neighbourhood is in a state of flux, the behaviour of such young people will tend also to include delinquent acts (see Shoemaker 1984).

While Shaw and McKay initially concentrated on the issue of a disorganised and transient population, the impact of the Great Depression prompted them to refine their analysis. They began to look beyond the link between immigration, settlement patterns, and crime. They also acknowledged the social strains caused by poverty and unemployment. Economic deprivation meant that, even where mainstream goals had been internalised, people were denied opportunities to achieve those goals. Thus a depressed and stratified economic structure could engender conditions that lead to a greater incidence of crime.

While depressed economic conditions, and overall diminished job opportunities, seem to provide a reasonable explanation for some types of criminal activity, how are we to explain the incidence of crime in periods of economic growth? This was the dilemma facing sociologists and criminologists in the 1950s.

The first two decades after World War II were characterised by low unemployment levels and high standards of living in the advanced capitalist countries. It was a time of general economic prosperity. Politically, the 1950s was stamped by the contours of the Cold War into which the two superpowers—the USA and the Soviet Union—were locked, along with their allies. This manifested itself in virulent anti-communist campaigns in the West, such as the public attacks on the left in the USA by the House Un-American Activities Committee, led by Senator Joe McCarthy, and in Australia the attempts by the Menzies government to ban the Communist Party of Australia. It was a time of general political conformity.

It was in this climate that Merton (1957) sought to offer an explanation for the continued existence of crime in the USA. In seeking to explain the prevalence of crime, he embraced the notion that crime rates are related to society's ability to establish norms that regulate the behaviour of the populace. Merton argued that crime can be understood in relation to two main variables: the **culturally defined goals** of a society; and the **institutionalised means** whereby one can attain these goals. 'Mal-integration' occurs when there is a disjuncture between the cultural goals and the institutional means.

Merton argued that all individuals basically share in the same cultural goal—the 'American Dream' of wealth, status, and success—but they have different institutional means available to them. In particular, some people experience blocked opportunities, and thus are unable to achieve their goals through normal or legitimate means.

In such circumstances, people are perceived as having the capacity to make meaningful choices as to how to negotiate their futures. That is, depending upon the opportunities available to them, people decide to accept or reject the cultural goals, and to accept or reject the institutional means to attain commonly accepted goals. The decisions one makes are determined or shaped by one's position or status in society. For example, those people at the lower end of the socio-economic ladder will experience a greater likelihood of blocked opportunities than those from better-off or wealthy families. This has an impact on behaviour.

Merton developed an abstract typology of responses to the means/ends equation. The typology described individual adaptations to goals and means. People can respond in five different ways to the structure of opportunities available:

1 **Conformism**—those who accept the culturally defined goals (e.g., financial success) and the institutionalised means of attaining them (e.g., education).
2 **Innovation**—those who accept the culturally defined goals, but who lack the institutionalised means to attain them. They therefore resort to innovative means to attain the goals, such as turning to crime (e.g., robbing a bank).
3 **Ritualism**—those who accept the culturally defined goals, but who know they cannot attain them. Nevertheless, they continue pursuing institutional means (e.g., staying at school when no jobs are available), regardless of the outcome.

4 Retreatism—those who reject both the culturally defined goals and the institutionalised means of attaining them. They retreat from society in varying ways (e.g., substance abuse).

5 Rebellion—those who substitute their own cultural goals and institutionalised means in place of the conventional goals and means in society. They create their own goals and means of achieving them (e.g., ecologically sustainable hippie lifestyle).

From the point of view of strain theory, the choices available to people reflect problems stemming from the structure of the society itself. That is, it is the relationship between cultural goals and institutional means that ultimately determines the kinds of opportunities and choices that are available to different groups of people.

Crime and culture

The structure of opportunities constitutes one part of the criminal behaviour puzzle. The other part, according to some theorists, is the ideas that people hold regarding what is acceptable or unacceptable behaviour. Specifically, attention was directed to issues of culture and the ways in which young people in particular learn certain ways of doing things and certain attitudes towards others.

The work done by Sutherland and Cressy (1974), for example, was directed at explaining the nature and development of youth subcultures. They argued that crime was cultural in nature, in the sense that it is learned behaviour. People in particular neighbourhoods, or particular social situations, learn about criminal behaviour by interacting with other people. The most significant interaction occurs within intimate personal groups, which of course includes peer groups.

Sutherland and Cressy developed the concept of **differential association** to describe a process in which behaviour is differentially associated insofar as some individuals will associate with carriers of criminal norms, while others will not.

They discussed the process that occurs when a criminal association does take place. The learning of criminal behaviour includes:

- the techniques of committing a crime (e.g., how to hot-wire a stolen car)
- the motives, drives, attitudes, and rationalisations associated with crime (e.g., stealing only Porsche cars, because 'the owners can afford it anyway')

- definition of the legal code as favourable or unfavourable (e.g., regarding the legal code relating to car theft as unfavourable, since people have car insurance anyway).

Differential associations may vary in frequency and duration, priority and intensity. Those persons who become delinquent or persistent offenders do so because of a greater number of definitions favourable to violation of the law over definitions unfavourable to violations. This in turn is shaped by group interaction. For example, an individual may associate with a delinquent group, and then later change that orientation by associating with a non-delinquent group.

The essential point of the theory is that criminal behaviour is learned. Because learning takes place in the context of specific types of group formation, and particular types of definitions of behaviour and attitudes, the issues of peer-group pressure and offending cultures are seen as of central importance.

The idea that people learn to associate certain classes of conduct, either legal or illegal, with the group's approval or disapproval, has obvious links to analysis of subcultures per se. That is, deviant or criminal behaviour is collective in nature, and is based on shared experiences and perceptions. From within the strain theory tradition, various writers have argued that the strain between cultural goals and institutional means is reflected in specific class cultures.

Albert Cohen (1955) argued that working-class subcultures can be seen as a product of a conflict between working-class and middle-class cultures. That is, such a subculture is an alternative cultural system that develops due to the blocked opportunities and low self-esteem experienced by working-class young people. Instead of measuring 'success' in conventional terms, then, the group focuses on alternative goals that are more directly related to their own class experiences. Whereas Merton's typology spoke of the disappointed individual, Cohen saw crime and delinquency in terms of collective behaviour associated with the different aspirations, expectations, and lived experiences of two different class groupings. For Cohen, the school was the point at which lower-class youth understood their choices were constrained by society.

Going one step further, Cloward and Ohlin (1960) put forward the view that, in fact, all classes have the same basic cultural goals (wealth, success, security), but that the working class as a class is disadvantaged in gaining these desired ends. Crime is indeed collective in nature (you learn from your peers), and some groups of working-class children who consider their opportunities to be blocked will adopt criminal or alternative opportunity structures as a result. In other words, illegitimate opportunity structures will develop in those situations where the culturally defined goals are still sought, but legitimate opportunities are blocked or absent. The issue here is not a conflict between middle-class and working-class cultures, but the relationship of certain subcultural practices to specific class backgrounds (i.e., a sense of injustice at the lack of opportunities).

Other explanations of subcultural form were provided by both Matza (1964) and Downes (1966). These writers argued that working-class young people neither rejected nor inverted the dominant culturally prescribed values of society. Instead, they saw working-class youth subcultures as simply accentuating particular 'subterranean values' (risk, adventure, fun) that are part of normal society, but which are sometimes taken too far. In response to restricted access to opportunity, the response of young people is to resort to forms of 'manufactured excitement' of their own.

CONTEMPORARY EXAMPLES

The appeal of strain theory is that it attempts to provide a sociological explanation for the causes of crime. As we have seen, crime is usually related to blocked opportunities, combined with the activities of particular subcultural groups.

There are several broad strands to contemporary strain theory. For example, there is a growing body of work in the area of **social ecology**. Part of this research looks at how aspects of the physical and social environment at the local level influence patterns of offending and the fear of crime. The emphasis is on exploring the spatial features of offences and offending by examining the natural and built environments, studying the actions of individuals and groups within certain places at certain times of the day or week, and evaluating the processes of social regulation as these pertain to specific city sites, residential areas, and commercial districts (see Evans et al. 1992; Bottoms & Wiles 1997). The intention of such research is to explain the uneven distribution and impact of crime, and to develop crime prevention and policing strategies that take into account characteristics of the local environment.

Another related approach is that which provides a theory of crime based upon analysis of community-level **social disorganisation**. Again, the main focus is on particular kinds of neighbourhood areas, such as inner-city ghettos. It is argued that, for example, persistent high crime among African-American youth is due to both structural and cultural factors. Specifically, a 'culture of violence' is sustained among the new urban 'underclasses' through 'structural disorganization and cultural social isolation that stem from the concentration of poverty, family disruption, and residential instability' (Sampson & Wilson 1993: 14). More generally, such perspectives stress the importance of considering the impact of 'neighbourhood effect' when it comes to crime. That is, the social status and crime rate of a neighbourhood have been shown to have an effect on a person's chances of becoming involved in offending behaviour regardless of their specific socio-economic status (Reiss 1986). For instance, a young person from a low-income background living in a high-crime area is far more likely to engage in offending behaviour than an identical person living in a low-crime neighbourhood. Thus, community context is seen as an integral part of why some unemployed and marginalised young people have a greater propensity to commit crime than other similarly positioned young people.

Social ecology and social disorganisation perspectives combined can provide important insights into how and why certain communities are stigmatised and disadvantaged as communities. For example, research undertaken in the United States (Wilson 1996), Germany (Heitmeyer 2002) and Australia (Collins et al. 2000) has pointed to the fusion of class and ethnic dynamics that have direct and indirect negative consequences for ethnic minorities. A crucial factor appears to be the location of specific minority groups in segregated ghettos, a process exacerbated by selected government policies and programmes. The result of a concentration of ethnic minority groups in heavily disadvantaged areas is the systematic exclusion of these groups from mainstream social, economic, and political life. It can also be associated with alternative forms of gaining social status, including the use of violence and reliance upon criminal or illegal activity.

An area of particular and growing interest to criminologists today is that of the study of **youth gangs** and youth in groups. This research has concentrated on providing detailed descriptions of specific types of youth group formations in places such as the USA (Klein et al. 1995; Huff 1996), Europe (Klein et al. 2001), Australia (White 2002), and Canada (Gordon 1995; Gordon & Foley 1998). This kind of work has generally attempted to provide more precise definitions of different types of youth groups, to examine the kinds of activities and associations associated with diverse group formations, and to explain the origins, dynamics, and changes in group formation as these relate to social, economic, and policing factors. Significant issues include not only those of poverty and unemployment, but racism and the impact of ethnic divisions and inequality on group behaviour. Attention is also directed at patterns of policing, and how these impinge upon different populations of young people in different ways.

A large body of literature has also emerged that is informed by what can be called **social development** theories. This literature deals with the personal, family, and social factors that influence the life chances and life decisions of young people. This research and theorising draws upon elements of strain theory, as well as ideas and findings more closely associated with biological and psychological research. For example, in a review of empirical research on the predictors and correlates of offending, Farrington (1996b) provides a systematic outline of the key 'risk factors' associated with youthful offending. Among the many factors cited are:

- prenatal and perinatal factors (e.g., early child-bearing, substance use during pregnancy, low birth weight)
- hyperactivity and impulsivity (e.g., hyperactivity–impulsivity–attention deficit, inhibition)
- intelligence and attainment (e.g., low non-verbal intelligence, abstract reasoning, cognitive and neuropsychological deficit)
- parental supervision, discipline, and attitude (e.g., erratic or harsh parental discipline, rejecting parental attitudes, violent behaviour)
- broken homes (e.g., maternal and paternal deprivation, parental conflict)
- parental criminality (e.g., convicted parents, poor supervision)
- large family size (e.g., insufficient parental attention, overcrowding)
- socio-economic deprivation (e.g., low family income, poor housing)
- peer influences (e.g., male group behaviour, delinquent friends)
- school influences (e.g., use of praise and punishment, classroom management)
- community influences (e.g., high residential mobility, neighbourhood disorganisation, physical deterioration, overcrowding, type of housing)
- situational influences (e.g., specific opportunities, benefits outweigh expected costs, seeking excitement).

The combination of these factors, and their association with certain categories of young people, are seen to explain variations in the propensity for criminal behaviour and criminalisation among young people. However, these risk factors are seen to coincide and to be interrelated in complex ways, and as such they do not yield easy or simple answers to the question of crime causation.

Researchers within this broad framework attempt to identify not only the range of 'risk factors' (such as drug abuse), but also those 'protective factors' (such as family cohesion) that influence whether or not an individual engages in criminal or antisocial behaviour (Catalano & Hawkins 1996). More generally, there is seen to be an overlap between offending behaviour and other types of problem behaviour, and a close connection between immediate social context and the developmental pathways of, in particular, serious and violent young offenders (Loeber & Farrington 1998; see also Rutter et al. 1998). This type of multifactoral perspective leans towards a quantitative and empirically based analysis of offending. As such, it pitches causal explanations not at the more general level of wider social structures, but at the immediate and observable features of society and behaviour. For instance, poverty is treated as a risk factor, rather than a phenomenon stemming from, and requiring investigation in terms of, systemic social inequality.

The sophistication and complexity of the explanations broadly influenced by strain theory are mirrored in the incorporation of elements of the theory into other distinctive explanatory models. For example, the notion that there are distinct criminal subcultures is an important component of republican theory (discussed in chapter 10).

CRITIQUE

Strain theory represents a broad array of differing perspectives. In the light of this, the critique offered here highlights some of the problems with the main thrust of strain theory. In general, for example, a critique is possible of strain theory's almost exclusive focus on working-class crime. Despite understanding the need to gauge levels of crime not reported to police within communities, strain theorists largely accepted the 'shape' of the official crime statistics, namely that the majority of offences are perpetrated by the working class. An exception to this was Sutherland (1983), who undertook ground-breaking work in the area of white-collar crime. The majority, however, accepted that the crime in working-class neighbourhoods was that which needed explaining and eradicating.

This reflected an acceptance of a consensus of values in society. Ultimately all people in society wanted to achieve the same goals and share the same lifestyle (again there are exceptions to the general view; see, for example, Miller 1958). In this way, strain theory accepts the status quo. Rather than seeing the goals and aspirations of society as moulded by those in positions of power, strain theory sees such aspirations as a genuine consensus of values. Others argue that this is not necessarily the case at all. The acceptance of the genuine nature of the consensus is subject to challenges today, for example, by many churches, which argue against the materialistic nature of the 'American Dream'. Still others argue against the notion of any consensus by looking at entrenched conflicts of values and interests, as indicated for example in the work of Marxist, feminist, and radical environmentalist writers.

The concept of a general social consensus has several consequences. First, it denies pluralism of values in society. By definition, since there is consensus, a conflict of values must mean that one group's values are wrong. Second, strain theorists tended to accept that the gender roles in society were part of this consensus. Working in the 1950s, Cohen, for example, felt that the major strain in the lives of young women was the tension associated with wanting an ideal husband (Naffine 1987). It did not occur to him that the roles of young women in the 1950s were imposed, or that, given the choice, they might have a genuine desire to pursue a career outside the home. Furthermore, Cohen's view was distinctly middle-class, since many working-class women needed to work to bring money into the family home. In working-class areas the strain of unemployment could be as great on working-class women as on their male counterparts.

It can also be argued that by accepting the status quo, in terms of 'core values', strain theory fails to take account of structural inequalities—the way the capitalist system by its very nature renders some people 'marginal' and so criminalises their activities. As theories in later chapters suggest, the system itself can be responsible for labelling some people and their activities criminal, while leaving alone other individuals whose activities are equally, or even more, harmful to society as a whole. The process of criminalisation is such that only those who challenge the status quo are labelled as criminal.

Without tackling issues relating to the inequalities of the system itself, some argue that strain theory simply attempts to adapt the individual to a system where structurally he or she has no place. Furthermore, there is often inbuilt resistance to this kind of change. Periodically, for example, the system will actively react against any (limited) attempts to 'adapt' marginalised groups and to provide them with equal opportunity. A good example of this 'reaction by the system' or 'backlash' is shown by the eventual collapse of the 'War on Poverty', a major initiative by the Kennedy, and later the Johnston, administrations in the USA. The aim of the initiative was to empower the poor in order to enable them to assimilate into the opportunity structure of American society. Part of the reason for the lack of effectiveness of this programme was the resistance by those in power to the new realities created by the movement towards empowerment. While various factors led to the demise of the 'War on Poverty', including some ill-conceived programmes it spawned, the resistance by the status quo—and particularly politicians who were now faced with an organised, aggressive inner-city urban population—was certainly a major factor in sealing its fate.

Finally, it can be argued that some variants of strain theory over-simplified the link between lack of opportunity and crime. Subsequent studies have shown the link between unemployment and offending to be a very complex one (see especially Weatherburn & Lind 2001). There are also numerous additional factors, such as attachment to school, family, and peers who also offend, which are not accounted for in many of the theories discussed above. While there may indeed be some generalised strain that underlies offending, how this affects individuals, and why some individuals respond with offending behaviour and others do not, is not explained adequately by strain and subculture theories.

Having said this, these theories did highlight aspects of offending that were clearly absent from psychological and classical perspectives. They raised the level of debate away from a focus on the individual, to the influence society has on the behaviour of the members of the working class who offend. In doing so it established a strong link between societal context and the nature of criminal or deviant activity. Furthermore, it recognised that criminal activity for those who lack opportunities is meaningful for those involved, given their reduced opportunities and/or peer-group supports. Finally, it opened the way for more progressive reforms politically, and against knee-jerk punitive approaches or intrusive psychological rehabilitation.

CONCLUSION

From a strain theory perspective, crime is seen to be more a matter of 'normal' people in 'abnormal' situations, rather than disturbed individuals acting out their pathology (Gibbons 1979). This is clearly a sharp break from individualistic perspectives that locate deviant behaviour squarely in the choices or defects of each offender. These theories took as a base the sociological concepts of Durkheim, which steered them away from look- ing at individual characteristics, and towards concepts such as anomie and social solidarity that could not be reduced to an individualistic frame of reference.

Within the aegis of strain theory there is a wide range of perspectives that share some similarities, yet also clearly differ in their detail and emphasis. Early theorists such as Shaw and McKay emphasised the disorganisation of the poor and lack of cohesive identity that lead to offending. Later theorists, such as Merton, emphasised the strain between goals and means, and the way criminal means would be used to attain goals in the absence of legitimate avenues, such as access to employment and career. Sutherland and Cressy shifted attention to the interaction between individuals that leads to offending behaviour, and looked at the way criminal associations supply the techniques, motivations, and rationalisations necessary to act criminally. Subcultural approaches, such as the work of Cohen, and Cloward and Ohlin, took association between individuals a step further and emphasised the formation of subcultures as a response to the lack of opportunity supplied by society to working- class youth.

The relationship between lack of opportunity, alienation, and criminal behaviour is, if anything, more important in the current economic climate. Levels of youth unemployment are high, and the inequalities between rich and poor continue to grow at an alarming rate. If strain theorists are right, then the levels of youth crime and the levels of gang formation should also increase. These concerns are, in fact, being reflected in the formation of new international networks of researchers. The

Eurogang Research Network, for example, comprises researchers from over 24 different countries spanning Europe, Russia, North America, and Australasia. A key task of this network is to provide grounded, specific research into the nature of youth group formations within the context of global processes relating to consumption, immigration, youth identity, employment trends, and educational opportunities (see also White & Wyn 2004).

Strain and subculture theories saw movement of analysis of criminal behaviour away from concentration on the conditions of the offender, to the circumstances of criminalisation itself—that is, crime as a social process in response to the inequalities in society. What was left unchallenged was the legitimacy of basic structures of society, and the way society itself influenced the way some activities were criminalised, and others not. This 'labelling process', the process of being seen as criminal, is the subject of the next chapter.

FURTHER READING

Cloward, R. & Ohlin, L. (1960) *Delinquency and Opportunity: A Theory of Delinquent Gangs*, Free Press, Chicago.

Farrington, D. (1996) 'The Explanation and Prevention of Juvenile Offending', in J. Hawkins (ed.) *Delinquency and Crime: Current Theories*, Cambridge University Press, Cambridge.

Merton, R. (1957) *Social Theory and Social Structure*, Free Press, New York.

Reiss, A. (1986) 'Why Are Communities Important in Understanding Crime?', in A. Reiss & M. Tonry (eds) *Communities and Crime*, University of Chicago Press, Chicago.

Shaw, C. & McKay, H. (1942) *Juvenile Delinquency and Urban Areas*, Chicago University Press, Chicago.

Sutherland, E. & Cressy, D. (1974) *Criminology*, Lippincott Company, New York.

Wilson, W.J. (1996) *When Work Disappears*, Knopf, New York.

CHAPTER 5

Labelling Perspectives

INTRODUCTION

The aim of this chapter is to discuss how labelling perspectives view issues relating to crime and criminality. Borrowing conceptually from sociological approaches such as 'interactionism', the labelling perspective introduces us to the idea that to understand crime we have to explore both objective and subjective dimensions of the criminal justice experience.

In the previous chapter we examined how strain theory explains crime in terms of blocked opportunities and cultural or learned behaviour. One of the hallmarks of positivist criminology—whether it be biological, psychological, or sociological—is that crime is basically seen as a given. That is, it is assumed that crime exists 'out there' in the real world, and that all we have to do is record it, through classifying behaviour and searching for determining causes. Such criminology assumes that much criminal behaviour is due to forces beyond our control (genetic, psychological, institutional). Generally speaking, it is further assumed that there is a consensus in society regarding core values and norms, and that the role of the social scientist is to provide an objective investigation into the factors that underpin why certain people commit crime.

The labelling perspectives challenge this view of crime and criminal justice. Instead, it is argued that crime is a **social process**. As such, it involves different perceptions of what constitutes 'good' or 'bad' behaviour (or persons), and particular power relationships that ultimately determine what (or who) is deemed to be 'deviant' or an offender. Crime is not an 'objective' phenomenon; it is an outcome of specific types of human interaction.

SOCIAL CONTEXT

The development of labelling perspectives within criminology was due to a combination of the influence of certain intellectual currents, and wider changes occurring in society generally. We shall explore the intellectual foundations of labelling theory in greater depth further on in the chapter. For now, suffice it to say that a central concern of the 'new deviancy' theory was the issue of subjective meaning, and how this impinged upon objective social relationships. Or, to put it differently, the concern was with how human beings actively create their social world.

Part of the impetus to the rise of labelling perspectives lies in the changes that were taking place in the advanced capitalist countries, particularly the USA, in the 1960s and 1970s. The dominant image of the 1950s was one of shared collective interests, consensus on core values, economic prosperity for everyone, and standards of 'deviance' and 'conformity' that were clear for all to see. The social order was thus viewed as monolithic—everyone was dedicated to common goals, and had a stake in the status quo. Any problems that did arise were able to be dealt with through adequate research and application of appropriate technical responses and programmes.

By the 1960s, however, the presumed consensus was disintegrating. The phenomenal popularity of Elvis Presley in the 1950s signalled a new cultural form that was premised upon energy, separateness, novelty, and rebellion. The birth of rock-and-roll music in the post-war period saw the creation of a leisure-based 'youth culture'; one that generally represented a sharp break with the existing 'culture' of the parents. Music, fashion, language, appearance, and activities—all were forged in a manner that departed from existing conventions (and, yet, in the end were linked to the creation of new youth-related and commercialised conventions). 'Deviancy' in the youth cultural revolution was consciously perpetrated and, simultaneously, hotly contested by the young themselves.

If conventional family relations involving the generations were undergoing massive change, so too they were put under pressure by the public campaigns of women, and gay men and lesbian women, to have their collective needs and human rights acknowledged in society. The Second Wave of feminism, in the form of a militant Women's Liberation Movement, actively challenged traditional, conservative notions of the female role and place in society. Similarly, conventional ideas regarding sexuality and sexual preference were subject to increasing analysis and condemnation by feminists and by gay and lesbian activists. Conflict went to the heart of mainstream society and, in particular, the basic assumptions concerning the 'American way of life'.

The idea of a uniform social consensus was further sundered by the coming to prominence of the civil rights movement. The radicalism of Malcolm X and Martin Luther King Jr, and the dream of creating a more just, equal, and free society for African Americans, were crucial components in a mass social movement for fundamental social transformation. The movements for equal rights, and indigenous rights, were echoed in Australia with the establishment of the Aboriginal Tent Embassy on the lawns of Parliament House in 1970. People of colour, native people, and migrant groups could no longer be easily silenced, nor could their demands be ignored. Social division was now on the political agenda.

The breakdown of convention, and the elevation of social difference to cultural and political prominence, was further entrenched through the fierce public resistance to the Vietnam War, particularly among the young, in a number of countries and especially in the USA and Australia, where conscription into the conflict was an ever-present reality for young people. The events of May 1968, in which students and then workers took to the streets of Paris and paralysed France for a period of weeks, underscored the fact that social change was unavoidable and was happening here and now.

One consequence of these great movements for change and reform was that social scientists started to rethink their conceptions of society, social order, and deviancy. Society was now seen as **pluralistic** in nature; made up of a number of diverse interest groups and classes. It was not immutable, but subject to constant pressures to change. Furthermore, what was deviant one day might not be the next. Likewise, what one group thought of as deviant might well be acceptable to another. Social reality thus is contingent—how we view the world very much depends upon where we are situated within that world.

One of the characteristics of the social movements of the time was the emphasis and stress placed upon human creativity, liberation, and free will. The libertarian ethos emphasised choice and rebellion over passive acceptance and conformity. Translated into social theory terms, this broad orientation was reflected in the idea that **meaning** is part of an ongoing social process. Social life is not fixed and immutable. It is made up of constant interactions between groups. The meaning we give to events and situations depends upon how we negotiate definitions of each event or situation.

BASIC CONCEPTS

Labelling perspectives generally start from the premise that crime and criminal behaviour are a social process (see chart 5.1). The focus of concern is with the nature of the interaction between 'offender', 'victim', and criminal justice 'officials'. What counts as a 'crime' is, in essence, determined by the activities of the criminal justice system and its officials; that is, the definition of particular behaviour or an individual as criminal depends upon who does the labelling. Official designations of 'crime' are thereby conferred by those who have the power to label.

CHART 5.1   Labelling Perspectives

Definition of crime	▪ defined by social action and reaction ▪ conferred by those who have power to label
Focus of analysis	▪ relationship between offender and those with power to label
Cause of crime	▪ stigmatisation and negative effects of labelling
Nature of offender	▪ determined (by) labelling process
Response to crime	▪ diversion from formal system
Crime prevention	▪ decriminalisation ▪ radical non-intervention
Operation of criminal justice system	▪ system should not have stigmatising effect ▪ greater tolerance and minimal intervention

The measurement of crime is a process in which the particular actions of certain people are defined by those in power within the criminal justice system as being 'deviant' or 'criminal'. This **institutionalist perspective on crime measurement** stresses that crime is not in fact 'objective': it is shaped by the nature of interactions and selective labelling by members of the criminal justice system in their dealings with the general public.

A key area of analysis is the relationship between the offender and those who have the power to label. The consequence of this relationship, and especially of the labelling process itself, is that stigmatisation can occur. Negative effects can arise from labelling, such that the person labelled takes on the role prescribed in the label. In other words, if a person is branded officially as a 'deviant', 'offender', or 'criminal', then this may result in the person acting in a manner that fits the label.

In effect, the labelling perspective points to the impact of labelling on the psychological and social development of offenders. The self-concept and social opportunities of the offender are determined or influenced by the labelling process. The stigma sticks to the offender, and it affects how others see them, as well as how they perceive themselves.

One result of stigmatisation is that some persons who have been negatively labelled not only engage in further criminal, offending, or deviant activity, but they also seek out or find comfort in the company of others who have likewise been cast as outsiders. Another consequence of the labelling process, therefore, is that it creates an impetus for similarly labelled people to associate with each other—generally in the form of delinquent or criminal subcultures.

From a labelling perspective, the potentially negative outcomes of the labelling process are seen to outweigh the necessity to intervene in the first place. That is, for young people in particular, the stigmatisation of official criminal justice intervention may well propel them into a criminal career for activity that, for most people, is generally transitory in nature.

The response of the criminal justice system to offending behaviour therefore should be based upon a policy of diversion from the more stigmatising aspects of the criminal justice system. The idea is that every attempt must be made to divert certain offenders from contact with the more formal elements of the system, and thus to reduce the chances of stigmatising them.

Less serious offences, for example, should not warrant arrest, court appearance, and incarceration. Rather, the response should be based upon the principle of (radical) non-intervention, or at the least minimal intervention. In a similar vein, in order to reduce the possibility of unwarranted or unnecessary stigmatisation there may be calls to decriminalise certain 'victimless' or 'non-predatory' activities.

Overall, there is a general demand that many different types of behaviour and activity should be tolerated by criminal justice officials. The power to label is substantial, and has lasting impacts. Therefore, it should be used judiciously and only where absolutely necessary.

HISTORICAL DEVELOPMENT

Labelling perspectives have a wide range of intellectual influences. These include social psychology, phenomenology, and ethnomethodology (see Muncie & Fitzgerald 1981; Taylor et al. 1973).

Broadly speaking, labelling perspectives have strong links to the 'symbolic interactionist' perspective in sociology. This perspective employs concepts such as 'self' and 'symbol' in order to explain social behaviour and social action. The logic of such a perspective revolves around the diversity of individual responses to social situations (see, for example, Berger & Luckmann 1971).

A **symbol** can be said to be anything that stands for something else (e.g., a badge, a gesture, a word). All human beings have to learn how to respond to different situations by accurately 'reading' the symbols around them.

The **self** is not a psychological concept (like personality), but refers to how people see themselves. This in turn is built through social interaction. In this sense we can talk about the 'looking-glass self'; that is, that your image of yourself is simply what you see of yourself reflected in those around you (see discussion of the work of Cooley and Mead in Coser 1977).

Part of human interaction involves **role-playing**. For role-playing to occur, each individual has to be able to 'take the role of the Other'—to see things as others see them. In other words, interaction can occur only because each person is able to attribute appropriate meaning to the symbols—words, gestures, and so on—of the other.

But the 'self' does not simply passively respond to events and people around it. It also plays an active part in selecting how it responds. How we respond to other people in our social interactions depends upon how we **define the situation**. The symbolic nature of behaviour means that the first stage of any interaction is one of definition. When people share the same definitions, communication is likely to be straightforward and clear, and we can now interpret the significance of the interaction itself.

The taken-for-granted world may appear to us as the 'real world' that exists outside us as hard, concrete objective fact. However, in actual fact we are collectively involved in constructing reality through the use of signs and symbols that each of us generally interpret the same way. The basis of our interaction with other people is the use of **typifications**, which are drawn upon as part of our recipe knowledge that we use in order to make sense of the world (Berger & Luckmann 1971).

The first step in communication therefore is one of defining situations in a process of interaction. Sometimes situations are misinterpreted if we define them incorrectly. For example, if we see two men embracing and kissing each other, a variety of explanations may suggest themselves: it could be a greeting (at an airport), a congratulatory gesture (on a sports-ground), or a love affair (in a club). What is important in terms of our behaviour is not the circumstances, but whether we have defined the situation in the same way—that is, whether we share the same definition of a situation.

From these types of propositions it is concluded that, at one level, it does not matter what the actual situation is: what matters is how we define it. For instance, a blazing light in the sky could be seen as a comet, or as a sign from a supernatural being. In either case, how we collectively define the situation will still have real consequences for our behaviour and actions.

While human beings are not passive, nevertheless how we are per-ceived by other people does have real and immediate effects on how we see ourselves and how we behave. This social process can be negative or positive. This has been demonstrated in work that has been done in the study of hospitals, asylums, schools, and prisons.

An important concept here is that of the **self-fulfilling prophecy**. The idea behind this is that who I am is determined by who defines my reality and how this is done. People who are labelled 'stupid', 'bright', 'dumb', 'genius', and so on will respond accordingly.

For example, in the so-called Pygmalion experiment, a group of school students was split into two. One half of the group was publicly labelled 'slow and stupid', while the other half was told they were 'brilliant'. After a while, the school grades of the two groups began to deteriorate and to improve respectively. The argument was put forward that each group had internalised the self-concepts framed for them, and had responded to the public labels by playing the role of 'stupid' or 'brilliant' (Rosenthal & Jacobson 1968).

It is further suggested that once a person has been labelled a particular kind of person, they are liable to be treated in a different kind of way from others who may engage in the same kind of behaviour, but who have not been so labelled. This general process can be represented as follows:

1 negative labelling
2 stigmatisation
3 new identity formed in response to negative labelling
4 commitment to new identity based on available roles and relationships.

Labelling perspectives in general are based upon this kind of processual model (see Rubington & Weinberg 1978). In essence, this says that in association with labelling, stigmatisation occurs. A person who is stigmatised is seen by others predominantly in terms of one particular character trait or behavioural pattern, based upon the content of the initial negative labelling.

For example, the negative label may be 'juvenile delinquent' because the person was alleged to have stolen an item from a shop. The person becomes subject to stigmatisation when the negative 'juvenile delinquent' label becomes a master public definition of 'what they are like'. Everyone then responds to the person according to the terms of the label, regardless of what the person may now actually be doing with their life, and with little regard for the other positive qualities they possess. Over time, if the stigma attaches, then you may commit yourself to the new label and hence change your identity to fit the label. Within labelling perspectives, labelling is usually seen to produce negative consequences.

The broad interactionist perspective thus focuses on how people typify one another (e.g., as 'mentally ill' or 'young offender'), how people relate to one another on the basis of these typifications, and what the consequences are of these social processes (Rubington & Weinberg 1978).

From the point of view of criminology, the influence of perspectives that wish to examine the 'social construction of reality' is manifest in two major questions:

1 How do individuals come to be labelled deviant or criminal?
2 How do individuals come to be committed to a deviant or criminal label, and ultimately, career?

Deviance or criminality is not something that is simply objectively given (as in the positivist framework); it is subjectively problematic (Plummer 1979). For example, it can be argued that deviancy itself can be the result of the interactive process involving individuals and the criminal justice system.

In early versions of the labelling perspective, it was asserted that deviancy is not an inherent property of behaviour. Rather, deviancy is something that is conferred upon an individual by society. According to Becker (1963: 9), the impact of **social reaction** to certain types of behaviour or particular categories of people is crucial to explaining the criminalisation process:

> Social groups create deviance by making the rules whose infraction constitutes deviance, and by applying those rules to particular people and labeling them as outsiders. From this point of view, deviance is not a quality of the act the person commits, but rather a consequence of the application by others of rules and sanctions to an 'offender'. The deviant is one to whom the label has successfully been applied; deviant behaviour is behaviour that people so label.

The focus of his research was people considered to be on the margins of society, and on the margins of conformity (e.g., the homeless, alcoholics, prostitutes). According to Becker, the key reason why these people are placed on the 'outside' is because their particular behaviour has been labelled deviant by more powerful interest groups in society. There is nothing in the behaviour itself that is necessarily 'deviant' or 'conformative': it only becomes so in the actual process of labelling.

The importance of this view was twofold: first, it called into question the social nature of the definitions of crime by alerting us to the variability in human behaviour; and second, it showed us that 'crime' is as much as anything a matter of who has the power to officially label behaviour or persons as criminal (see Cicourel 1976). According to labelling theorists, the use of self-report and victim surveys indicates that crime and victimisation are ubiquitous—that is, they are found in all social classes and across gender and ethnic boundaries. Hence, the crucial issues are who gets labelled by whom, and what are the consequences of this labelling.

One explanation of the importance of labelling on people's future behaviour was provided by Lemert (1969). In this case, the main concern is with the social-psychological level of analysis. That is, we want to know the reasons why a person engages in a deviant act to begin with, and furthermore, what maintains their commitment to deviant activity. According to Lemert, in order to describe the process of labelling we can distinguish between primary deviation and secondary deviation.

Primary deviation refers to initial deviant behaviour. The proposition here is that most of us at some stage in our development engage in activities regarded as deviant (e.g., underage drinking, smoking cannabis, petty shoplifting), but we do so because of a wide variety of social, cultural, and psychological reasons. Little is said about the primary causes of deviant behaviour, except that these are wide-ranging and involve a multitude of individual factors. However, the important point is that at this initial stage of deviation, when people engage in deviant activity they do not fundamentally change their self-concept; that is, the individual's psyche does not undergo a symbolic reorientation or transformation (e.g., we do not see ourselves as a drunk, a pothead, or a thief). There is no change in identity, and deviance is seen as nothing more than a passing event.

The main focus of labelling perspectives is with **secondary deviation**. This occurs when the individual engages in some kind of primary deviation (e.g., shoplifting) and there is an official reaction to that behaviour (e.g., the police are called in). If a person is apprehended by the police, they may be officially labelled as 'deviant' (e.g., 'young offender'). The individual may begin to employ a deviant behaviour or role based upon this new status, which has been conferred upon them by state officials, as a means of defence or adjustment to the overt and covert problems created by the public social reaction to their original behaviour. For example, the person may start to 'act tough' to counter ridicule from peers, taunts from neighbours, and persistent surveillance by police when they go out. Secondary deviation is said to occur when, because of the social reaction to primary deviation, the person experiences a fundamental reorientation of their self-concept, and thus their behaviour.

Labelling perspectives were to have most application in the area of juvenile justice. It was argued that young people are particularly vulnerable to the labelling process, and thus more likely to respond, for better or worse, to official social reaction. In their work on juvenile delinquency, for instance, Sykes and Matza (1957) and Matza (1964) described the motivational accounts provided by young people themselves as to why they engage in certain types of activity. They argued that young people use certain **techniques of neutralisation** as a way of denying the moral bind of law (e.g., 'they started it', 'no one got hurt'). Furthermore, Matza argued that the actions of the juvenile justice system, and especially youth perceptions of the competence of officials and the application of sanctions, also affect the 'will to crime' of young people and form part of the ways in which they neutralise their moral restraint.

In studying the values, perceptions, and emotions of young people, Matza (1964) explored the reasons that propelled some youth into further criminal activity. Although most people at some stage engage in some form of criminal, antisocial, or deviant behaviour, not all young people experience offending and criminal justice in the same way. Matza found that juveniles generally 'drift' between the two poles of conventional and unconventional behaviour (including crime), without being fully committed to either. In the end, most young people drift towards conventional lifestyles and behaviours as their permanent pattern. However, if during the teenage years of drift there is official intervention and social reaction to specific kinds of unconventional behaviour, this may well precipitate the movement of the juvenile into a more permanent state of delinquency.

The idea that young people who are subjected to public labelling may be propelled into criminal activity or careers also features in the work of Schur. The solution, according to Schur (1973), is to adopt a policy of **radical non-intervention**. This means that we should take a hands-off attitude to juvenile offending as far as possible. Young people should be free from official intervention, and they should be diverted from the formal systems of juvenile justice in order to avoid stigmatisation.

CONTEMPORARY EXAMPLES

Labelling perspectives have become an ingrained part of how we think about juvenile justice institutions and processes (see Cunneen & White 2002). As will be explored in more detail later on, many of the core ideas of labelling perspectives have spurred further conceptual development in the areas of 'restorative justice' and 'reintegrative shaming' that are at the heart of the republican theory of criminal justice (chapter 10).

Cultural criminology

The idea of reaction being important to crime is also found in the work of Katz (1988). In an unusual twist to the labelling perspective, Katz has argued that knowledge of labelling processes (and in particular, the notion of shaming) may itself constitute part of the impetus to engage in deviant or offending behaviour. Katz was interested in the relationship between crime and the emotional states of offenders. He turned his attention to the **seductions of crime** and the compulsions that are felt by people as they engage in various types of criminal projects. Crime, in emotional terms, is exciting and exhilarating. It represents a transcendence of the mundane, an opportunity to creatively explore emotional worlds beyond that of 'normal' rational behaviour. Part of the thrill of crime is seen to lie precisely in the risk that one will be shamed if caught. Thus, being successful in activity such as shoplifting or joyriding is not only about 'getting away with it'; it is also about avoiding the shame they would feel if they did get caught. These risks thus constitute an important part of the excitement of the deviant experience. If an arrest does occur, this is seen by Katz as a kind of 'metaphysical shock' in that it implies that persistence in the activity would now signal a commitment to a deviant identity. This, in turn, would undermine the emotional impact of knowingly being deviant, particularly since such thrill-seeking deviance is seldom tied to the notion of criminal identity or criminal career.

As with the themes and issues raised by Matza, for Katz (1988) it is important to examine the lived experiences of criminality, to consider the emotional and interpretive qualities of crime. Emotions such as humiliation, arrogance, ridicule, pleasure, and excitement are often central to why we act as we do. Indeed, the study of the emotions of crime is capturing greater interest within criminology, particularly since criminal behaviour is deeply and ambiguously emotional. It is argued that different states of emotional arousal, from fear and anger through to pleasure and excitement, have major bearings on individual and group behaviour, and for the policies and practices of criminal justice institutions (see De Haan & Loader 2002). Locating activity within an emotional universe is one of the characteristic features of what is broadly known as cultural criminology.

Cultural criminology refers to a body of scholarship that tends to focus on the pleasures, excitement, and opportunities for 'psychic resolution' involved in certain modes of criminality (Hayward 2002: 80; Ferrell & Sanders 1995). The focus, therefore, tends to be on the varied emotional dynamics and experiential attractions that constitute an essential element of much crime and antisocial behaviour. For example, Presdee (2000) writes about the spectacle of violence in popular movies, sexual activities such as sadomasochism, the attractions of rap and rave, and so on. Ferrell (1997) describes the liberating feelings and sense of power and resistance associated with graffiti. A common theme in much of this work is that deviance offers the perpetrator a means of 'self-transcendence'—a way of overcoming the conventionality and mundaneness of everyday life (Hayward 2002).

More sophisticated accounts also make the link between the loss of ontological security (a sense of place and belonging) at an individual level that makes people feel at risk in an unstable world, and achieving a sense of 'controlled sense of loss of control' by engaging in risky practices (see Hayward 2002). Consider car surfing for example. This involves a person standing on top of a speeding car and putting oneself at considerable personal risk in so doing. So why do it? The emotional answer is that it is fun and exciting; the analytical answer is that it represents a choice to engage in a controlled sense of loss of control. According to cultural criminologists, as everyday life becomes more routinised, sanitised, and criminalised, so too there will be greater propensity among people to transgress the boundaries of what is deemed to be acceptable behaviour.

In addition to having a major influence on perspectives such as Marxist, feminist, republican, and cultural criminology, the labelling approach has had a marked impact at the level of policy development. This is particularly the case with respect to young people and children. For example, diversion programmes operate in many jurisdictions. These take the form of pre-court programmes (such as police cautioning schemes) and alternatives to court (such as juvenile conferencing projects). The emphasis here is to divert the young person away from the more formal aspects of the criminal justice system, and therefore to reduce the likelihood of stigma and negative labelling.

Another example of the systemic response to labelling perspectives is the way in which a number of jurisdictions attempt to protect the young person from being stigmatised and penalised for the rest of their life for offences committed when they are young. This can take the form of the destruction of official records once a juvenile has reached a certain age and has not reoffended. Limitations on publicity in cases heard before the Children's Court, and restrictions on the taking of bodily samples and fingerprints from children and young people, are similarly designed to keep the young person at arm's length from the official criminal justice system.

One of the more unusual applications of labelling theory was the Tattoo Removal Scheme. This was part of a young offender programme in the State of Victoria in which attempts were made to reshape the public image of certain young people. The presence of tattoos was seen as part of the problem for these young people. They were too easily branded as 'crims' or 'toughs', and this fed into a long-term scenario of heightened police intervention, offending activity, and criminal careers. In order to reduce the stigma attached to these young people, the detention centres introduced a scheme whereby they could have their tattoos removed (Ross 1985). Again, the idea here is that how 'others' respond to a person is an integral part of how people see themselves and how they behave. This example also points to the changing nature of symbols. Tattoos were once a symbol of deviance, but are now highly desirable, with tattoos common among young people—not only those who are viewed as 'troublemakers'.

CRITIQUE

One of the first criticisms that often comes to the mind of students is the fact that the labelling perspective does not provide any explanation as to why people offend in the first place—so-called 'primary deviation'. The theory concentrates on social reaction to deviant behaviour. While this is true, those using the labelling perspective argue that they did not in fact set out to explain why primary deviation occurred. They do not see labelling theory as a discrete theory but rather as a perspective, a part of the overall picture that is able to explain the negative consequences of criminal justice intervention.

Some would argue, however, that there is a problem with focusing exclusively on crime as defined by social reaction. There are a number of crimes that are characterised by high social agreement concerning both their harmfulness and their criminality. Crimes such as rape and murder are seen to possess intrinsic qualities that make them a part of criminal law across cultures (Hagan 1987). Focusing exclusively on social reaction with respect to such crimes would seem to distort the reality of such criminal behaviour.

So, while labelling theory seems plausible in explaining minor delinquency, there are some crimes, such as rape and murder, where the labelling perspective is less useful. It is hard to conceive of these crimes as purely defined on a subjective basis, or as simply a by-product of the confirmation of a 'criminal identity' by the state. While some serious offences, such as murder, are committed by those with an extensive history within the criminal justice system, and could be seen as a result of secondary deviation, for others murder is a first offence. It is hard in these cases to conceive of these as resulting entirely from secondary deviance.

Nonetheless, even under the terms of the labelling perspective itself, it is not always clear what gives people the capacity to reject particular labels. While some seem to succumb to labels and easily slip into deviant identities, others reject the labelling process even after repeated contexts where 'labelling' has taken place. There is extreme variability in how people respond to labels in practice. This has many implications for labelling theory, and republican theory, which we shall consider in chapter 10. Fundamentally, labelling is unable to explain what gives one person the capacity, or the will, to reject the label, while another lacks such a capacity.

There is, then, considerable variability in how people respond to a labelling process. For example, an individual may persist in shoplifting in the absence of overt or immediate social reaction. This same individual, when caught, may cease shoplifting precisely because of the stigma of being caught (and possibly not even because they think that what they were doing was 'wrong'). Others, such as political activists, may be arrested several times for their activities, yet continue to protest. This is because they see official policy—such as the destruction of the rainforest or bias against homosexual lifestyle—as the deviance, not their behaviour. They actively reject the labelling of the criminal justice system. Finally, for some people the act of going through the criminal justice system and its labelling processes may be seen as an important rite of passage, as has been suggested is the case with some indigenous young people in northern Australia (see Johnston 1991). The labelling perspective cannot explain this phenomenon on its own, since it is bound up with broader issues such as colonial relationships, and in particular the relationship between Aboriginal people and the police.

However, it is important not to oversimplify the labelling process, for example, by suggesting that it only takes one event and a person is labelled for life. The process of acquiring labels is far more subtle, and, as Plummer (1979) points out, labels are used by a wide range of institutions, such as family and school, which extend far beyond the reaches of the criminal justice system. By the time someone reaches the criminal justice system they may well have an entrenched set of negative labels. It may be this labelling process, not that which occurs in the criminal justice system, that determines the fate of a young person. Labelling by the criminal justice system remains important, however, since as Polk (1993, 1994a) points out, it can wield only negative labels—'graduating' from a criminal justice institution has very different connotations in mainstream society to graduating from high school.

For this reason there has been much discussion of the concept of 'net-widening' in the literature. Those with concerns about the policies that emanate from labelling theory argue that diversion, rather than turning people away from formal involvement in the criminal justice system, actually draws more people into its purview. Thus, the negative labels wielded by the system reach further into the juvenile population. This is particularly the case where diversion results in greater intrusion into individuals' lives, for example, through the use of juvenile conferencing in cases of minor offending (see Alder & Wundersitz 1994; Cunneen & White 2002). 'Failure' in the context of such diversionary programmes can mean re-entry into the justice system, possibly with harsher penalties involved. Alternatively, this possibility is minimised where diversion involves no further action, such as in the police cautioning programme in New Zealand.

The concept of diversion then needs critical evaluation. Cohen (1985) argues that analysis of diversionary programmes reveals several recurrent problems. First, diversionary programmes can be more intrusive of individual lives (denser nets). Second, people may be brought into the criminal justice system where previously they would have had no contact (broader nets). Finally, while the institution of social control may change, the nature of social control may remain—that is, control that marginalises and alienates the person (different nets). For example, the criminal justice agencies may be replaced by some form of medical or psychiatric control.

Ultimately, however, to explain criminality it is necessary to go beyond interaction at the level of individuals and social groups. Explanation of how power is wielded within the labelling perspective is limited to the immediate institutional level (e.g., the individual police officer), which begs analysis of the wider distributions of power in society. The analytical gaze of the labelling perspective is on the 'underdogs' and their reaction to their position, not on how they are positioned, and regarded by the more powerful in society.

CONCLUSION

The labelling perspective can be seen as a radical break from earlier positivist and classical explanations of criminality and criminal behaviour. It was the first time that the notion of a consensus in society was challenged by criminologists and sociologists. With this challenge came the understanding that 'crime' and 'criminal' were themselves subjective, and depended as much on context and social reaction to give them meaning, as on the nature of the actual behaviour.

Labelling theorists were ultimately concerned with the nature of action and reaction that resulted in an individual taking on a deviant identity, and pursuing a deviant lifestyle. The central problems that inform the labelling perspectives have been usefully summarised by Plummer (1979: 88) and include:

- What are the **characteristics** of labels, and their variations and forms?
- What are the **sources** of labels, both societally and personally?
- How, and under what **conditions**, do labels get applied?
- What are the **consequences** of labelling?

Through these questions, crime is seen as a process. Becoming successfully labelled as 'criminal' involves taking on a negative label that is primarily applied by the criminal (or juvenile) justice system. This system is full of symbols, or cues, that denote who is criminal (the one in the dock) and who sits in judgement on them (those on a raised platform, the judge or magistrate). The consequences of this process include an individual taking on a criminal identity and then acting according to the expectations of that label; that is, committing more offences. Labelling theory has important issues to raise about the social reaction process, and how best to intervene or not to intervene.

Finally, the labelling perspective raises the importance of power and competing interests in society. This combination of the power differential and conflict of interest between some groups in society often results in the powerless being labelled as deviant. Those without power are thus more vulnerable to the labelling process. It is this issue of the power differential in society that is taken up in radical and feminist theories.

FURTHER READING

Becker, H. (1963) *Outsiders: Studies in the Sociology of Deviance*, Free Press, New York.
Cicourel, A. (1976) *The Social Organisation of Juvenile Justice*, Heinemann, London.

Hayward, K. (2002) 'The Vilification and Pleasures of Youthful Transgression', in J. Muncie, G. Hughes & E. McLaughlin (eds) *Youth Justice: Critical Readings*, Sage, London.

Katz, J. (1988) *Seductions of Crime: Moral and Sensual Attractions in Doing Evil*, Basic Books, New York.

Plummer, K. (1979) 'Misunderstanding Labelling Perspectives', in D. Downes & P. Rock (eds) *Deviant Interpretations*, Martin Robertson, Oxford.

Presdee, M. (2000) *Cultural Criminology and the Carnival of Crime*, Routledge, London.

Sykes, G. & Matza, D. (1957) 'Techniques of Neutralization: A Theory of Delinquency', *American Sociological Review*, 22: 664–70.

CHAPTER 6

Marxist Criminology

INTRODUCTION

The labelling perspective represented a major challenge to existing orthodoxies of crime, particularly positivist assumptions regarding the straightforward existence of crime as fact. Labelling perspectives instead saw the creation of crime as an active social process. When such notions were first mooted in the 1950s and 1960s, a number of significant questions were raised that created further critical waves within criminology. For instance, why are some groups in society labelled more than others, and why are some groups more vulnerable than others to the labelling process? One answer to such questions was provided by perspectives that analysed the structure of society itself as a major source of inequality and differential treatment. These were the Marxist and broad conflict perspectives in criminology.

This chapter will focus predominantly on the **Marxist perspective** in criminology. The key aspect of this approach is that it views crime as an outcome and reflection of basic class divisions in society. The focus of analysis, therefore, is on power and inequality, especially insofar as these embody class-related processes associated with the overall distribution of social wealth.

The chapter begins with a brief discussion of the differences and similarities between a Marxist and a broad conflict perspective within criminology. This is followed by a review of the core concerns of Marxist writers, and the particular attention they pay to crimes of the powerful, as well as crimes of the less powerful. The relationship between economic, political, and criminal processes is a central theme of the chapter.

SOCIAL CONTEXT

Terms such as 'critical', 'conflict', and 'radical' have all been applied inter-changeably to theories that acknowledge the importance of power and social inequality in the construction of criminality. However, the termi-nology can be misleading. Regardless of the label, there exist important conceptual boundaries between liberal-conflict theories and Marxist analyses of crime.

The work of social scientists in the 1950s was largely conservative in nature. Writers of the period had either overtly bought into the Cold War ideology, which defended the 'American way of life' (based upon defence of capitalism), or were afraid to voice a critical response to such ideology. Their fear was created by state-sponsored attempts to stifle social criticism that bore any resemblance at all to communist ideas, such as the House Un-American Activities Committee in the USA. This situation was similarly reflected in the criminological writings of the time, many of which were premised upon the idea that there was a consensual social order and a core set of societal values. Deviance meant deviation from consensus and the presumed accepted core values and norms.

This **consensus perspective** adopted a functionalist approach in which everything was conceived as operating to sustain society as a whole. We all have shared values and shared interests in society. If an individual deviates from the social norm, then we bring them back into line, thus restoring the equilibrium. In this fashion, individuals are socialised into the core set of values and common interests. This view of society characterised most of the criminological perspectives until the 1960s.

The 1960s was a period that saw sustained critique of many of the dominant social institutions. There was a general rebellion against the norms, values, and activities of mainstream society. This took the form of resistance to the Vietnam War in Australia and elsewhere, of student militancy, the rise of the Women's Liberation Movement, demands for civil rights by Black and indigenous minorities, and so on. By this stage, as well, the anti-communist fervour had died down, thus permitting a more open and critical analysis of society. The readiness to adopt a con-flict perspective of society is reflected in the literature of the time. It is essential to note here that a conflict perspective is not necessarily radical; it does not necessarily have to question the status quo, including the processes and institutions of society.

In the 1960s, labelling theory emerged as the precursor to more profound critiques of the existing orthodoxies; it questioned the prevailing world views, and emphasised that not all was as it appeared to be. Indeed, some of the writers who had subscribed to the consensus view of society, such as Lemert, changed their views and began conceiving of society in **pluralistic** terms (see Pearce 1976). Society was no longer seen as a homogenous, unitary whole, but one made up of various competing interest groups. One could identify diverse ethnic, class, and religious groupings; divergent economic and political interest groups; conflicting lifestyle approaches; and subcultural values.

The recognition of social difference was translated at the level of theory into several conceptions of the relationship between social interests and power. Some theories suggested that competing groups are more or less equal in power, and that power is more or less evenly distributed throughout the social structure. Other theories suggested that conflict exists between different elite groups in society. These theories were based on the assumption that there will always be powerful minority groups, and the less powerful majority. The question then was: What is the nature and composition of those elites in society who are able to move up or down the power hierarchy?

While these **conflict perspectives** acknowledged the competitive nature of society, they were not necessarily radical. In many cases, for example, they still assumed a basic consensus in society in relation to the appropriate means of dispute resolution. That is, a 'consensus' still existed, but this related to the **methods of resolving disagreements**, rather than to a commonality of values and interests. The basic institutions of society therefore were not challenged. The state is seen as essentially neutral and detached from the competing interest groups. An appropriate forum for change, for example, would be the existing parliamentary procedures. At any time, there is conceived to be a plurality of opportunities to move in and out of parliament. The balance of power is therefore in a constant state of flux.

Radical pluralists held a different view of competing interest groups in society. Becker (1963), for instance, observed that there is not a constant movement up and down the power ladder. Instead, it is always the same composition of people on the bottom; it is always the poor, the Black, and the disadvantaged. A key concept here is that of the 'underdog' (see Pearce 1976). According to this view, the solution to the problem was **to assist the disadvantaged**—who were locked out of the process of acquiring wealth in society—via the assistance of piecemeal management programmes. This strategy does not challenge society's basic institutions, however: it merely tries to ameliorate the more blatant negative aspects and inequalities of the system.

Marxist conceptions of society are rooted in the analysis of **social power**. A crucial aspect of the theory is the notion that power is concentrated increasingly into fewer and fewer hands; there is a ruling or capitalist class. There is therefore not a plurality of power. Those who ultimately wield power are said to be those who own the means of production—the factory owners, landowners, and media owners; it is these individuals who will dictate the nature and shape of society.

A liberal-conflict conception of the state sees it as a coordinating body within society. It recognises that conflict exists within society between competing groups, but sees the state as acting in the capacity of a neutral arbiter or umpire, independent of and not aligned to any particular class interest. Marxist theory disagrees with this view. From the more radical perspective, power is concentrated in a capitalist society, and the state and its personnel are not neutral. The argument here is that if one conducts a class analysis of the state's personnel and analyses critically the state's policies, including economic and military ones, it becomes apparent that the state is far from neutral and impartial.

Ultimately, the state apparatuses (the courts, judiciary, police, prisons, and community programmes) operate in the interests of capitalism. Questions were therefore raised in relation to the criminalisation process: Structurally, if the state reflects the interests of capitalism and the capitalist class, then who is subject to what kind of state sanctions, and why?

BASIC CONCEPTS

Marxist conceptions of society are based upon an analysis of structural power in society (see chart 6.1). As mentioned, those who wield decisive power in a society are those who own and control the means of production—the factory owners, the landowners, the media owners, and the owners of information technology. An individual in a class society is defined not so much by personal attributes or by reference to universalising statements regarding 'choice' and 'determinism', but by their position and opportunities in society as dictated by class forces.

CHART 6.1   Marxist Criminology

Definition of crime	■ human rights conception ■ class interests
Focus of analysis	■ economic and state crimes of the powerful ■ economic and socio-cultural crimes of the less powerful
Cause of crime	■ institutionalised inequality, exploitation, and alienation ■ marginalisation and criminalisation of working class
Nature of offender	■ choices of offender dictated by structural imperative to maximise profit, or by subsistence pressures ■ alienation
Response to crime	■ challenge state repression of working class ■ expose extent and nature of social harm by the powerful
Crime prevention	■ radical democracy ■ collective ownership and control over means of production ■ redistribution of societal resources according to need
Operation of criminal justice system	■ democratisation of institutions ■ public accountability ■ upholding of human rights ■ law reform to reflect working-class interests

To understand crime, we need to examine the actions of the powerful in **defining and enforcing a particular kind of social order**, and the activities of the less powerful in the context of a social structure within which they have fewer resources and less decision-making power than the owners of the means of production. Power is concentrated in a capitalist society, and the activities of the state reflect the interests of capital-in-general in fostering the accumulation of capital, in maintaining the legitimacy of unequal social relations, and in controlling the actions of those who threaten private property relations and the public order. The general tendency of state institutions (such as the police, the judiciary, the prisons, and community programmes) is to concentrate on specific kinds of behaviour (usually associated with working-class crime) as being more 'deviant' and 'harmful' than other kinds of destructive or exploitive behaviour (usually associated with crimes of the powerful), which is deemed to be less worthy of state intervention.

In determining what is 'crime', the initial difficulty is that if the laws reflect the interests of the ruling class, then many types of social harm may not be incorporated into the criminal law if they go against capitalist interests. In such circumstances there is a need to establish wider criteria relating to the nature of offences. Thus, for example, crime has been redefined in a broader sense to encompass any activity that interferes with **basic human rights** and causes **social injury**.

Marxist criminology directs attention away from an exclusive focus on 'street crimes' or working-class crime, towards the social harms perpetrated by the powerful within society. It attempts to demonstrate how **class situation is linked to specific types of criminality**.

According to the Marxist view, a broad distinction can be made between the crimes of the powerful and the crimes of the less powerful:

- **Crimes of the powerful** are linked to both a personal desire to augment one's wealth and a structural imperative to get an edge in the overall capitalist economic competition. They include economic crimes (e.g., fraud, violation of labour laws, environmental destruction) and state crimes (e.g., misuse of public funds, violation of civil rights, corruption).

- **Crimes of the less powerful** stem from a combination of economic and social motivations. In the first instance, they are related to efforts to bolster or supplement one's income relative to subsistence levels; in the second, they may represent antisocial behaviour linked to varying types of socio-cultural alienation. They include subsistence-related crimes (e.g., shoplifting, workplace theft, welfare fraud) and socio-cultural crimes (e.g., vandalism, assault, public order disturbances).

Thus, the cause of crime is found in the structure of unequal class relations in a society. It is institutionalised inequality, the intrinsic economic exploitation of workers by the capitalist class, and the alienations associated with consumer capitalism that form the context for criminality under capitalism. In essence, where you are located in the class structure will influence the kinds of criminal activity you engage in, the propensity for you to engage in such activity, and the intensity of that involvement.

The pressures and limits of circumstance—and thus **offender choice**—vary according to class position. For example, economic forms of criminality involve different motivations, propensities, and characteristics, depending upon class background and circumstance. Crimes perpetuated by the working class are largely the result of a need to ensure economic subsistence; that is, a need to live. This situation can be contrasted with motivations based on accumulation rather than subsistence.

Hence, the choices open to an offender are dictated by wider structural imperatives to maximise profit, or by immediate subsistence pressures. In addition, both individuals who are powerful and those who are less powerful in society can be deeply alienated from other members of the human community.

For a Marxist, to respond to crime is to expose the extent and nature of the social harm perpetrated by the powerful in society. It is argued that crimes of the powerful have a much greater economic and social impact than 'street crime' and working-class crimes generally, and that if coercion is to be used it should be directed at those doing the **most harm**.

Simultaneously, effort is put into challenging the manner in which the state apparatus is used to **repress the working class**. This extends to such issues as public-order policing—especially of the unemployed, poor, and minority groups—and the policing of class conflict in the form of union strikes and industrial disputes.

In ideal terms, the operation of the criminal justice system should be based upon: full **public accountability** of each apparatus of the state (e.g., the police, courts, prisons); a genuine upholding of human rights; law reform that is designed to protect the interests of the working class (e.g., enshrining the right to strike); and a **democratisation of institutions** (e.g., by a combination of participatory involvement of citizens and election to decision-making positions within the criminal justice system).

The best form of crime prevention is one that addresses the basic problem of a concentration of wealth and power into a small number of hands in society. Crime is seen to flourish in a context of inequality and structural pressures towards capitalist accumulation and profit. Alternatively, it is felt that much crime can be eliminated or reduced through the extension of radical democracy throughout society and its institutions, the **collective ownership and control over the means of production** (e.g., various forms of nationalised industry), and a redistribution of societal resources according to **human need**.

HISTORICAL DEVELOPMENT

Within the Marxist framework it is argued that history can be seen in terms of a succession of different 'modes of production' (see, for example, Cornforth 1987). Each mode of production encompasses particular forces of production (e.g., tools, techniques), relations of production (e.g., lord–serf, capitalist–proletariat), and social institutions (e.g., monarchy, parliamentary democracy). So, as societies move from, for example, feudalism to capitalism, we see a shift in the mode of production across these areas: from agriculture to industry; from power concentrated among the aristocracy to power concentrated among the bourgeoisie or capitalist class; from institutions built upon the notion of the divine right of monarchs to those based upon rule of law that binds the ruler as well as the ruled.

The emergence of different modes of production has been associated with the rise of different kinds of class societies, where the central dynamic of each society is that of the expropriation of surplus from the direct producers and into the hands of those who own and control the overall means of production. For instance, in a slave-based economy (as in ancient Greece or Rome) the slave owner appropriates the surplus product of slave labour; in a feudal society the lord appropriates the surplus product of the serf; and in capitalist society the factory owner appropriates the surplus labour of the worker. Hence, the concept of economic exploitation and class struggle are central to the Marxist view.

In order to place the rise of conflict approaches and Marxist criminology into perspective, we need to acknowledge the impact of recent historical developments. In the last century and a half, for example, we have witnessed the birth and growth of a new class—the working class or proletariat—and with this the rise of distinctively working-class political organisations (e.g., trade unions) and theories (e.g., social democracy, socialism). In particular, the philosophies and analyses provided by Marxism and anarchism voiced the concerns of working people to forge a new kind of social order in which the working class, rather than the capitalist class, was in power. Revolutionary ideas were in a number of instances accompanied by actual revolutions. Some of these were successful (as in the overthrow of the Tsar in Russia in 1917) and some were not (as in France in 1871 and Germany in 1918–19).

As the twentieth century unfolded, rebellion and revolution were to be features of many peasant and working-class revolts around the world. Class conflict was an ingrained part of life for many people. Class conflict was manifest in the form of periodic economic recessions that disproportionately affected the working class (e.g., in Australia in the mid 1800s, the 1890s, the 1930s, and the mid 1970s), and in the form of struggles over industrial issues (e.g., strikes and lock-outs) and political activism (e.g., with the formation of the Australian Labor Party and later the Communist Party of Australia). It was a time of conflict, revolution, and change.

Early Marxist writings on crime in the first few decades of the twentieth century discussed the ways in which crime is an outcome of the precipitating economic and social conditions of capitalism. Bonger (see Taylor et al. 1973), for example, argued that 'criminal thought' is generated by the conditions of want and misery foisted upon sections of the working class, and is also the result of the greed that underpins the capitalist competitive process. In Australia, the work of Wood on convict history provided an important stepping stone for later radical historians who likewise saw crime as stemming from the twin evils of poverty and a savage and unjust criminal code (see Garton 1991). However, generally speaking, these writings went against the mainstream of criminology of the time. It was not until the 1970s that Marxist criminology was incorporated into the field as a significant and popular perspective in its own right.

During the 1960s and 1970s, American criminologists such as Quinney and Chambliss directly challenged the prevailing approaches in criminology. Clear distinctions were drawn between a conservative ('functionalist') and a radical ('conflict') perspective on the nature of crime and law enforcement. It was argued that where there are class divisions in a society, you will find different capacities to determine the content of the laws of that society. The powerful ruling class will be able to shape the criminalisation process in such as way as to protect its own collective interests, which reflect the interconnection between this class and a particular state form (see Chambliss 1975b; Chambliss & Mankoff 1976; Quinney 1970, 1974).

How issues are constructed, how crime is defined, and how crime is responded to all relate directly to one's position in the class structure. If social power is concentrated in the hands of those who own the means of production, then they will influence and generally dictate what behaviour will be defined as criminal and what will not. For example, shoplifting may be considered theft, but false advertising may be viewed as only a trade practices violation. Similarly, those with power are capable of influencing the nature of societal reaction to behaviours deemed to be socially harmful; for example, whether to prosecute industrial homicide as murder or simply to see it as accidental or a product of negligence.

In developing a new typology of crime—one that dealt with both crimes of the powerful and crimes of the less powerful—Quinney (1977) argued that analysis of the relationship between class, state, and crime is essential. It was put forward that, on the one hand, there are **crimes of domination**. These are crimes committed by the capitalist class, the state, and the agents of the capitalist class and the state. They include crimes of control (e.g., police brutality, violation of civil liberties), crimes of government (e.g., warfare, political assassination), and crimes of economic domination (e.g., pollution, price-fixing). On the other hand, there are **crimes of accommodation and resistance**, which are associated with the working class. These include predatory crimes (e.g., burglary, robbery), personal crimes (e.g., murder, assault, rape), and crimes of resistance (e.g., workplace sabotage, protests).

Criminality is intimately tied to class position, and the logic of a system that is geared towards capital accumulation rather than the meeting of social need (see Greenberg 1993). According to Quinney (1977: 60) crime must be understood from the point of view of the political economy of capitalism:

> Those who own and control the means of production, the capitalist class, attempt to secure the existing order through various forms of domination, especially crime control by the capitalist state. Those who do not own and control the means of production, especially the working class, accommodate and resist in various ways to capitalist domination.

A crucial concept within the Marxist framework is that of **surplus population**, in that much of the existing forms of criminalisation and public concern with 'street crime' are seen to be targeted at those layers or sections of the population that are surplus to the labour market and the requirements of capitalism generally (Spitzer 1975). A broad political economic analysis of capitalism set the scene for research and writing on more specific aspects of class conflict and class processes relating to crime.

For example, arising from concerns with class and class analysis of society, attention was drawn to the specific ways in which the activities of working-class juveniles have been subject to particular processes of criminalisation. The research of the Birmingham Centre for Contemporary Cultural Studies in England, for instance, re-examined the issue of youth subcultures from the point of view of the unequal material circumstances of working-class boys and girls (Hall & Jefferson 1976). It was argued that class was central to any explanation of the experience of 'growing up', and that the relationship between young people and social institutions such as school, work, and the legal system is characterised by different forms of class-based resistance to the relations of power and domination. Certain youth subcultures were seen to 'solve', in an imaginary way, problems experienced by working-class young people (e.g., unemployment, educational disadvantage) that at the material level remained unresolved (Clarke et al. 1976; Brake 1985).

From the point of view of social control and policing, various studies pointed to the ways in which the media portrayed certain types of youth subcultures, which in turn led to a form of 'deviancy amplification' (Cohen 1973; Young 1971). That is, the sort of public labelling that pertained to some groups of young people actually generated further 'deviant' behaviour in the group so labelled. More generally, the link was made between the actual experiences of working-class young people—culturally, socially, and economically—and the manner in which the state, particularly the police, intervened in their lives both coercively (e.g., arrest rates) and ideologically (e.g., through the promulgation of 'moral panics' over their behaviour and attitudes).

By providing a structural perspective on social institutions, social processes, and social outcomes, Marxist approaches argued that revolutionary or profound social transformation is needed if 'crime' is to be addressed in a socially just manner.

CONTEMPORARY EXAMPLES

In Marxist criminology the concern is to highlight the inequalities of a class society (e.g., wealth and poverty; business profits and low wages), and to show how these impact upon the criminalisation process. The powerful are seen as designing the laws in their own collective interests, while having greater capacity to defend themselves individually if they do break and bend the existing rules and regulations. The less powerful in society are propelled to commit crime by economic need and social alienation. They are also the main targets of law enforcement and wider criminal justice agencies. This is reflected in statistics that show an overrepresentation of the unemployed and poor in prisons, in police lock-ups, and in the courts.

Due to a range of academic institutional factors (e.g., the rise of postmodernism as a perspective) and external political changes (e.g., the collapse of Stalinism, the demise of large Marxist-oriented political parties in the West), the Marxist perspective waned within criminological circles in the 1980s. In its stead there developed a broader and more inclusive radical approach that we describe in chapter 11 as critical criminology, and various liberal strands of criminology such as Left Realism and republican theory. Nevertheless, there are ongoing attempts to restate and make applicable the basic propositions of Marxist criminology today, especially in the light of the increasing polarisation of wealth and poverty on a world scale, and the further concentration and monopolisation of production.

The ongoing contribution of a Marxist framework to understanding contemporary developments in society, and criminal justice specifically, has long been highlighted in the work and writings of Jeffrey Reiman (1998). Reiman first published his book *The Rich Get Richer and the Poor Get Prison* in 1979. As the title suggests, the book is an analysis of the economic biases, ideological processes, and social inequalities associated with the criminal justice system. In later editions, the book includes an appendix that provides a detailed outline of the Marxist critique of criminal justice. Marxism as an analytical framework may have declined in popularity among academic intellectuals, but Reiman argues (1999) that the issues with which it is concerned have not lost any of their potency or relevance.

As Reiman (1999: 1) puts it: 'Economic bias is still with us. What has changed is that the attention and concern that was once focused on economic bias as a serious problem that threatened to undermine the legitimacy of the criminal justice system has steadily diminished.' For Reiman, economic bias has continued and, in some respects, deepened. The lack of attention to the contours and dimensions of this bias among social scientists and political leaders is explained in terms of the power of ideology, and specifically what he refers to the 'angle of moral vision'. Reiman says that the 'awareness' of economic bias may well still be there, but its 'acceptance' indicates that differences in wealth are perceived simply as morally irrelevant differences (1999: 4). Thus, analytically

Marxism is seen to continue to provide important insights into class inequality, and the ideologies and institutions that sustain this. The political attractiveness and criminological implications of the perspective, however, tend to be bound up with the degree of social upheaval and social movement within society at large. In other words, the social context within which Marxist analysis takes place forms an important part of how it is received in the wider intellectual and political communities.

An article by White and van der Velden (1995) provides another example of contemporary Marxist writing on issues of class and criminology. It argues that there are typical patterns of crime associated with specific classes. This is because class position embodies diverse material circumstances and capacities of people to marshal economic and political resources, and this in turn depends upon one's relationship to the means of production. To put it differently, the wealth and power one determines the kind of crime in which one might engage. Thus, the crimes of the capitalist class are linked both to augmentation of personal wealth and to attempts to secure an advantage in the process of 'doing business'. This translates into various types of criminal fraud and illegal business transactions. By way of contrast, working-class criminality is seen as based on subsistence, designed to supplement income or in some cases to be of a survival nature (e.g., theft, shoplifting). Further, working-class crime also includes a range of activities that reflect the various alienations experienced by workers, such as vandalism, rape, racist attacks, and so on.

The impact of the crimes of the powerful is often diffuse, yet they affect a large number of people directly or indirectly simply because of the capacity of the capitalist to do harm on a large scale. For example, tax avoidance or environmental destruction may have a considerable social cost, but not be 'visible' in the public domain in the same way as 'street crime'. In defending themselves against prosecution, the powerful have greater social resources at their disposal with which to protect their interests. Furthermore, the sheer costs associated with investigation and prosecution of white-collar and corporate crime often make it prohibitive for the state to proceed, or to cast a wide net to catch other violations similar to the exceptional few that are prosecuted. Crimes of the powerful may have significant structural effects in terms of lives lost and financial impacts. Because such crimes are usually directed in the first instance against other capitalists or against the rules governing the marketplace, they are rarely perceived by the general public as being of special interest to them personally (except in the case of events such as industrial homicide).

By way of contrast, the crimes of the less powerful tend to be highly visible and to be subjected to wide-scale state intervention involving police, welfare workers, social security officials, tax department officials, the courts, prisons, and so on. A feature of relative powerlessness is that the crimes committed tend to be individualised and thus to have a discrete impact. There is usually one victim (or a few), whether personal or business or household, and the impact of the offence is limited to the actual household or person violated. The response of the major institutions in society is largely oriented towards stopping these kinds of crimes, regardless of the comparatively greater amount of damage caused by crimes of the powerful. The lack of access to resources, such as control of the media and legal experts, means that working-class people are more vulnerable to apprehension, prosecution, and punishment at the hands of the capitalist state. They are exposed to societal control mechanisms in such a way that they feel the full force of the state for any transgression they might commit.

In this analysis, issues of the regulation of an 'underclass' and the policing of working-class communities is bound up with the cyclical and long-term deterioration of the social and economic conditions of life for the majority in capitalist society (see White & van der Velden 1995). The structural conditions producing working-class crime (e.g., unemployment, cutbacks in welfare spending) are seen to have implications, as well, for the capacity of the state to respond other than coercively to 'street crime'. Because the state is undergoing a fiscal crisis (a crisis around a real or perceived lack of government funds), it cannot use welfare-type measures as a means to deal with the social fall-out arising from capitalist restructuring. Harsher 'law-and-order' strategies will thus only make worse the political isolation, socio-cultural alienation, and economic immiseration of the marginalised layers of the working class, thus causally feeding the very criminality that the campaign for enhanced social control is designed to overcome.

Most criminological theories focus their attention on those crimes perpetrated by the working class. Marxist theory, however, redirects our attention away from 'street crimes' and compels us to examine crimes of the powerful. The question then arises of how we are to do this, given the concentration of power and the ability of the powerful to define crime in their interests. For example, within capitalist society there are contested definitions concerning criminal behaviour (what ought to be criminalised), and instances where criminal offences exist but are not enforced (what is actually criminalised). In other words, the criminality of this behaviour is perceived as ambivalent within the capitalist system— there is uncertainty whether or not an activity is really criminal—and whether or not the powerful in some instances should be labelled as criminal (e.g., industrial homicide).

Alternatively, Marxists argue that there is a need to broaden the definition of crime. This entails establishing wider criteria relating to the nature of offences (see Schwendinger & Schwendinger 1975). The definition of crime would accordingly extend to encompass any activity that interferes with one's human rights, including things such as racism, sexism, and so on. Ultimately, Marxists argue that wherever economic exploitation exists, a crime has occurred.

CRITIQUE

Despite the overview given above, it is clear that Marxist criminology— like many other strands of criminology—has variations on a particular theme. The theme here is that capitalist exploitation leads to criminal behaviour and criminalisation of one group (the workers) to a greater extent than the powerful in society. While there are considerable areas of agreement between Marxist criminologists, there are also considerable areas of disagreement.

One concern of some Marxist criminologists relates to the use of the term 'criminal'. For example, Steinart (1985) argues that the term 'crime' has lost any useful meaning it might once have held. It is too imbued with the capitalist ethos, so that the symbolic emotive aspect of the label cannot be separated from its capitalist connotation. For this reason the term is of no use to Marxists. Rather, he argues that the term should not be used; instead, the aim of Marxist criminology should be to highlight those who are harmed the most (the proletariat) and devise policies that have the sole aim of reducing harm, without recourse to criminal law or criminal process. Such a position is labelled as 'left idealist' by those advocating Left Realism, a theory discussed in chapter 9.

While some would see this position as extreme (including many Marxists), it does overcome a central problem in Marxist criminology;

namely, how to define crime. Is there a qualitative difference between the harm that is labelled 'criminal' and other sorts of harm? Traditional perspectives in criminology insist that crime consists of both 'the harm' and 'the guilty mind'. One of the problems with this definition is that 'the guilty mind' takes actions out of context, in particular a context where the powerful dictate the conditions under which the powerless act. Furthermore, harm in the white-collar area results, in many cases, from many negligent minds rather than one guilty mind. For these reasons Marxist criminologists have moved away from the notion of *mens rea*, and focused on the degree of harm.

The problem then becomes what harm to define as criminal. This has led, as we have seen, to very broad definitions of what constitutes criminal activity: for example, 'any activity that interferes with one's basic human rights', or 'wherever economic exploitation exists', a crime has occurred. Some would argue such definitions are so broad that they lose any useful meaning (Cohen 1993), and alienate wide sectors of society that may be sympathetic to the general thrust of Marxist criminology. This raises big issues for criminology generally; that is, the terms 'crime' and 'non-crime' are dichotomous, whereas in reality degrees of harm can be considered along a scale. Definitions of crime that are broad (or narrow) do not solve this problem of trying to squeeze a variable that exists on a continuum (such as harm) into dichotomous categories, such as criminal/not criminal.

Furthermore, Cohen (1988) argues that there is a tendency for those who argue for greater use of the criminal law against white-collar crime, such as the Marxists, to forget the problems associated with using the criminal law to curb harmful behaviour. Earlier research has mapped out a multitude of problems associated with processing people through the criminal justice system, such as the problems associated with stigmatisation and the costs involved in criminal prosecutions. There is also the issue of the politics of criminalisation. Any push to criminalise behaviour is subject to political contingencies that result in unintended consequences of reform: instead of ameliorating the harm, it may indeed exacerbate it.

Marxists have been subjected to further criticism as well. It has been argued that aspects of Marxist writing in criminology have a romantic image of the criminal as 'primitive class rebel'. These conceptualisations understate the real harm caused by such 'rebels'. Those who are the victims of antisocial behaviour, often poor themselves, suffer considerable hardship at the hands of those who commit 'street crime'.

Some Marxists have been criticised for conspiratorial overtones in their analyses regarding, for example, the direct involvement of members of the ruling class in dictating the operational activities of the police (Hall & Scraton 1981). Critics argue that there are many examples where laws are enacted to fetter the activities of specific capitalists (e.g., insider trading). There are many laws in existence that restrain the activities of individual capitalists, which would seem to refute the Marxist argument of the criminal law always defining the activities of the powerless as criminal and never those of the powerful.

This criticism, however, highlights a debate within Marxism itself concerning the precise nature of the state. Some, such as Miliband (1969), have argued that the state can be viewed as an instrument of class rule by virtue of the close social relationship between the top members of the state apparatus (such as high-level bureaucrats and members of the military establishment) and members of the capitalist class (such as bankers, media owners, industrialists, and other corporate leaders). Others such as Poulantzas (1972) have argued that the state exists to promote the interests of capital-in-general, not individual capitalists. In the end, both Miliband and Poulantzas would be unfazed by the criticism above that laws impact negatively on individual capitalists. They would see that the state exists to maintain conditions for capital accumulation, and defend those conditions, whether threatened by individuals of the ruling class or the proletariat. However, the state, by defending the conditions of capital accumulation, ultimately enhances the prospects of the ruling class as a whole.

In terms of crime, it is clear that one cannot reduce crime to a simple equation with poverty or alienation. If this were so, then we would need to explain why it is that not every person living in poverty commits crime, and why some people who appear to be well-off do engage in crimes such as vandalism, homicide, etc. This does occur. However, Marxists are more interested in general trends and broad predictions, based upon the notion that social context shapes the choices or options actually available to a person. The choices for the poor concerning whether to steal or not are categorically different to the choices for the rich; furthermore, these conditions are structurally determined.

Not all criminal laws can be defined as 'class' laws, however, in that some deal with class-neutral questions such as rape. This suggests that power may not be totally encapsulated or explainable in class terms. Power and powerlessness can exist in a sense outside the class structure, such as the power of men over women. Similar concerns have been expressed in relation to issues of racism and the relative position of different ethnic groups in society. In either case, however, there are usually strong class factors that shape the contours of the power relationship between men and women, and different ethnic and 'race' groups.

There are many diverse interpretations and explanations for crime from within the broadly Marxist framework. Some of them offer rather simplistic formulations (e.g., the ruling class directly defines what is criminal or not) and some of them provide detailed, sophisticated accounts as to how class power is exercised via the state to enforce basic class rule (e.g., through analysis of personnel, decision-making processes, limits to reform). Overall, however, it can be said that the strength of such approaches is that they attempt to locate social action within the wider structural context of a class-divided society. In doing so they elevate the issue of power and control to the foreground of criminological analysis, and they stress the ways in which social background and social processes give rise to certain propensities (on the part of the powerful and on the part of the less powerful) to engage in criminal activity.

CONCLUSION

Marxists argue that within contemporary capitalist societies, the capitalist mode of production operates at many levels, both national and global, and this has an impact economically, socially, and politically. There is a concentration of wealth and power into the hands of transnational corporations, which control both material and cultural production. The penetration of capitalist relations and enterprises (e.g., in Russia), and the concentration of economic power into fewer hands (e.g., Murdoch), is apparent on a world scale. Internationally and at the national level, the number of poor is growing and the rich are getting richer.

Marxist criminology argues that the concentration of wealth and power into the hands of a small capitalist class has ramifications for the definition of, and responses to, crime. If power is concentrated in the hands of those who own the means of production, they will influence, and to a certain extent dictate, what behaviour will be defined as crime and what will not. Those with power are likewise capable of influencing the nature of societal reaction to behaviours deemed to be criminal. There is thus an ability here to influence how the state will intervene, for example, on issues relating to environmental destruction.

According to a Marxist perspective, if we wish to examine crime and class in the global context, we must determine who it is that controls the finances (e.g., the banks, the International Monetary Fund); we must evaluate trade agreements that define how the benefits of trade are to be distributed, and the conditions of trade that will be adhered to; and we must consider the impact of mass production and technology (including new information technology) on the lives of workers. Class divisions exist both within and between countries. The existence of the rich and the poor, the divide between the North and the South, are symptomatic of processes of polarisation that fundamentally determine the distribution and definition of crime. For a Marxist, the fundamental questions revolve around the implications of such divisions for the nature and causes of crime, and for the manner of state intervention into people's lives.

FURTHER READING

Greenberg, D. (ed.) (1993) *Crime and Capitalism: Readings in Marxist Criminology*, Temple University Press, Philadelphia.

Quinney, R. (1977) *Class, State and Crime: On the Theory and Practice of Criminal Justice*, David McKay Company, New York.

Reiman, J. (1998) *The Rich Get Richer and the Poor Get Prison*, Allyn and Bacon, Boston.

Schwendinger, H. & Schwendinger, J. (1975) 'Defenders of Order or Guardians of Human Rights', in I. Taylor, P. Walton & J. Young (eds) *Critical Criminology*, Routledge and Kegan Paul, London.

Spitzer, S. (1975) 'Toward a Marxian Theory of Deviance', *Social Problems*, 22: 638–51.

White, R. & van der Velden, J. (1995) 'Class and Criminality', *Social Justice*, 22(1): 51–74.

CHAPTER 7

Feminist Perspectives

INTRODUCTION

The intention of this chapter is to discuss and review issues pertaining to feminist perspectives in criminology. To do this adequately, we need to know something about the position of women and girls generally within the broad criminological discipline, and how gender differences or similarities have been theorised within the field.

The previous chapter outlined the impact of class structure on the construction of criminality, and fundamental motivational distinctions were drawn between crimes of the powerful and those of the powerless. Generally, crimes of the powerful are said to be committed in order to enhance competitive advantage or to augment personal wealth. Additionally, these individuals are said to possess, or have access to, social resources that enable them to resist detection or prosecution attempts. By contrast, working-class crimes are tied to issues of economic subsistence and alienation—be it economic, social, political, or cultural. Furthermore, it is the activities of this class that are excessively regulated; given the lack of access to social resources, they are in the most vulnerable position.

This chapter shares some themes in common with Marxist criminology. Namely, feminist criminology has been centrally concerned with issues of power, the distribution of economic and social resources, and the differential position of selected groups in society, which has implications for their activities as either 'offenders' or 'victims'. According to feminist criminology, the sexist nature of the criminal justice system is an ingrained part of that system, and is long overdue for reform.

SOCIAL CONTEXT

Marxist criminology put questions of power on the agenda in a forceful way during the 1970s. Feminist criminology also looks at who holds and wields power in society, and questions how this impacts on women. Feminist criminology developed in the late 1960s and into the 1970s, and was closely associated with the emergence of the Second Wave of feminism at this time. History reveals that women have long been oppressed as a group, denied rights, and subjected to violence. The new movement was called the Second Wave of feminism in recognition that the First Wave of feminism had surfaced in the form of the suffragette movement towards the end of the nineteenth century. This movement had been expressly concerned with attaining political power through gaining the vote for women.

The advent of the Second Wave of feminism in the 1970s saw the formation of a dynamic social movement that projected many issues into the public domain, highlighting both the structural oppression of women and the general abuses and crimes directed at them. In its radical phase, the Second Wave of feminism was called the **women's liberation movement**. The social agenda was radical social transformation. The key demands were:

- equal pay
- equal education and job opportunities
- free contraception and abortion on demand
- free 24-hour nurseries, under community control
- legal and financial independence
- an end to discrimination against lesbians
- freedom from intimidation by the threat or use of violence or sexual coercion, regardless of marital status
- an end to the laws, assumptions, and institutions that perpetuate male dominance and men's aggression towards women.

Feminist Anthology Collective (1981)

In any discussion of feminism, there is a fundamental distinction to be made between sex and gender. This distinction is likewise at the nub of explanations of male and female offending and victimisation. **Sex** (male/female) is a biological classification indicated primarily by genital characteristics. **Gender** (masculine/feminine) is a social construct, not a biological given. Concepts of masculinity and femininity are part of the learned culture of the actor indicated by dress, gestures, language, occupation, and so on.

In a review of feminist thought and criminology, Daly and Chesney-Lind (1996: 343) describe what they see as the key defining elements of feminism as a mode of analysis:

- Gender is not a natural fact but a complex social, historical, and cultural product; it is related to, but not simply derived from, biological sex difference and reproductive capacities.
- Gender and gender relations order social life and social institutions in fundamental ways.
- Gender relations and constructs of masculinity and femininity are not symmetrical but are based on an organising principle of men's superiority and social and political-economic dominance over women.
- Systems of knowledge reflect men's views of the natural and social world; the production of knowledge is gendered.
- Women should be at the centre of intellectual enquiry, not peripheral, invisible, or appendages to men.

Feminism has much to contribute to our understanding of both biological and social constructions of the female (see, for example, Eisenstein 1984). Early feminist works, for instance, looked at sex roles and distinguished between the differences between males and females in a biological and social sense; they essentially sought to explore whether sex roles are biological or social.

This questioning was followed by a period in which feminists looked not at the polarisations between men and women, but rather at the similarities. The focus of analysis here was on androgyny. Males and females were said to exhibit characteristics that were similar as a whole. For example, rock stars such David Bowie, Grace Jones, and Michael Jackson at times have presented an androgynous image that combined elements of 'femininity' and 'masculinity'.

Another approach adopted a women-centred analysis, which explored the specifically different characteristics of women stemming from their biology or physiology. The emphasis here was on the fundamental, special divisions that separate men and women. For instance, the ability of women to give birth—to perpetuate the human race—was viewed as rendering women essentially superior to men in regard to aspects of caring, sharing, and loving another person.

Regardless of specific orientation, feminism deals with the structural position of women in society. For example, there is a call for greater autonomy and the advocacy of rights for women in social, political, and economic spheres. Feminist movements were initially motivated for change because of a perceived inequality of autonomy and rights. This can be generalised to all women in society or can be applied to specific categories of women. Aboriginal women, for instance, tend to be over-represented in the criminal justice system. Some groups of women therefore experience specific concerns related to or stemming from their ethnicity, class position, and national background.

Feminism itself has many different strands, and this has implications for how we view the world and respond to it. There are a number of competing explanatory frameworks focusing specifically on the place of women in society that need to be acknowledged (see Eisenstein 1984; Tong 1989; Segal 1987). These various feminist strands are primarily concerned with autonomy, rights, and power. The different perspectives within feminism broadly include the liberal, Marxist, radical, socialist, and cultural approaches, which are each discussed below.

Liberal feminism

This views the individual as the most important part of society. There is talk here about rights, dignities, and freedoms of the individual. The hallmark of this perspective is the need to value reason, not to discriminate against anyone. In the view of liberal feminists, the question of rights is paramount in the context of competitive views of the individual. Hence, the laws should be changed to ensure that women have equal rights. For example, it is seen as necessary to change legislation in order to provide equal opportunities in the sphere of paid work. There was a recent example of the assertion of such rights in a Western Australian case of female construction workers. The argument was that sexist violence (e.g., pornography and abusive language) existed in many forms on the work-site, and that female workers should not be exposed to this. The Equal Opportunities Board decided in this instance that the women were being denied the right to participate in the workforce.

Marxist feminism

This perspective is not so much concerned with traditional rights, but instead analyses the structural position of women in society in terms of paid and unpaid labour. The key category of employment for women is seen to be that of domestic labour, which is unpaid. This situation is viewed as exploitative. Even in those instances where women participate in the paid workforce, they tend to be lowly paid relative to their position and their male counterparts, and to be concentrated in insecure positions such as part-time and casual work. The argument advanced here is that if we want to deal with gender inequality then we need to do something to fundamentally transform class societies such as capitalism that are organised around the exploitation of female (and male working-class) labour.

Radical feminism

This stresses the common experiences of women; it is basically involved in collective consciousness-raising about the oppressions shared by all women. The assertion here is that all aspects of women's lives (both personal and political) are touched and shaped by patriarchal relations. The personal is viewed as inherently political. Women are viewed as an oppressed class, and all women are said to be subject to the oppressive structures of male domination. At the same time, all men share in some way in the benefits of that oppression. This approach examines the historical exclusion of women from political, social, and economic spheres. The social institutions of home, the law, the workforce, the courts, etc. are examined in order to expose the victimisation of women across all spheres and institutions of life. The issue of male violence—physical, verbal, and psychological—is of major significance.

Socialist feminism

This agrees that in both the public and private spheres women have been, and continue to be, exploited and oppressed, but this is viewed within the framework of capitalist society. There is an emphasis here on the necessity of examining the commodification of women's bodies as a capitalist enterprise; for example, the pornography and advertising industries.

It is contended that the nature of a class-divided society and the issue of male domination need to be considered in tandem. Women as a broad social category are subject to oppressive images and practices, but the specific nature of concrete instances of exploitation and inequality needs to be examined from the point of view of capitalist accumulation. In essence, the social and economic needs of women have been subordinated to the requirements of profit-making institutions, a process that directly affects many men as well. It is possible, therefore, to think of alliances with certain sections of the male population on some issues as a means to institute social change to the benefit of women.

Cultural feminism

This adopts a women-centred analysis that is often not tied to any specific economic or political programme. It concentrates instead on the development of a separate women's culture and the special nature of women's relationships to each other, society, etc. This perspective manifests itself philosophically in the appeal of New Age religion, magic, and mysticism. Women are seen as intrinsically and fundamentally different from men. They are seen to exhibit a number of gender-specific traits (such as caring and sharing attitudes) that are positive feminine features that make them somehow superior morally to their male counterparts. Alternatively, male traits such as violence and egoism are constant dangers to women individually and collectively. Hence, for many women, the solution is to separate themselves from male society, and thus domination, as far as they can. As part of this, it is also important to develop and expand a 'female discourse' or construction of the social world that sees things in specifically female gender terms.

Female crime

Each of the above perspectives has implications for how we view female crime and respond to it. We must further understand that how we respond to 'crime issues' is determined by the way in which the law positions women in society. It is essential here to note that the language adopted within the law is generally male-gendered language, which clearly advances the rights of 'man' but makes little if any mention of the rights of women.

Criminological theorising did not escape this gender-based critique (see, for example, Allen 1990). A couple of important observations in that regard can be made:

- There has been sheer neglect of women in criminological thought and enquiry, in part due to the male domination of academic criminology both historically and in the present. This is an important point, since what results is necessarily a male perspective of the world and the selection of issues perceived to be important by males.

- The criminal justice system is also dominated by male personnel—judges, barristers, solicitors, prison officers, and police. Again, it can be argued that the composition of institutional workforces can have a significant impact on how that workforce pursues its tasks in practice.

Hence, in terms of theory and research and at the level of the practitioner, the system is dominated by men; there is obvious male structural domination. This is not to say that there have not been periods where individual men have challenged overtly sexist practices. Judges, magistrates, and barristers have indeed done so, but this has not necessarily produced changes in the overall structural domination (i.e., the way institutional practices themselves are systematically biased against women). Similarly, individual women are directly involved in policing and other justice-agency practices, but in doing so may simply serve to reinforce the conservative views of ideal female sexual behaviour. For example, the policing of morality and behaviour of female children during the period of the 'child savers' movement at the turn of the nineteenth century was both conservative and spearheaded by women (Platt 1977). Such practices did not challenge the position of women in society in any way.

The neglect of women within the discipline of criminology is a reflection not only of the composition of the criminal justice system, but also of the picture portrayed by criminal statistics. Women do not appear to be as statistically significant a problem as men. They appear generally to commit fewer crimes, and the crimes they do commit appear to be less serious than those committed by men; they are less violent. Furthermore, in examining victimisation statistics, although there are female-specific categories of victimisation such as rape and domestic violence in which women appear overrepresented, females do not appear to be victims of homicide to the same extent as males. As a consequence of such observations, investigators within the criminological field have often regarded it as unimportant to look at female offending or female victimisation.

When seeking to examine female offending, there has been the additional problem of applying male correlates. Theories of offending have generally been conducted within a male framework and constructed in male terms. Since mainstream criminological theories reflected a male experience, it was difficult to apply them to females; for example, strain theory's concept of opportunity structures and cultural goals (see Naffine 1987). The limitations of mainstream criminology are discussed further below. For now it is important to acknowledge the need for, and significance of, a perspective that argued that female crime was tied to wider structures of gender and power in society.

BASIC CONCEPTS

The feminist perspectives are based on the premise that women are structurally disadvantaged in the present society (see chart 7.1). That is, male domination and female subordination are an entrenched part of patriarchy, which expresses fundamental inequalities between the sexes. Sexual inequality and the disempowerment of women are embodied, as well, in the legal and criminal justice systems.

CHART 7.1   Feminist Perspectives

Definition of crime	▪ male violence ▪ institutionalised inequality and discrimination
Focus of analysis	▪ unequal position of women in society ▪ victimisation of women ▪ victim status of female offenders
Cause of crime	▪ criminality is a function of patriarchy ▪ result of social oppression and economic dependency on men and state
Nature of offender	▪ sexualisation of offences and victimisation according to gender criteria (e.g., 'femininity')
Response to crime	▪ social empowerment of women ▪ confrontation of institutions of male domination
Crime prevention	▪ economic, social, political power and equality ▪ anti-sexist training programmes for judiciary and other sections of criminal justice system
Operation of criminal justice system	▪ provision of gender-specific services and support systems within criminal justice (e.g., jails) and welfare spheres (e.g., refuges)

Feminist criminology defines crime in terms of gender-based and gender-related types of activities. Specifically, a major concern is with the nature of **male violence** as this impacts upon both female offenders and female victims, and the ways in which forms of **gendered inequality and discrimination** are institutionalised throughout society. A substantial part of feminist criminology has been directed at exposing the 'hidden' levels of violence against women, and the structural oppressions that they have had to face over long periods of time.

The main focus of analysis, therefore, is the unequal position of women in society, the specific kinds of crimes committed against women as women, and the status of female offenders in the context of wider social inequalities and gender-based oppressions. Crime against and involving women is seen to be the result of **social oppression** and **economic dependency** upon men or the welfare apparatus of the state.

The way in which women, as victims and offenders, are processed by the criminal justice system is described in terms of the **sexualisation thesis**. This refers to the notion that when the criminal justice system and its agents deal with women (in whatever capacity) they do so on the basis of certain gender-related criteria. That is, the behaviour, marital status and appearance of women are constantly linked to particular ideas regarding the preferred forms of 'femininity'. In this way, what is labelled 'criminal' or an act of 'victimisation' depends to a large extent upon the perceived sexual behaviour and social status of the woman in question.

It is argued that there is a **double standard of morality and power** with respect to women in the criminal justice system. Men and women are treated differently on the basis of gendered stereotypes. Furthermore, in many cases this leads to inequitable and unfair treatment of women who present themselves as offenders or victims before the system. One manifestation of this double standard is the fact that the senior members of the police, judiciary, and correctional apparatus are men, and that generally speaking they reflect existing prejudices regarding women's roles, status, and position in society.

From the point of view of feminist criminology, there need to be major changes to the existing criminal justice system and to society as a whole. The problem is ultimately seen as one of **social empowerment** of women as a broad category, and of confronting the negative and restricting nature of male domination as evident in the present institutional set-up.

To prevent crimes against women, and to forestall many of the crimes committed by women, it is necessary to have greater economic, social, and political equality. Institutional reforms could include: affirmative action policies to advance the position of women within the criminal justice and judicial systems; anti-sexist training for lawyers and judges; and law reforms that recognise and acknowledge the gendered nature of the social world. The criminal justice system needs an overhaul with respect to the provision of gender-specific services and support systems in areas such as detention (e.g., trauma counselling, skills training), and more resources are needed in the wider 'welfare' domain (e.g., rape crisis centres, refuges).

HISTORICAL DEVELOPMENT

In the historical development of feminist criminology there are two points to note at the outset. The first is that while female offenders were generally ignored in mainstream analysis, there were instances when they were specifically examined. However, this was a rather small and neglected area of criminological theorising. Second, the critique offered by feminists was that such theories as did exist were either overtly sexist in nature, or extremely limited in what they could say about the nature of female involvement in the criminal justice system.

When attempting to explain female crime as a distinct and specific social phenomenon, the mainstream theories accepted the narrow, conservative view regarding the place and position of women in society, and more often than not did so on the basis of a form of **biological reductionism**. This refers to instances where female experiences and behaviour are reduced to the imperatives of biology—the (biological) sex of a person is seen to dictate or determine appropriate social roles and practices in terms of one's gender (social constructions of femininity).

A key contribution of feminist criminology has been to critique one-sided, distorted views of women in the traditional literature that did exist on female offending. The basis of the critique had to do with the conflation of sex and gender (failure to distinguish the biological and the social) in much of the analysis on offer, and the misogynous (women-hating) character of some of the writing. Here we can point to several different theories that have ultimately based their conclusions upon the idea of innate female social characteristics linked to female biology.

Biological explanations

These explanations view female crime as stemming from biological causes (see, especially, Smart 1976; Naffine 1987). Most focus on sex-specific biological differences as the standards by which to compare men and women, and as explanations for particular kinds of activity. They vary in substantive emphasis, but the overall message of biological determinism remains the same:

- Early theories argued that the true, biologically determined nature of women was antithetical to crime. Such views were based upon stereotypical notions of women as being passive, non-aggressive creatures. Criminality was linked to 'maleness' and 'masculine' traits such as aggression and physicality. Therefore the female offender, who was seen as exhibiting male traits, was considered doubly deviant, both socially and biologically—she was an exception to the usual sex of the offender and, as a woman, she went against her biological nature and thus was not fully female.

- Some theories discussed female criminality in terms of the physiological differences between the sexes. In this case, women conceal their offending behaviour (and thus have lower rates of report and detection than males) and use their sexuality to attain (presumed) greater leniency by the police and the courts; they do this because their nature is inherently deceitful and manipulative. This in turn is linked to their physiological make-up, in that women are capable of concealing their sexual arousal (unlike men) and thus in the most intimate human acts they have the opportunity and ability to manipulate those around them.

- In some recent theories, research on hormonal disturbances and social behaviour has tried to establish a link between pre- and post-menstrual activity, and the propensity of women to engage in criminal activity. In a similar vein, it is sometimes argued that post-natal depression is responsible in some instances for infanticide. In other words, as the female body fluctuates in terms of hormonal activity, the woman may engage in a wide variety of antisocial and criminal activity.

Socialisation theories

A common way to explain female crime is to point to differences in the ways in which men and women are, or should be, socialised (Smart 1976). These types of explanations are generally closely tied to specific notions of appropriate sex roles. The problem is usually seen as inadequate socialisation, leading to a violation of the behaviour appropriate for members of the female sex. Again, very often the approaches reduce crime causation to essentially biological factors.

- Some theories see deviancy or delinquency as a form of 'acting out' on the part of young women. It is stated that women have traditionally been socialised to be passive and need affection, and that this explains their lower crime rates. However, if they have been abnormally or poorly socialised, then they may be susceptible to manipulation by men, and this manipulation can result in sex-related deviancy such as prostitution.

- A variation of this theory argues that the key issue is the under-socialisation of individual female offenders. The maladjustment of the offender to mainstream social norms manifests itself in the form of sexually inappropriate conduct, such as promiscuous sexual relations. The desire of girls and women for acceptance and approval may result in gratuitous sexual relationships because this is seen as the only way in which the young women can assert themselves (i.e., through their sexuality).

- Some theories begin by arguing that crime is due to the disconnection felt by some women. The psychological absence of love produces instability in these females and this in turn leads to various 'acting out' behaviours of an antisocial or deviant nature. The argument assumes that emotionality is an inherent biological feature of the female sex. Women are said to have a need for dependencies because they are primarily emotional creatures—again a biological reductionist argument.

Feminist responses

The response of feminist writers to these kinds of biological explanations and socialisation arguments is that they represent a 'double standard' in terms of morality and power. Underpinning this double standard is a blurring of the distinction between 'sex' and 'gender'. Females are presumed to have a fixed biological nature, which is indistinguishable from their fixed social role. Any maladjustment to this stereotypical femininity is said to be the consequence of biological defect or inherent biological weaknesses of the female sex. Women's social nature is given naturally by her biological being.

The crucial issue from a feminist perspective is that of relative social power and access to community resources (Alder 1994). The criminalisation process itself is heavily laden with sexist assumptions that reinforce and reproduce structural inequalities of gender in society (Gelsthorpe & Morris 1990). Sexist assumptions determine how offending behaviour is constructed, and how victims are portrayed (see chart 7.2). The central proposition of much feminist analysis is that women are treated differently in and by the criminal justice system because of the persistence of traditional gender-role expectations regarding 'appropriate' and 'feminine' behaviour for women (and men).

Underpinning this gendered division of the sexes is the question of **power**; that is, society is male-dominated, and this is reflected in a myriad of social institutions, including the law and the criminal justice system. Thus, feminist jurisprudence has been concerned to demonstrate the gender biases built into the very processes of the law (for example, the 'reasonable man' argument in legal reasoning), as well as specific overt instances of gender inequality (for example, laws that allowed rape in marriage). The status of women as 'property' and as 'rights holders' has been examined historically and as part of an ongoing struggle to assert women's place and position in a patriarchal system and society (Scutt 1990; Graycar & Morgan 1990; Naffine 1990).

The nature of **female offending** is placed into a wider social, economic, and political context, rather than one that reduces female experience to biological or psychological determinants. Women who commit homicide, for instance, have very often been victims of violence themselves. Similarly, women who commit social security or other minor forms of fraud and theft usually do so, not for themselves, but to support children and dependants. Hence, the generalised violence against women as a social category, and the relative disadvantages they suffer economically, are explored as vital preconditions to any personal or individual offending behaviour.

In the case of **victimisation**, much attention is paid to the ways in which crimes against women have historically either not been considered as crimes (e.g., domestic violence) or are subject to trivialisation and sexual bias (e.g., rape trials involving sex workers). It has been argued in some cases that a woman who has been victimised is herself judged in relation to a man, rather than a specific offensive action. For example, a married woman subjected to injury may be seen in terms of a 'serious crime' insofar as it affects her status as her spouse's 'sexual property' or 'homemaker'. An unmarried woman who has a sexual history of multiple partners may be treated by the courts as having actually provoked a criminal assault. Questions of what is an 'offence' and who is a 'victim' are thus often intertwined with gender stereotypes and biases that reflect a general inequality between the sexes in society.

CHART 7.2   Women and Crime

	Women as offenders	Women as victims
Nature of crimes	■ Sex-specific offences, e.g., prostitution, infanticide ■ Sex-related offences, e.g., shoplifting, fraud	■ Sex-specific offences, e.g., rape, sexual assault ■ Sex-related offences, e.g., consumer rip-offs
Mainstream explanations	■ Related to issues of female sexuality, e.g., biological drives and hormonal activity ■ Related to notions of gender, e.g., constructions of 'feminine' behaviour, and socialisation into these ■ Categories of 'mad' and 'bad' based upon essentially passive and/or deceitful nature of women	■ Categories of 'deserving' and 'undeserving' victims based upon sexuality and relationship to men, e.g., married ■ Related to notion of 'weaker' sex and dominant sex roles and social functions, e.g., housewife ■ Sex-specific victimisation explained in terms of male biological drives, e.g., rape and 'provocation'
Feminist explanations	■ Double standard of morality, e.g., sexualisation of offences for women but not men ■ Prior status of women as victims, e.g., of persistent abuse, of economic dependency ■ Attempts to control and regulate female behaviour by criminalising certain offences as sex-specific ■ Different social opportunities linked to male-dominated institutions and cultures	■ Emphasis on women as victims of male violence generally ■ Sex-specific victimisation linked to patriarchal cultures and institutions ■ Relative powerlessness of some women to protect themselves from personal and property crime ■ Traditional gender-role expectations shape victimisation process

A fundamental question assessed by feminist criminology is how the **sex variable** has been dealt with by the various perspectives:

- There are theories that ignore the sex variable altogether; the vast majority of traditional criminology appears to do this, since it deals only with male criminality and ignores the specific conditions under which women exist in society; that is, the female experience.
- There are then theories that conflate or blur the distinctions between sex and gender. Females are presumed to have a fixed biological nature and/or role(s), and any maladjustment to this stereotypical femininity is said to be the consequence of biological defect. Women's nature is seen as naturally given by her genitals.
- There are theories that ignore the impact of gender relationships. There is a discussion here of women, but the male/female experience is presented as androgynous. These theories neglect the impact of sex relationships on people.

Feminist criminology wanted to explore issues relating to women and looked initially at sex-role differences. Smart (1976) stated that there was a double standard operating in society in relation to morality and power. This was particularly indicated in the nature of offences with which women were charged; primarily sex-specific offences such as infanticide and prostitution (women's crime). The legal framework—both historically, and as revealed by the official statistics—has similarly treated the category of prostitution as relating to women. We know male prostitutes exist, but prostitution is not constructed as a male-specific offence.

There are also **sex-related** offences such as shoplifting—of the total number of crimes reported by the official statistics, a proportionately higher incidence of shoplifting offences are committed by females. The nature of the goods stolen also appears to be gender-related—for example, perfume, lipstick, and tampons.

In terms of activities pertaining to young offenders, historically men have been picked up for certain 'conventional' violations of the law, while young women were seen as delinquent because of their presumed immorality or promiscuity (see Alder 1985; Cunneen & White 2002; Chesney-Lind & Shelden 1992). It is thus presumed that men are in court because of their criminal offending, while females are there because they have slept around—clearly there are double standards operating. Gender is also tied to other offences; for example, passing fraudulent cheques and social security fraud tend to be female offences.

CONTEMPORARY EXAMPLES

If we examine contemporary female offending, some interesting pictures emerge:

- A significant proportion of offenders are single parents, of low educational standing, and unemployed; many have been victimised through male violence, such as rape, sexual abuse, incest, etc. There is also an overrepresentation of indigenous women in the system.
- Feminist theorists state that there are obvious double standards operating in terms of how women and men are treated, both as victims and offenders. This can be highlighted once again by referring to the example of prostitution. Why is it that the female service providers are charged with solicitation and offences associated with prostitution, while the male service recipients are not? While there is a dual relationship between servicer and servicee, rarely is the male patron implicated.
- With respect to the offence of rape, again for many years and still today, there are many myths relating to the nature of rapists. The stereotypical rapist has customarily been portrayed as a violent sexual psychopath and serial offender. Thus the individual is disturbed, and/or the victim has been seen to act to arouse the uncontrollable desires of the male attacker (e.g., by wearing inappropriate clothing). This image reduces rape to an individualistic biological problem, disregarding societal explanations that view rape as relating to social power.
- Likewise, in terms of victims, there has been a league table established in relation to the worthiness or otherwise of the victim status; distinctions are made as to who is or is not to be believed. As conveyed in a judge's comments in Victoria, claims of rape made by a nun or married woman are to be believed, while those made by a prostitute are to be treated as dubious. Such distinctions misconstrue the nature of the issue—the exertion of violence and power, and actual evidence of harm.

Such double standards of power and morality are represented as the **sexualisation thesis** by feminists; that is, women who deviate from what is construed to be the norms of sexuality and morality are seen to be offenders (see Chesney-Lind 1974; Smart 1976).

In particular, when such offenders are young, they are viewed as being immoral or in moral danger. This has been a traditional way of bringing young women into the system; that is, through a category of welfare provision (what are called 'status offences' in the USA) rather than criminal offence. Hence, they did not necessarily have to have done anything illegal to warrant state intervention. Young women who were considered to be sexually promiscuous (thus 'exposed to moral danger') were incarcerated in juvenile institutions 'for their own welfare'. Historically, intervention was often followed by physical examination and subjection to 'treatment' regimes. Institutionalisation aimed to impart necessary instruction in domesticity; adolescent girls were taught to play their 'natural' subservient role as the servers of men. They were released when considered to be 'of a marriageable age'. Men have not been classified, diagnosed, and treated in the same way. Their sexuality has been encouraged, because it is viewed as a 'natural' part of manhood.

The clause in child welfare provisions concerned with 'moral danger' has historically resulted in long periods of incarceration for considerable numbers of young women in Australia (Jaggs 1986). It is important to recognise that in Australia such provisions were not part of the criminal law as such, but were part of the child protection legislation. In reality, such treatment regimes translated into harsher penalties than those given for offending behaviour. Such provisions, it should be added, no longer exist, but they form an indelible part of the history of women's involvement with the criminal justice system.

It should be noted that not only the justice system, but psychiatric, welfare, and other relevant establishments all tried to reinforce these conventional boundaries and distinctions. Women who transgressed the boundaries of dominant conceptions of femininity were seen as falling within one of two categories—they were either **mad** or **bad**. The policing of female behaviour occurs not only in the legal and medical arena, but also in the wider social community. This is evident, for example, in the examination of the nature of the interactions between men and women in youth centres (Nava 1984). The policing of females is widespread, with the objective of preserving the good sexual reputations of the women. Derogatory language—such as 'slut', 'slag', etc.—is commonly used as a tool to regulate female behaviour.

In recent times, there has been a critique of the sexualisation thesis. Carrington (1993) criticises the sexualisation thesis on the grounds that from the mid 1970s there have been equal proportions of males and females appearing before the courts. She discusses the notion of the sexualisation of offending, but looks also at the nature of penalties imposed. She examines the notion that young women are prosecuted primarily on the grounds of their immorality and are dealt harsher sentences because of this. She argues instead, however, that when welfare intervention occurs, irrespective of whether the offender is male or female, harsher sentences are received, because the actions are initiated by the welfare–helping professions.

Carrington also challenges the sexualisation thesis on another ground. If the sustenance of male patriarchy is the objective of the legal system, then one would expect the system to be dominated by men. She claims we should instead look at the composition of all those seeking to control women's behaviour—welfare workers, youth and community workers, social workers, and so on. If we do, we see that a large proportion of those who are the gatekeepers and custodians of female behaviour are women. And among those who wield derogatory and negative labels are young women themselves. Research by Lees (1989), for example, found a liberal use of such terms by adolescent girls within the schoolground setting, as well as stereotyped labelling by women teachers of their students.

The impact of 'race' or ethnicity on female offenders is also raised by Carrington as part of the critique of the sexualisation thesis. In particular, concern is expressed regarding why working-class and Aboriginal young people are overrepresented in the crime statistics. These are the types of questions asked by a number of contemporary feminist criminologists (see Gelsthorpe & Morris 1990). A more sophisticated and complicated analysis is obviously required: it should focus not just on sex differences, but also on differences of class and ethnicity.

Carrington's rejection of the sexualisation thesis has not been entirely convincing, however. In a recent review of Australian feminist criminology, Alder (1994) argues that the sexualisation thesis itself should not be oversimplified. While acknowledging differences between women's experiences, Alder argues that the power of the sexualisation thesis lies in linking the similarities of women's experiences. Women's offending behaviour, and their subsequent involvement in the criminal justice system, form but one part of their lives. If we were to examine the totality of women's lives, in all their complexities and diversities, both the similarities as argued by the sexualisation thesis, and the differences as argued by Carrington, can be supported. Alder goes on to argue that contemporary feminism cannot be oversimplified and parodied any longer as somehow merely advocating a simple relationship between gender and experience. Nonetheless, exploration of the diversity of women's lives reveals consistent themes of surviving, coping, and thriving within patriarchal structures, all of which demand further attention and analysis.

Recent feminist work has tended to focus on two key substantive areas for investigation (Daly & Chesney-Lind 1996). These are, first, explaining and responding to **men's violence** towards women (which encompasses issues such as pornography, rape, and prostitution); and second, thinking about the problems associated with **equality and difference** as these manifest in the legal and criminal justice systems (which encompasses issues such as legal equality, affirmative action, specific needs of female prisoners, and so on). In analysing these kinds of issues, feminist criminologists have employed a wide array of analytical methods and concepts, as shown in accounts that utilise Foucauldian analysis of knowledge and power relations involving men and women (for example, Carrington 1993), and those which focus on 'deconstruction', a technique to explore the workings of language—including non-verbal communication—in conveying meaning (see Young 1990). As suggested by Naffine (1997), contemporary feminist criminology cannot ignore these recent theoretical and methodological insights into the social world, but nor can it ignore the limitations (and strengths) of any one particular perspective or approach.

Feminist criminology is diverse, particularly when reviewing the contemporary debate. Feminists focus on the creation and construction of female offending via the sexualisation thesis, but they also seek to explore the area of victimology, particularly in relation to the victimisation of women. Feminists have long been associated with activism, as well as theoretical debate. In particular, feminist criminologists are concerned to change the law to promote a recognition of issues of violence directed against women. This has led many to argue for the harsher enforcement of laws against perpetrators at the operational level, and a call for greater sensitivity of police to these crimes. However, others see limitations to this, arguing that calling for greater use of the criminal law in a patriarchal system to defend and protect women is fraught with problems (Edwards 1990).

CRITIQUE

Various issues have been the subject of intense discussion and debate within feminist criminology. For example, it has been noted that some feminist approaches do not deal adequately with questions relating to class, ethnicity, and 'race' in discussions of the female offender and the female victim. Yet, as various studies show (e.g., Carrington 1993), the 'race' of a person is a crucial factor in terms of overall representation of some groups within the criminal justice system. Likewise, the class background of the offender or victim has significant consequences with regard to the actual nature of the criminalisation and the victimisation process.

A second area that is generating more attention is the notion that feminist criminology needs to do more than provide a woman-centred analysis: It needs to foster a non-sexist criminology that focuses more broadly on gender relations in their entirety. Specifically, it has been suggested that issues of female and male criminality need to be examined in terms of the social constructions of both 'femininity' and 'masculinity', and with regard to the relationship between each of these social constructions (Gelsthorpe & Morris 1990; Cunneen & White 2002). Naffine (1997: 91) makes the telling comment that: 'As feminist criminologists have shifted our understanding of women, repudiating the female stereotypes, revealing the differences between women's understandings of their own lives and the orthodox (male) accounts of them, so man (whose meaning is so intimately linked with woman) has been altered too.' The idea that women and men need to be understood in terms of their mutual relationship to each other is evident in the literature associated with feminism as such. It is also apparent in the criminological work that has been influenced by feminism but that focuses specifically on men and the male experience (see Polk 1994b; Messerschmidt 1986, 1997; Jefferson 1997). Recent years have seen a burgeoning interest in, and debates over, how best to conceptualise the relationship between men and violence. Work by theorists such as Connell (1995, 2000) has consistently pointed to the ways in which certain forms of 'hegemonic masculinity' are played out, and resisted, in specific historical situations. In many instances, how diverse masculinities are positioned in relation to each other (and in relation to various femininities) have been shown to have major implications for youth crime, homophobic violence,

violence against women and children, and male-on-male violence (see Connell 2002; Tomsen 2002; Mason 2002).

Generally, as Naffine (1997: 2) argues, the message conveyed in mainstream criminology is that 'feminism is about women, while criminology is about men'; but the analytical and political challenges of feminism are nevertheless highly influential throughout the field.

One area where this influence has been greatly felt is in victimology. For example, conventional and some feminist notions of women-as-victims have been subjected to various criticisms. There is the argument that victims should not be viewed merely as passive, but need to be empowered by extending to them the alternative term of 'survivors'. This term is said to imply active response. Hence, debate within the feminist movement has served to push the boundaries as they relate to women, both as victims and as offenders.

More generally, the issue of power, and how this is manifested institutionally, remains an area where more research and discussion are also required. This is particularly so with respect to feminist conceptualisations of the state. Meanwhile, an immediate problem confronting feminist writers and activists is that of the conservative backlash against many of the concepts and issues raised by feminists generally. The profile of female victims, and the dilemmas and inequities surrounding the processing of female offenders, have been actively raised by feminist criminologists. But in the light of contemporary calls for greater 'law and order', there is a fear that such work will be subverted and/or swamped by the simplistic moralising, and simplistic answers, of the New Right.

CONCLUSION

In summary, the feminist perspectives within criminology challenge the male biases and neglects of mainstream criminology. It is identifiably part of Second Wave feminism, which has been part of the social landscape since the 1960s. Within criminology, criticism is levelled at historical and contemporary examples of the double standards applied to women and men in the criminal justice system. As well, active intervention has been called for in areas such as inappropriate responses to female offenders (e.g., imprisonment), law reform that prevents discrimination against women (e.g., equal employment opportunity), the legal recognition of certain crimes against women (e.g., sexual harassment), and active enforcement of laws to protect women from male violence (e.g., domestic violence, incest, rape).

Feminist criminology cannot be seen, however, as a single theoretical perspective. As outlined in this chapter, there are many strands of feminism, from radical feminism and socialist feminism through to liberal and cultural feminism, each having a distinctive voice within criminology. Taken as a whole, feminist criminology has radically altered the nature of the criminological debate. Challenges highlighted by feminists have influenced debates within left-leaning perspectives such as Left Realism and critical criminology, as well as conservative and liberal theories such as New Right criminology and republican theory. Thus, as well as constituting an identifiable perspective within criminology in its own right, feminist criminology has significantly influenced the wider criminological debate.

FURTHER READING

Carrington, K. (1993) *Offending Girls*, Allen & Unwin, Sydney.
Daly, K. & Chesney-Lind, M. (1996) 'Feminism and Criminology', in P. Cordella & L. Siegal (eds) *Readings in Contemporary Criminological Theory*, Northeastern University Press, Boston.
Naffine, N. (1987) *Female Crime: The Construction of Women in Criminology*, Allen & Unwin, Sydney.
Naffine, N. (1997) *Feminism and Criminology*, Allen & Unwin, Sydney.
Scutt, J. (1990) *Women and the Law*, Law Book Company, Sydney.
Smart, C. (1976) *Women, Crime and Criminology: A Feminist Critique*, Routledge and Kegan Paul, London.
Tong, R. (1989) *Feminist Thought: A Comprehensive Introduction*, Unwin Hyman, London.

CHAPTER 8

New Right Criminology

INTRODUCTION

The 1960s and 1970s were broadly characterised by rapid social change and heightened political conflict, which manifested themselves in the rise of radical theories about society in the social sciences, including criminology. By the 1980s, however, a major change in thinking had occurred in society at large. Conservative politicians and political ideologies dominated the electoral landscape across many countries, and 'law and order' emerged as a predominant issue, along with that of high levels of unemployment.

The aim of this chapter is to outline the main currents of **New Right criminology**. This particular approach or perception of crime has both a populist dimension (related to the political process) and an academic dimension (related to the work of criminologists). The fundamental ideas of New Right criminology are based on two themes: placing responsibility for crime squarely on the individual, and reasserting the importance of punishment in responding to crime.

The chapter makes a broad distinction between 'right-wing libertarian' views and those of 'conservatism'. These describe essential differences in the political perspectives contained under the New Right criminology umbrella. The chapter also discusses those traditional academic approaches within criminology itself that reflect and are reflected in the general New Right perspective. In particular, the ideas of 'social control theory' and of 'opportunity-rationality theory' will be discussed.

SOCIAL CONTEXT

The phrase 'New Right' refers to a particular political orientation, rather than to a systematic, coherent theory in its own right. A conservative perspective in criminology—directly opposed to the liberalism of strain theory and labelling perspectives in particular—arose at a time when the long boom of economic prosperity in the advanced capitalist countries was coming to an end. The mid 1970s saw a world economic recession, followed over the next two decades by periodic, and in some instances devastating, economic slumps.

In these new times there was likely to be an increase in property and personal crime at both corporate and street level. The alienation and marginalisation of a significant layer of the population, many of them young people, was associated with a range of antisocial and deviant behaviour. For example, 1977 saw the rise of punk rock music and the overt rebellion of many young people against both the commercial music industry for its insipid conformity and slick production values, and the power-brokers and 'respectable' members of society who had done so little to stem the tide of youth unemployment and yet condemned the ripped shirts of the poor.

Politically, by the 1980s there had been a swing to the right at the level of policy formulation and development, regardless of the political party in power. The economic ideas of Margaret Thatcher in the UK and Ronald Reagan in the USA, the advent of 'Rogernomics' (named after the Treasurer) in New Zealand, and the approach adopted by Hawke and Keating in Australia all signalled an **economic rationalist** platform for dealing with contemporary issues. This emphasised the notion of 'economic efficiency' above all else in policy development, and in each case led to tax cuts for both individuals and corporations, while at the same time universal provision in the allocation of the welfare services and benefits was curtailed. According to the economic rationalists, the wealth created by these measures would benefit both rich and poor. Many argue, however, that the net effect was to exacerbate the growing distance between the rich and the poor in society.

Simultaneously, efforts were made to neutralise any resistance to the economic restructuring that aimed to increase competitiveness and efficiency. Conservative parties in particular made concerted attempts to drastically reduce trade union power. For example, Reagan smashed the air traffic controllers' strike in the USA, while Thatcher took on the miners' union in the UK. In Australia, union power was curbed more subtly and, some would argue, more effectively. The Prices and Incomes Accord between the Australian Labor Party and the Australian Council of Trade Unions was used to defuse any possible union militancy. Nonetheless, strong-arm tactics were also used against 'recalcitrant' elements; notably the army was used to break the airline pilots' strike, and the police and courts were used to deregister the Builders Labourers Federation.

The 1980s saw an emphasis on controlling union power and enhancing wealth creation. In the 'decade of greed', much media prominence was given to business entrepreneurs, many of whom gained near folk-hero status. Labour and financial markets were deregulated, and the idea of a 'free economy and a strong state' (Gamble 1988) was entrenched in places like the UK through the rhetoric of defending the 'people's capitalism'. Market structures were opened up in order to stimulate greater economic activity. In reality, in most cases it was the strong who stood to benefit most, while the rest would have to work that much harder to gain a share of the societal wealth. State agencies that were seen to impede economic growth were more closely scrutinised. Welfare provisions were often downgraded or targeted at a minority of the most impoverished in society, and those institutions that maintained public order and protected private property, such as the police, were strengthened.

In the context of increasing economic hardship and an ideological swing to the Right, supported largely by an economic rationalist mentality, there was a rise in 'law-and-order' politics, both domestically and internationally. For example, internationally, the former concern with the preservation of 'human rights' propounded by world leaders was quickly transformed into an emphasis on terrorism and the drug trade, and the necessity to combat these 'by any means necessary'.

Domestically, the law-and-order push assumed the tone of a 'war on crime' and an attack on the disorder of society. This translated into a call during the 1980s for increased police personnel, powers, and resources; for longer jail sentences; the provision of more prisons; stronger discipline within families and schools; and a return to more traditional values generally. For young people there was the demand for 'greater responsibility', which translated into more punitive attitudes in the area of juvenile justice.

New Right criminology tends to revolve around the individual in society, and to provide a moralistic and punitive approach to issues of crime and criminality (Young 1981). While academic studies have provided sophisticated defences of these ideas (Tame 1991; Buchanan & Hartley 1992), in the public domain the get-tough approach has generally been associated with populist appeals to the public at large. This has proved to be electorally expedient and attractive, even if the consequences of the adoption of such measures leave something to be desired.

Populism is not a political ideology as such, but is a loosely defined mood. It appeals to people on the basis of 'us' versus 'them'. The 'us' is always viewed as virtuous. The 'them', whoever they are, are viewed as being parasites and destructive to the social body. In terms of crime, the essence of populism exaggerates the dangerousness of crime, and the foreign or alien nature of the criminal. The criminal is seen to be outside the society—its networks, institutions, communities, mores, values, methods of income, and ways of life. Insofar as the criminal is not seen to be bound by normal social rules of conduct, so too it is argued that normal rules of order should not necessarily be adhered to if criminals are to be brought to book for their offensive activities.

The rhetoric of populism is one that reduces all crime problems to simple solutions. Offenders are made entirely responsible for their actions, particularly since they exist outside the mainstream institutions of society. They are not seen as members of the 'community' and, indeed, are sometimes presented as not being members of the human race (e.g., they are described as 'animals' or 'savages'). Insofar as this social distancing occurs at the level of rhetoric and policy development, it is not a great leap to encourage ever-more draconian solutions to the crime problem. If the problem is constructed as being one of 'us' against 'them'—as a 'war', which implies violence and destruction—then redemption of the situation is seen to lie in enhanced state power.

The 1980s saw populist rhetoric about crime used actively as a major electoral tool, particularly in the UK. **Authoritarian populism** refers to a process in which crime is ideologically conveyed in a series of moral panics about 'law-and-order' issues (Taylor 1981; Hall 1980; Hall et al. 1978). The extent and seriousness of crime is highlighted (but not necessarily backed up by statistical or other research findings) and this, in turn, is used to justify harsher penalties, and the assertion of state authority in more and more spheres of everyday social life. As part of this process, specific groups or categories of people are singled out for special attention: young people, Aborigines, welfare recipients, striking workers, and sole parents. Thus, 'we' are protected by having ever-greater state intervention into the affairs of 'them', the most likely candidates for membership of the criminal class. Again, the rationale behind such intrusion is usually a combination of protection of private property, and the differential treatment that should be meted out to the moral and immoral in society.

The broad appeal of authoritarian populism is due in part to the pervasive influence of the print and electronic media in conveying particular types of images regarding crime in society (Grabosky & Wilson 1989; Ericson et al. 1991; Males 1996). For example, Hogg and Brown (1998) have identified the key assumptions in what they call 'law and order commonsense', many elements of which are perpetuated by the media. The assumptions include:

- crime rates are soaring
- crime is worse than ever
- the criminal justice system is 'soft' on crime
- the criminal justice system is loaded in favour of criminals
- there should be more police
- police should have more powers
- courts should deliver tougher penalties
- the greater satisfaction of victims demands more retribution through the courts.

These general elements of law-and-order commonsense are seemingly routine aspects of the way in which the electronic and print media portray crime. By and large, crime is sensationalised in and by the media. The flooding of the media with stories of 'street crime' has, however, real and pertinent effects: heightening the fear of crime, feeding the stereotypes regarding the 'typical offender', exaggerating the extent of extremely violent and serious crimes, and fostering acceptance for policies that appear to 'get something done' about the crime problem. The politically important role of New Right criminology is thus related to the basic electoral appeal of authoritarian populist rhetoric.

BASIC CONCEPTS

The main elements of New Right criminology include a combination of conservative moralising and free-market competitive ethos. These sometimes contradict each other at the level of specific policies. However, the overriding message is that there is a need to 'get tough on criminals', to hold them responsible for their actions, and to punish the wrongdoer in a consistent manner.

New Right criminology is opposed to perspectives that emphasise 'treatment' and 'reform' rather than punishment. It opposes the views of orthodox positivist criminology, which have a deterministic view or model of the causes of crime; rather, it asserts that **people do make choices**, and that they therefore must pay for these choices. In a nutshell, the argument is that if you 'do the crime', then you must 'do the time'.

The New Right criminological perspective includes several strands: some deal with more philosophical views regarding the nature of human activity, and some with specific areas of interest such as retributivist concerns with sentencing; the range extends to economic analyses of the causes and social responses to crime. For present purposes, however, we will illustrate the broad orientation of these kinds of perspectives by examining two general views on the nature of crime and crime control—right-wing libertarianism and traditionalist conservatism. Each is concerned with the **punishment and disciplining of offenders**, but the overall analysis of crime in society does nevertheless differ.

Right-wing libertarianism

The right-wing libertarian perspective harks back to the days of classical liberalism, characterised by competitive free-market capitalism and minimal state intervention, including welfare provision (see chart 8.1). In this approach, human beings are conceived of as rational entities with free will. It is based upon a moral philosophy of egoism (selfishness), in which the only constraints on behaviour are that there should be a duty not to initiate force over others.

The notion of a **competitive ethos** pervades this perspective. This is usually tied to the idea of rights to private property as being the first virtue of the legal and criminal justice system. Accordingly, crime is defined in terms of the infringement of private property, including infringements of one's physical self. Generally this approach defines crime in restrictive terms, as only those acts that violate the 'natural rights' of others.

Since human nature is conceived of as being possessive and individualistic, and since crime is conceived mainly in terms of private property, then the role of the state should be restricted to those instances where other people actually come to harm by one's social actions. In other words, there should be **minimal state intervention** in one's life. What intervention that there is should be tightly focused on enhancing and protecting individual liberty and protecting private property.

The cause of crime is seen to lie with the individual. In reinforcing notions of individual selfishness, rights, and individuality, this perspective simultaneously asserts that criminological theorising of the recent past has made excuses for individuals, by taking away people's **responsibilities for their actions**. It is argued, for example, that to speak of biological drives or social determinants such as poverty takes away any notion of choice in the selection of behaviour and activity.

Thus, individuals should be held fully responsible for their actions. Crime is seen fundamentally as a matter of **rational choice**, involving various incentives and disincentives. Since individual liberty is highly valued, however, the perspective believes that so-called 'victimless crimes' should be **decriminalised** insofar as they do not directly affect those beyond oneself. In other words, anything goes—people should have complete liberty to do as they want, as long as they do not infringe upon the property or person of others in an illegal way.

CHART 8.1   Right-wing Libertarianism

Definition of crime	▪ (restrictive) only those acts that violate the 'natural rights' of others
Focus of analysis	▪ individual liberty and protection of private property rights
Cause of crime	▪ matter of rational choices involving incentives and disincentives
Nature of offender	▪ fully responsible for their own actions
Response to crime	▪ retribution, deterrence, incapacitation, and punishment insofar as individual held responsible
Crime prevention	▪ decriminalisation, minimal state intervention, moral call for taking of personal responsibility and self-control
Operation of criminal justice system	▪ reduction in number of laws relating to 'victimless crime' ▪ greater use of incarceration and detention ▪ use of restitution to compensate victims ▪ support for privatisation of security, law enforcement, prisons

Where harm to another individual does occur, as in the case of the commission of an offence, then the offender should be punished. The perspective generally favours the promotion of retribution, deterrence, incapacitation, and punishment in its response to crime. It is informed by a **just deserts** philosophy, whereby punishment should be proportional to the crime. Furthermore, it favours the enforcement of **restitutive measures** with respect to the victims of crime; that is, compensation should be paid by the offender to the victim for any harm which they may have caused in the course of the offence.

In response to perspectives that see behaviour mainly in terms of psychological or social influences, this approach calls for a **moralising** of society. Morality is seen in this context to be rooted in the individualistic ethos of personal responsibility and self-control. In return for minimal state intervention, it is essential that people use their liberty in accordance with the law. Where this is not so, then they should have to shoulder the penalty themselves.

In line with a general libertarian philosophy that de-emphasises the state, this approach also supports the idea that security, law enforcement, and prisons should be **private** rather than public institutions. This reflects a broad ideological commitment to the so-called free market as the best and most efficient avenue for the provision of social services.

Traditionalist conservative

The traditionalist conservative perspective on what constitutes a crime takes a broader view than the right-wing libertarian one (see chart 8.2). The conservative view of crime includes not only that activity which endangers property or the person, but also that which offends morality. Hence, attacks on certain traditional values and people's general respect for authority may be viewed as criminal.

From this point of view, crime is not only a matter of 'free choice' but also is linked to certain intrinsic aspects of humanity. In particular, people are seen to possess certain 'natural urges' that go against the more civilised or divine purposes of society. Whether it be a concept of 'original sin' or a secular theory of human nature that sees people in a negative light, the idea is that all people are somehow **inherently evil or flawed**.

In order to constrain the 'natural' urges to do wrong, it is necessary to establish a strong order based upon personal sacrifice, self-discipline, and submission to authority. **Order** must take precedence over all else, including justice. Crime is said to be caused by the unwillingness of people to accept discipline, the undermining of traditional loyalties—such as to the (patriarchal) family—and the pursuit of immediate individual gratification without appropriate hard work.

According to this approach, punishment is an essential part of deterrence. This is so not only because it establishes personal responsibility for one's actions, but also because it has an important **symbolic impact** on society as a whole. That is, punishment has to be seen in terms of its effect on the establishment of moral solidarity through stigmatisation. Punishment is, in effect, a form of social **retribution**, and may thus represent a response that is not proportional to the offence (in fact it may be much greater) due to the important symbolic role of punishment in bonding community members together.

Strong emphasis is placed upon the importance of **morality** in the maintenance of social authority. Thus, if someone does something deemed to be wrong or harmful, then they must be punished swiftly and appropriately in order to set the moral standard. Simultaneously, it is important to set clear moral standards and guidelines to conduct.

CHART 8.2   Conservatism

Definition of crime	■ (expansive) violations of law, and acts that offend morality as well
Focus of analysis	■ personal discipline and self-control
Cause of crime	■ lack of self-discipline, undermining of traditional loyalties, lack of respect for authority
Nature of offender	■ inherently 'evil' or flawed
Response to crime	■ need for strong coercion, general deterrence strategies, assertion of authority
Crime prevention	■ importance of traditional morality in maintenance of social authority, emphasis on self-discipline and submission to authority
Operation of criminal justice system	■ expansion of laws relating to 'moral' issues such as pornography ■ harsher penalties to enforce the legal and moral code ■ order to take priority over justice ■ emphasis on conformity to established traditions and social roles

The traditionalist conservatives generally possess anti-libertarian views with respect to pornography, sexual behaviour, drug use, and abortion; that is, they favour intervention in areas regarded as victimless crimes. Indeed, the conservative point of view often favours **increased state intervention** in everyday social life because it is felt that only strong coercive measures will ultimately keep people in line and teach them the discipline they require to live as members of a civilised community.

HISTORICAL DEVELOPMENT

The New Right perspective has historical links with several different traditions within criminology. The right-wing libertarian approach is clearly identified with a classical criminological perspective. The emphasis on individual choice and responsibility, punishment and proportionality, and protection of liberty and property all have their echoes in the previous discussions of the social contract.

The traditionalist conservative approach has also been reflected in sociological and criminological theorising. For example, the emphasis on punishment as a means of reinforcing moral boundaries echoes aspects of Durkheim's work. As Garland (1990: 28) puts it, Durkheim saw punishment as a social institution intimately concerned with morality and social solidarity: 'The existence of strong bonds of moral solidarity are the conditions which cause punishments to come about, and, in their turn, punishments result in the reaffirmation and strengthening of these same social bonds'. Durkheim was thus concerned with exploring conceptually the nature of punishment, particularly in relation to the ideas of the 'collective conscience' and the role of passion and sentiment in social life. However, unlike Durkheim, conservative traditionalists promote a single moral 'rightness' that pertains to society as a whole, whereas Durkheim was at pains to point out that morality varied between different societies.

More recent work has elements of both descriptive and proscriptive analysis. The emphasis on discipline, coercion, and self-control in the traditionalist conservative approach, for instance, is mirrored in the concerns of control theory. Whether it emphasises bio-social processes (as in Eysenck's work) or socialisation processes (see Nettler 1984), a social control perspective argues that the nature of crime is intertwined with the connection between individual and society.

Control theory as formulated by Hirschi (1969), for example, is premised upon the idea that it is an individual's bond to society that makes the difference in terms of whether or not they abide by society's general rules and values. From this perspective, all people are inherently antisocial, and thus all people would commit crime if they so dared. It is the nature of the bond that children have with their society that ultimately determines their behaviour (Empey 1982; Nettler 1984).

Hirschi (1969) theorised that the social bond is made up of four major elements:

- **Attachment**—the ties of affection and respect to significant others in one's life, and more generally a sensitivity to the opinion of others.
- **Commitment**—the investment of time and energy to activities such as school and various conventional and unconventional means and goals.
- **Involvement**—the patterns of living that shape immediate and long-term opportunities; for example, the idea that keeping busy doing conventional things will reduce the exposure of young people to illegal opportunities.
- **Belief**—the degree to which young people agree with the rightness of legal rules, which are seen to reflect a general moral consensus in society.

It is the combination of attachment, commitment, involvement, and belief that shapes the life world of the young person, and that essentially dictates whether or not they will take advantage of conventional means and goals of social advancement, or whether they will pursue illegal pathways to self-gratification.

It is up to society, and its agents, to step in and ensure that its younger members are imbued with the right bonds. In other words, there is a high degree of intervention necessary if children and young people are to be guided the right way, and if they are to follow paths that uphold social values, but that ultimately go against their essential antisocial nature. Without adequate socialisation—a strong social control presence of some kind—criminal behaviour would be common.

CONTEMPORARY EXAMPLES

In related and more recent work, Gottfredson and Hirschi (1990) argue that the central issue in explaining crime is that of self-control; that is, people differ in the extent to which they are restrained from criminal acts (see also Wilson & Herrnstein 1985). This, in turn, is linked to the question of social bonding, and especially the problem of ineffective child rearing. The theory incorporates elements of other theories and perspectives: classical theory, in its acceptance of the idea that people are basically self-seeking; bio-social positivism, in its focus on the importance of proper 'conditioning' or training of the young; and sociological perspectives, which look to the nature of the family as a key variable in the development of self-control.

The theory does not analyse specific social divisions (e.g., class, gender, ethnicity), but rests upon a conception of human nature that sees all people as essentially driven by the same kinds of 'universal tendency to enhance their own pleasure'. Given this, the crucial issue is then one of how best to socialise all people to conform to society's values and to engage in conventional law-abiding behaviour.

In policy terms, the answer to juvenile crime lies in redressing the **defective social training** that characterises offenders who have in some way 'lost control'. In other words, the emphasis from a practitioner's perspective will be to reattach the young people to some kind of family, to recommit them to long-range conventional goals, to involve them in school and other constructive activities, and to have them acquire beliefs in the morality of law (Empey 1982: 269).

Importantly, the control perspective is premised upon the idea that 'deviancy' stems from lack of self-control, and that this is fundamentally a matter related to the processes of socialisation. Whereas Gottfredson and Hirschi emphasised the significance of relationships within the family, other contemporary criminologists have concentrated on making changes to the costs and benefits of crime.

Much work, for example, has been done in the general area of **opportunity-rationality theory**. This approach reflects the libertarian emphasis on choice and responsibility for one's actions. It is postulated that crime cannot be understood apart from the nature and distribution of opportunities for both crime and non-criminal behaviour. Thus, when people find themselves in situations in which they have opportunities to commit crime, the decision to do so or not to do so is a rational one (see Barlow 1993).

In fact, from the point of view of rational choice theory we need to assume that most 'criminals' are rational agents who can be deterred from committing additional crimes by an increase in the punishment they might expect to receive (Buchanan & Hartley 1992). In economic terms, the idea here is that individuals will always act in such a way as to maximise their own benefit. They are responsive to incentives and disincentives. From an economic rationalist position, therefore, the best criminal justice policy is one that prevents the commission of crime at the least financial cost. For example, according to the advocates of this approach, the most economically efficient way in which to manage the crime problem is to privatise institutions such as prisons, and to increase the probability of detection and conviction of offenders.

The broad philosophical orientation of rational choice theory is also closely related to the adoption of crime prevention techniques directed primarily at **opportunity reduction** (see Felson 1994), rather than the structural reasons for offending behaviour or the criminalisation process itself. Analysis of particular activities and locations can form the basis of a strategy designed to change the risks and costs associated with certain behaviours. In this way, the potential offender is deterred from making the decision to commit crime in certain areas, against certain targets.

A third perspective identified with New Right criminology is that of **underclass** explanations (Herrnstein & Murray 1994; Murray 1990). In this view, the problem resides in the behaviour of certain population groups, particularly the poor, the homeless, single mothers, and, in the case of the USA, African-Americans (see Mooney 1998; Fraser 1995). The problem of crime and deviancy is thus seen to lie within the identi-fied populations themselves. The 'underclass' comprises those sections of the poverty-stricken who, through their own volition or choice, or by genetic default, engage in criminal activity, substance abuse, illegitimate births, and deliberate non-participation in paid employment. Essentially, the so-called underclass is presented here as a 'moral' category, given that the emphasis is on behaviour (rather than structural conditions such as lack of jobs) and disapproval (rather than understanding of social hardship).

A summary of common themes in New Right writings on the underclass is provided by Lind (1995). The nature of the problem, from a right-wing perspective, is a combination of lack of economic incentives (e.g., welfare dependency), a culture of poverty (e.g., familial breakdown and inappropriate role models), intellectual deficiencies (e.g., hereditary genetic inferiority), and low standards of morality (e.g., illegitimacy via sole parenting). The proposed solution is to make members of the 'underclass' more responsible and accountable for their own welfare and lifestyle choices. In effect, the demand is for the withdrawal of government support for the disadvantaged, coupled with efforts to resocialise people into new value and moral systems.

Whatever the specific theories that have been developed over the years, it appears that many writers have adopted a New Right criminological position simply due to the perception that 'nothing else has worked'. The so-called new realists, for example, have observed the deficiencies of a system partly built upon 'treatment' and positivistic assumptions, and concluded that it is time to reassert order and authority across our social institutions (see Tame 1991; Wilson 1975). Given the trends towards economic and social polarisation, and given the apparent electoral appeal of law-and-order scapegoating, it is also the case that New Right criminology dovetails with New Right politics generally.

From the point of view of crime control and public order, the direction of policing and punishment fostered by New Right criminology is towards more active containment of, and control over, what are seen to be criminogenic populations—the 'dangerous classes' of the late modern era. The practical implementation of criminal justice policy is based upon the regulation of those population groups most closely identified with the 'underclass'. For instance, intervention is increasingly concerned with identifying, classifying, and managing groups in the community that are assessed on the basis of 'risk' and 'dangerousness' (see Feeley & Simon 1994). This is associated with various kinds of pre-emptive action and incapacitation strategies, such as 'zero tolerance' policing and 'three strikes and you're out' punishment. The emphasis is on attacking the 'signs of disorder' through confrontational policing strategies (in which any behaviour, activity, or group deemed to be antisocial is not to be tolerated by authorities), and by locking up those who transgress the criminal and moral norms of society (through committing them to long prison terms). Getting 'tough on crime' is part of a generalised escalation in the punishment ethos. For all the criminological talk about 'rationality', it would appear that, increasingly, criminal justice policy is marked by sensationalist hyperbole and, indeed, a high degree of irrationality about crime and what to do about it.

CRITIQUE

A critique of New Right criminology stems from the way in which theories within this perspective ignore issues of power in their assertion of choice and free will. In this way the critique of New Right criminology mirrors, to some extent at least, criticisms of classical criminology. On 'rational' criteria, there is much to criticise in New Right criminology, particularly in its populist political guise.

On a theoretical level New Right criminology does not analyse the nature of choice within a society that is characterised by inequality, as opposed to equality. It does not address concerns about the ethnic and 'racial' divisions in society, and the way in which certain groups, such as indigenous people, are systematically overrepresented in the criminal justice system. The explanation that such overrepresentation can be explained purely by a 'choice' to offend does not seem to take us very far. Much New Right criminology simply ignores issues of 'race', ethnicity, gender, and class by prioritising the individual, along with individual choice and individual values.

Where levels of analysis other than that of the individual are evident, it is clear that they rest on a particular set of values that does not include significant sectors of society. For example, control theory talks unproblematically about inculcating majority values, expressed through belief in the rightness of legal rules that are seen to reflect a general moral consensus in society. The interdependence of individuals that prevents criminal behaviour is premised upon adherence to the moral consensus. Non-adherence predisposes an individual to criminal offending. Within multicultural societies such as Australia, Canada, the USA, and the UK, there are major problems if the notion of consensus is defined in the narrow terms that traditional conservatives tend to use.

Many of the policies proposed by New Right theories have themselves been discredited. In particular, the capacity of harsh, or even proportional, punishment to deter individuals from reoffending has been the subject of long debate. There is substantial evidence that imprisonment in particular is counterproductive, and serves only to exacerbate, not diminish, rates of offending. Prison (and the 'big stick' in general) is both ineffective and expensive.

Furthermore, the debate concerning the need for harsher penalties has negative consequences in and of itself. For example, it engenders a fear of crime, which is out of all proportion to the realistic possibility of victimisation. The problem of how to deal with the fear of crime—independent of how to deal with crime per se—is an urgent issue facing many people today.

Finally, crime itself is defined narrowly. For the majority of New Right theorists, the major concern is with 'street crime'. Crimes of the powerful and crimes of the state are hardly mentioned. Where they are mentioned, the state is seen as able to deal adequately with the problem, since there is no conception that the state itself may favour the powerful over the powerless.

The popularity of the law-and-order debate, and with it the popularity of New Right criminology in general, cannot be accounted for adequately by reference to a rational 'scientific' debate. It is best explained by the need of societies for symbolic assurances of certainty in the face of growing economic uncertainty. The symbolic and political nature of the crime debate is well evidenced through the popularity of New Right criminology. It provides government with a justification to capture the emotional needs of an electorate within a capitalist democracy. The potency of the symbol of 'law and order' is not lost on governments increasingly at the mercy of unpleasant financial and employment trends in the economic sphere.

A further, and worrying, aspect of the authoritarian strand within New Right circles is the merging of global and international developments with national and domestic concerns. This is most evident in the ways in which the so called 'war on terrorism' has seen even greater collaboration between military, police, and secret services; a greater propensity to do away with long-established human rights and civil rights protections (in the name of homeland security); and the putting into place of informal and formal sanctions designed to ensure public 'unity' in support of war efforts (both within and without national borders). Politically, the pursuit of 'security' has been accompanied in the United States by what has been called 'prescriptive patriotism', an orchestrated patriotism that is 'aimed at closing down debate and dissent through the imposition of a prescribed allegiance' (O'Leary & Platt 2001: 42). Crime and deviance is thus defined almost exclusively in terms dictated by ruling elites, who mobilise public opinion in ways that allow for the silencing of dissent, the imprisonment of those who have not been formally charged with a crime, and the vilification of minority groups.

Similar types of processes are also apparent with regard to immigration controls and border protection. Once again, the treatment of asylum seekers, especially in countries such as Australia, has frequently been characterised by systematic denial of human and legal rights, an emphasis on illegality of entry, the selective rejection of refugees by possible host nations, and the enforced detention of those who survive the journey to new lands (see Weber 2002; Pickering & Lambert 2001). The symbols of the New Right are basically constructed around notions of social difference, which are in turn interpreted as evidence of social deviance. This applies to 'deviants' inside a country, as well as those outside.

Despite the negative aspects of New Right criminology, there are elements that are of importance to the criminological debate. While it asserts issues of individual responsibility, it also highlights individual rights and, in particular, the right to feel safe and secure. The rights of victims, which had been ignored by the majority of criminologists, are brought to the fore within this perspective. Victims' rights and needs can no longer be ignored within criminological theory. Finally, the phenomenon of New Right criminology is a timely reminder of the political nature of crime and crime policy. Criminological theory has to come to grips with political realities if its policy proposals and strategic plans of action are to go beyond mere conjecture.

CONCLUSION

New Right criminology refers to a particular political orientation, rather than to a systematic, coherent theory in its own right. For this reason there is a broad range of theoretical perspectives that are brought together in this chapter, from authoritarian populism and right-wing libertarian perspectives through to traditionalist conservatism and control theory. Despite the differences of these approaches, all can be characterised by a focus on the rights, responsibilities, and free will of the individual who offends. Each has a particular moral stance that upholds the status quo of society and the right of those with power to dictate what constitutes the moral consensus.

Each strand of New Right thinking also tends to see human nature as ultimately depraved. Without sufficient deterrent measures put in place by the state, or strong social bonds as defined by control theory, human nature would automatically lead to antisocial and criminal behaviour. Overlaid on this perspective of human nature is the need for society to clearly define right from wrong, to reward the right, and, more importantly, to punish the wrong. Without such an approach, a general breakdown in law and order would result.

Like many criminological theories, the popularity of New Right criminology cannot be divorced from the broader political environment. The political popularity of the law-and-order debate and calls for tougher punishment on a political level are legitimised through many of the perspectives outlined above. The prominence of the law-and-order debate, as fostered by New Right ideas, led directly to the emergence of a new theoretical perspective on the left, namely Left Realism. It was the success of the New Right at a popular level that led sections of the Left to 'take crime seriously'. To do so they recognised that issues such as victims' rights and the popularity of a strong response to criminal behaviour resonated with community concerns, and were thus important.

FURTHER READING

Buchanan, C. & Hartley, P. (1992) *Criminal Choice: The Economic Theory of Crime and Its Implications for Crime Control*, Centre for Independent Studies, Sydney.

Feeley, M. & Simon, J. (1994) 'Actuarial Justice: The Emerging New Criminal Law', in D. Nelken (ed.) *The Futures of Criminology*, Sage, London.

Gottfredson, M. & Hirschi, T. (1990) *A General Theory of Crime*, Stanford University Press, Stanford.

Herrnstein, R. & Murray, C. (1994) *The Bell Curve*, Basic Books, New York.

Lind, M. (1995) 'Brave New Right', in S. Fraser (ed.) *The Bell Curve Wars: Race, Intelligence and the Future of America*, Basic Books, New York.

Murray, C. (1990) *The Emerging Underclass*, Institute of Economic Affairs, London.

Nettler, G. (1984) *Explaining Crime*, McGraw-Hill, New York.

Tame, C. (1991) 'Freedom, Responsibility and Justice: The Criminology of the "New Right"', in K. Stenson & D. Cowell (eds) *The Politics of Crime Control*, Sage, London.

CHAPTER 9

Left Realism

INTRODUCTION

Left Realism is best seen as a response to two conflicting perspectives on crime that emerged strongly in the mid 1980s: New Right criminology and Marxist criminology. The previous chapter outlined the political popularity of the conservative political perspective with its strong emphasis on 'law and order'. Left Realism was concerned that the political debate was being dominated by the right wing, which had a destructive impact on the lives of the working class. It attempted to capture the political debate by focusing, like the conservatives, on the victims of so-called street crime. However, Left Realists wanted to highlight the fact that the majority of victims of street crimes were from the working class, not the middle and upper classes. In doing so, Left Realism wanted to reorient the law-and-order debate—away from the middle-class fear of the working class, and towards a consideration of how the working class itself suffers from crime.

Left Realism saw radical criminology as unable or unwilling to ameliorate this suffering of the working class because it failed to take crime seriously. This failure further meant that such criminological analysis was unable to provide the antidote to the conservative 'law-and-order' politics that dominated crime policy. Left Realists contrasted the political popularity of the conservative Thatcher government in Britain with the political marginalisation of the radical perspective, or 'left idealist' view (as it was labelled by the Left Realists). The reason for such marginalisation, they suggested, was the lack of practical suggestions put forward by Marxist criminology to deal with crime in the inner city.

155

This chapter will outline the origins of Left Realism and the nature of the response it made to 'law-and-order' politics from a left perspective. It has received considerable criticism, mainly from the left, and has undergone considerable revision. The major revisions within Left Realism will also be outlined in this chapter. What is central to the Left Realist endeavour, and common to all permutations of the theory, is its pragmatic core. Left Realism sees itself as both a reasonable and practical response to the problem of crime in inner-city communities.

SOCIAL CONTEXT

In terms of social context, Left Realism can be seen as a concern within (initially) British criminology with the policies of neo-conservatism in general and the Thatcher government in particular. It was avowedly political in that it saw itself as a political response to the law-and-order agenda of the right. It was this response to the law-and-order debates of the early 1980s that galvanised the thinking of Left Realists. Prior to this time they had been writing as predominantly Marxist or radical criminologists debating with other radical criminologists from within the same essential paradigm.

In attempting to enter into the political discussions of law and order, the Left Realists joined in the conservative debate about **crime control**, which was less concerned about the causes of crime. In doing so, they confirmed that conservative politics had successfully defined the crime problem as one where there were clear distinctions between those who were criminal and those who were not. In this conception, crime was a unitary phenomenon defined by common sense. With this in mind, crime policy was properly concerned with controlling crime, not with reducing conditions that might give rise to criminal behaviour, such as inequality and unemployment.

This emphasis on controlling crime, rather than on dealing with the causes of crime, could be seen clearly in the contribution Left Realist writers made in response to the **riots** experienced in Britain in 1981. These riots occurred in areas of poverty and high levels of unemployment, such as Brixton, but it was not this unemployment and deprivation per se that captured the imagination of the Left Realists. These theorists argued that while poverty and deprivation were a precondition of riots, and more generally of increases in crime, they were not a sufficient cause. Poverty and unemployment could be associated with quiescent fatalism and the acceptance of adversity, as much as with rebellion and violence (Lea & Young 1982). Left Realists argued that the riots had their genesis in three factors: West Indian counterculture; the political marginalisation of the inner city; and, crucially, the police methods of dealing with people who lived in deprived neighbourhoods.

The explanations by the realists for the existence of a violent and aggressive counterculture are similar to the explanations of the strain theorists, which were outlined in chapter 4. Left Realists argued that countercultures thrive where the expectations of material rewards engendered by the education system and the mass media are manifestly not available to certain sectors of society. In particular, successive generations of West Indian immigrants in the UK saw themselves as discriminated against and alienated from the mainstream culture. In the face of this lack of opportunity, a counterculture developed—based on a 'hustling' mentality and street culture—that was competitive, disorganised, and antisocial. Along with poverty and unemployment, the existence of this counterculture produced extremely high rates of inner-city crime. In opposition to Marxist criminologists, who downplayed or denied the existence of rising rates of street crime, Left Realists argued that street crime was much higher than police figures suggested.

Those who lived in the decaying inner city lacked access to an effective voice within the political process; this exacerbated the alienation that people in those neighbourhoods experienced, and spawned the counterculture. Those marginalised within the inner city had no access to traditional centres of power within society, such as those controlling capital or the trade unions. Such people were locked out of the world of production and, with this, access to the political system was also denied. Left Realism suggested that the return to violence, epitomised by the riots, was the politics of last resort. Economic marginalisation exacerbated political marginalisation.

The marginalisation felt by people in these neighbourhoods was not addressed by government or state agencies. Rather, the methods used by the arm of the state that had the greatest impact in the area, namely the **police**, were disastrous. Left Realists argued that in deprived neighbourhoods police deliberately shifted away from 'consensus' policing (policing for the community), which might have at least gone some way to reducing alienation in these communities. Instead, police used military tactics, 'swamp' procedures, and 'stop and search' provisions that allowed on-the-street searching of any suspicious-looking person. These tactics had the effect of blurring the distinction between offender and non-offender to a point where, Left Realists argued, any action by police became perceived as a symbolic attack on the community as a whole. It is at this point that any consensual relationship that existed between the police and the public breaks down, and actions by police can trigger rioting (Lea & Young 1982).

The analysis of the riots in the UK set the scene for the early formulations of Left Realism, and defined the theory as one primarily concerned with the control of crime, rather than amelioration of the preconditions of crime. Relief of the preconditions of the counterculture, for example, was not the primary policy goal of the theorists. Rather, they took as central planks the second and third strands of analysis outlined above—political marginalisation and policing reform. The political dimension was addressed by alignment with the British Labour Party and the production of policies with which the left could intervene effectively in the law-and-order debate (Lea & Young 1984). The substance of the policies provided by Left Realism predominantly addressed the third strand of analysis, that of policing reform, and the creation of consensus-style policing within inner urban areas.

The focus on policing was seen as justified because of perceived omissions by Marxist criminology concerning the reality of crime in working-class areas. The theory argues that the major concern of the working class and marginalised poor in the city was not the crimes of the powerful, as suggested by Marxist criminology, but the property offences, robbery, and domestic violence that were experienced as an everyday reality. The victims of such crimes, as well as the perpetrators, were predominantly the poor and vulnerable sections of society. The radical criminological focus on crimes of the powerful and crimes of the state 'missed the point' and failed to accurately represent the needs of the working class. Furthermore, when 'street crime' was mentioned by radical criminology it was too often romanticised: street criminals were characterised as 'latter-day Robin Hoods' rather than as perpetrators of criminal behaviour that was seriously antisocial and destructive. So, for Left realists it was the street crime of inner-city neighbourhoods that should form the predominant focus of criminology.

BASIC CONCEPTS

Left Realist criminology is characterised by its pragmatic focus on crime control (see chart 9.1). Because of this, it is not concerned with lengthy analyses of what crime actually is. Rather, it is content to define crime as that contained in the legal code. This can be seen as partly a result of the major means of data collection used by the Left Realists—namely, local crime victim surveys (see for example Jones et al. 1986). Local crime victim surveys target specific inner-city locations, and ask residents about their victimisation from criminal activity, and what residents would like done about it. As a result, the definition of crime is driven by the definitions of crime that are reported on the survey. Local residents are more likely to see crime as defined in traditional terms, and so Left Realism itself defines crime in traditional terms.

CHART 9.1   Left Realist Perspectives

Definition of crime	▪ as contained in legal code, with main focus on street crime
Focus of analysis	▪ crime by and against working class, with working class as both offender and victim ▪ use of crime victim surveys
Cause of crime	▪ relative deprivation ▪ ineffective methods of policing
Nature of offender	▪ most crime is intra-class ▪ offenders must be held responsible to a degree for their own actions
Response to crime	▪ develop more effective policing, and greater community control over criminal justice agencies
Crime prevention	▪ reduce alienation of community from the criminal justice system ▪ adopt problem-solving approaches ▪ take crime seriously
Operation of criminal justice system	▪ active cooperation between police and community members ▪ meeting of victim needs ▪ crime prevention programmes

The local crime victim survey is the major tool of analysis of Left Realists. Because the emphasis is on addressing the concerns expressed by inner-city populations, analysis is directed towards concerns raised about crime in local areas as expressed through the crime surveys. In particular, this perspective is noted for concern about **intra–class crime**; that is, criminal behaviour by the working class against the working class.

More recent analysis has focused on the 'square of crime'. This consists of two dyads. One is concerned with the **criminal act**, which comprises offender and victim. The other is concerned with **social control**, which comprises social action (e.g., the actions of police and 'multi-agencies') and social reaction (e.g., the reaction of the public). A complete analysis of crime, according to Left Realists, should focus on both dyads (Young 1991).

The causes of crime as perceived by the Left Realists span both the conditions endemic to inner-city working-class areas, such as poor facilities and lack of jobs, and the response by the criminal justice agencies, notably the police, which exacerbate the problem of crime by their heavy-handed responses. The cause of crime, according to Left Realism, results from the amalgamation of three aspects: the **relative deprivation** of those in working-class areas, which gives rise to countercultures; the lack of access to the political sphere, which spawns **feelings of powerlessness**; and **dissent and police responses** that antagonise local populations and cause further breakdown in these communities. This leads to rising crime rates in these areas. The level of crime, according to Left Realists, is higher than that in official figures, and is rising in areas of high social breakdown (Young 1991).

Concern with the suffering of the victims of crime has led Left Realism to adopt a less-than-sympathetic view of the offender. Offenders are **responsible for their behaviour**, which is antisocial and destructive, and causes great hardship within already impoverished areas of society. However, unlike New Right criminology, Left Realists do not see offenders or offending totally as a result of free will. The motivation to offend springs from the relative deprivation in these areas. Young people and ethnic minorities are led by the broader culture to expect material reward, yet their situation within the social order prevents them achieving that reward. Further to this, social cohesion in these areas has broken down. Left Realists argue that in other times of great hardship, such as the depression of the 1930s, there was a working-class solidarity and working-class culture that saw people pull together. Today inner-city areas with a high crime rate lack **social solidarity** that could insulate against feelings of deprivation. The result is anger and frustration, particularly in young people.

So, how do Left Realists see effective responses to these problems? The primary response has been in the area of **police and policing**. Crime can be controlled by a police force that is responsive to the needs of the local community (Kinsey et al. 1986). Furthermore, the community needs to be in control of the police force: police should respond to local city councils rather than a distant bureaucracy at the state or national level. Local communities need effective political responses to their concerns, which can be brought about by giving greater power to local councils to control criminal justice agencies. More recent writing in the area of Left Realism has dealt with what to do once offenders are apprehended. However, in areas such as penology (the study of corrections), Left Realism has largely 'borrowed' from the liberal analysis, which emphasises the need for **community-based corrections**.

Crime prevention, then, will be achieved by reducing the alienation of the community from the criminal justice system. This will not be achieved, though, by the agencies themselves deciding what is in the best interests of these high-crime areas. Policies are needed that will reduce the alienation of the community from the criminal justice system. These policies will give the **local communities an active voice** in how the police, in particular, go about dealing with people in local areas. Local communities should be able to decide what the problems are that the police should tackle, and then should be able to work cooperatively with police to solve these problems.

The criminal justice system under a Left Realist policy agenda would involve active cooperation between community members and police. The system would be geared towards the concerns of **local communities** rather than driven by a broader, and more partisan, political agenda. The law-and-order debate would then be immune from capture by political concerns aimed at providing a 'quick fix', such as military-style policing, which is ultimately a symbolic and destructive solution.

HISTORICAL DEVELOPMENT

The historical development of Left Realism can be seen as two 'waves'. The first came out of the analysis of the Thatcher years by Left Realists in the mid 1980s; the second, more comprehensive, theory arose in response to a critique of early formulations of the theory, mainly from the so-called left idealists. Before describing these two waves, it is important to describe the way in which data is gathered for analysis and theorising under a Left Realist perspective. Left Realism prides itself not only on development of a paradigm with which to understand the problem of crime and criminality, but also on development of the research instrument that underpins this theorising—the local crime victim surveys.

Local crime victim surveys can be differentiated from broad-based crime victim surveys undertaken at state or national levels. The aim of these local surveys is to understand the problem of crime and victimisation within specific locations. These locations are the poorest and most marginalised. In the UK, for example, the first survey was undertaken in Islington, a predominantly Black working-class area in London. The aim of the surveys is to monitor people's needs concerning crime, and then develop policies that accurately reflect those needs. Questions in the surveys concern themselves broadly with issues of victimisation and relationship with criminal justice agencies. The surveys purport to measure some 550 variables (MacLean 1993).

Importantly, the surveys are seen as a complete method in themselves of obtaining the necessary information on which to base theory and policy. This can be contrasted with the traditional methods of radical research—case studies and ethnographies (interview and participant observation). Left Realists claim that the victim surveys generate better empirical data, which is then more authoritative in the public sphere.

There are, however, significant shortcomings in victim survey data. Among these shortcomings is the problem of reporting only on those crimes that are included on the survey; white-collar crimes, for example, were omitted from early studies. Furthermore, other crimes, such as domestic violence, pose problems for those using a survey format due to the sensitivity of the material. In addition, the surveys were not used to explore the various meanings of the label 'criminal', and terms such as 'violence', 'vandalism', and 'sexual assault'. While there may be consensus regarding their seriousness, there may be little agreement concerning what these terms actually mean (Hogg 1988). Finally, asking about what people want done about crime may not elicit the most useful response. Organised burglaries may result from the influence of the receiver of stolen goods, not the actual burglar. Arresting one burglar is unlikely to stop burglaries from happening if it is the receiver of stolen goods who provides the primary influence for the offending (Hogg 1988).

Left Realism has attempted to deal with some of these criticisms, primarily through redesigning the survey instrument. Successive waves of victim surveys have resulted in successive refining of the theory itself. It is to the major developments that we now turn.

Early versions of Left Realism

The first formulation of Left Realism was well summarised by Russell Hogg (1988), and is substantially reproduced here. The main points are outlined below, in each case pointing to the similarities to, and differences from, mainstream radical criminology.

- Crime is a major problem, especially personal violence and property crime, and is a problem of growing proportions.

By denoting 'crime' as the major focus, Left Realists were reasserting the centrality of 'crime' as a unifying focus for criminology. Although Marxist criminology, as well as labelling theory, had gone to great lengths to highlight the contextual nature of labelling an event 'criminal', Left Realists saw crime as a unitary concept, something 'out there' and measurable. Furthermore, unlike Marxist criminology, Left Realism emphasised 'street crime' and played down white-collar and state offences. Finally, this differed from Marxist criminology in that it saw crime as increasing. Some Marxist criminologists are less convinced of an increase, and see the rise shown by statistics as more likely a result of a 'law-and-order' panic, than any real increase in the rate of offending.

- Official crime statistics considerably underestimate the problem due to the levels of unreported crime, which is in large part a result of public alienation and frustration with the ineffectiveness of criminal justice agencies, particularly the police.

Here Left Realism is somewhat similar to mainstream radical theory in that it asserts that the community is alienated from the criminal justice system (in this case, the police). However, unlike radical criminology, Left Realism argues that there is even more crime, defined in traditional terms, than suggested by police statistics.

- Most personal crime (robbery, assault, burglary, etc.) is intra-class and disproportionately afflicts the poor and their neighbourhoods, thus compounding the inequalities and exploitations they already suffer.

The similarity with mainstream radical theory here is that it is the working class that primarily suffers exploitation and hardship. However, unlike some Marxists, Left Realists argue that the victimisation is primarily intra-class: that is, the working class preys on the working class. This is a marked diversion from traditional Marxist criminology, which emphasises that the ruling class preys on the working class.

- The police are both extremely inefficient at dealing with inner-city crime and are endemically hostile and discriminatory with regard to the inner-city populace (especially youth and ethnic minorities).

Much of this resonates with a traditional radical view with respect to the endemic hostility between police and the working class. Unlike traditional Marxists, who see police as an instrument of class control and maintenance of the status quo, Left Realism sees possible positive roles for police. Police might well be useful, if only they were more effective.

- The mutual antagonism between police and local communities sets in train a vicious circle of non-cooperation whereby the alienated community does not report crime to the police, and the police respond by heavier proactive and discriminatory police strategies, which alienates the community further.

This elaborates on why the police are ineffective, and underscores the futility of current policing methods in attempting effective control of crime. Marxist criminologists would argue, however, that the purpose of discriminatory policing is not crime control, but control of the working class. For Marxists, then, such discriminatory policing is fulfilling its purpose if it is effective in 'quieting the masses'.

- Inner-city working-class communities are deeply concerned about local crime, want effective policies to control it, and see the police as central to crime control.

This is crucial to the Left Realist position. Left Realism takes the working-class communities' opinion at face value and reasserts the position that the communities themselves see police and police response as key elements of crime control in inner-city areas. Left Realists argue that these sentiments must be listened to, and acted on, if radicals are to claim any credibility in attempting to help these communities. If the communities say police are potentially useful, the task for criminology is to assist in making police more responsive to the communities' needs, not to decry the police existence.

- Effective policing requires that police concentrate on those crimes that the public see as most serious, that they cease alienating the public by heavy-handed intrusive strategies, and that they be brought under local democratic control through elected police authorities.

This is the last major argument of the early formulations of Left Realism. It argues that crime can be controlled within working-class communities to some extent. This must be achieved through active cooperation between the police and the policed. This differs from the general thrust of Marxist criminology, since it places prime emphasis on the possibility of reform within the capitalist system that would benefit the working class in the long term, and also argues that reform of police is possible.

This early version of Left Realism caused much debate. It became clear that the theory was too narrow, and too fixed on issues of policing. The key criticisms of this first attempt hinged around four major areas, and arose in part from weaknesses in the research instrument, the local crime victim survey.

The first criticism concerned the problem of using 'crime' as the unifying focus. While Left Realists asserted the need to 'take crime seriously', critics asked which crime should be the major focus and, more importantly, what was meant by the term 'crime'. Critics argued that the theory treated definitions of crime as if they had common meanings that were universally accepted. Such an assumption is anathema to many on the left who assert that the term 'crime' has no common meaning. Further, popular definitions of crime are too heavily influenced by the state to be of constructive use. Terms such as 'vandalism' and 'graffiti' are used in the political sphere for political ends. The theory failed to take account of the political dimension of terms concerned with crime and criminality.

Furthermore, the use of politically tainted terms allows popular misconceptions of crime and criminality to continue. In particular it exacerbates the problem of stereotypic impressions of who 'we' are (the goodies), as opposed to 'them' (the baddies). Critics argued that Left Realism tended to treat the results of the victim surveys as if they represented a true picture of crime, and what crime is. Public concern must be understood as the result of a political process, and in particular a result of the active influence of the police and the media in shaping popular conceptions of crime and criminality.

Besides the problems of the definition and meaning of the term 'crime', critics also pointed to the narrow scope of victimisation covered by Left Realism. Concern was expressed that only certain forms of victimisation were considered as important. The most notable omissions were in the area of white-collar crime. Certain forms of white-collar crime also disproportionately affect the working class, most notably industrial pollution and negligence, loan sharking, and false advertising.

Great criticism was also levelled at the narrowness concerning effective responses, notably the almost exclusive focus on policing. This partly resulted from the emphasis of the surveys themselves. Early surveys placed a great weight on what the victims felt should be done about crime. Critics argued that this allowed the assumption to remain unchallenged that in order to reduce crime one must necessarily focus on police action. Effective reduction strategies may mean something else entirely: in particular, solutions may lie outside the criminal justice system. A good example of this arises within Australia. Aboriginal communities recognise that the problem of violence within their communities is a result, in part, of the availability of alcohol. Some of these communities have taken action to limit the availability of alcohol, in some cases restricting sales in multiracial towns such as Tennant Creek. This is seen to be far more effective than direct police action. Police action, however well intentioned, may simply exacerbate the violence, since the cause lies outside police control.

Critics also argue for greater attention to the possible consequences of greater cooperation between the public and the police. Police responding to complaints may be ineffective in solving burglary, as mentioned above, if the primary problem is one of receiving stolen goods. Left Realists argue that changes in policing style—so that it is reactive, cooperative, and accountable—will increase the flow of information to police and dramatically improve clear-up rates. However, the opposite might occur if, for example, clear-up rates were substantially boosted by verballing (i.e., untrue police testimony).

If policing strategies did lead to greater numbers of arrests, Left Realism had also left open the question of what to do with offenders once they had been apprehended. They had not considered what was appropriate in dealing with offenders in terms of a humane penal policy. Furthermore, penal policy—in particular, the greater use of jails—is very expensive, and Left Realism had not come to terms with methods of funding an increase in the size of the system. There were fears that this vacuum in theorising would result in the familiar conservative plea for harsher penalties.

The second wave of Left Realism

Left Realism has made attempts to come to terms with the criticisms levelled at the theory as it was initially expressed. In collection of data, analysis, and policy-making there has been considerable revision of the original theory.

In terms of data collection, Left Realists have undertaken a second wave of surveys. They argue that the notion of 'victim surveys' is now a misnomer, since they now attempt to deal with a far broader range of issues. Among the new questions considered are those concerning self-report data, public evaluation of police service deliveries, police public encounters, public attitudes to adequate punishment, and avoidance behaviour with respect to some crimes. Left Realists have also retreated from seeing the survey as the sole focus of data collection. They now argue that, while these surveys are important, it is necessary to supplement the data gathered in this manner with other forms of empirical inquiry. Positivist methods of data collection (such as psychological testing, for example) are seen as relevant, along with traditional radical research methods such as case studies and ethnography.

In theory at least, Left Realism has widened the focus beyond exclusive concentration on the offender towards a broader emphasis, which they conceptualise as the **square of crime**. The square of crime, as we have seen, involves two dyads. The first concerns social control, and comprises police and other agencies of social control on the one hand, and the public on the other. The second concerns the criminal act, and comprises the offender and the victim. The current aim of Left Realism is to address all parts of the square, in that all aspects need to be addressed in theory, research, and policy. Further to this, each aspect should not be taken as a separate entity, as the interaction between each element is crucial to understanding crime and crime control. Crime rates are, according to Left Realists, a product of the four aspects of the square of crime (Young 1991).

This proposal by Left Realists of the centrality of the 'square of crime' directs attention to the criminal act and its context by its emphasis on four separate but interrelated dimensions: the police, the public, the victim, and the offender. They argue there needs to be analysis of the state and the problems of defining crime within a political system, as the left argues, but there also needs to be realistic account taken of the 'reality' of crime and the offender–victim dyad. This means researching appropriate responses that can address the needs of victims, as well as supporting programmes and policies that both reduce offending before it occurs (crime prevention), and respond effectively when offences do occur.

Left Realism has also broadened its focus in terms of the crimes that are considered of major concern. Recent volumes contain analyses of white-collar offending and issues of gender that are more explicitly brought into the Left Realist fold (Lowman and MacLean 1992). Importantly, Left Realism has also acknowledged the need to discuss penal reform.

However, much of this writing has not come from the Left Realists themselves, but from authors with particular research interests that are used to 'fill the gaps' of earlier versions of the theory. In addition, when theorising is undertaken by those readily identified with Left Realism, such as Roger Matthews (1989) in the case of penal reform, the suggestions that are mooted do not differ significantly from liberal suggestions in the same area.

Left Realism has then shifted ground from identifying with radical or Marxist criminology to a position that is more easily described as social democratic or liberal. That is, it is more concerned with a reform agenda that deals with the issues of crime and crime control within the current social system than with suggesting that the system itself is the root of the problem and should be changed. In doing so, it borrows heavily from theories and research that are characteristic of the middle ground, such as strain theory, labelling, and certain strands of radical criminology. By shifting ground in this way, Left Realism loses some of its identity and at times becomes indistinguishable from the theories it replaces, or purports to supersede.

CONTEMPORARY EXAMPLES

This section looks at Left Realism in Australia. It is important to point out that Left Realism per se does not exist as an independent entity within Australia. Nonetheless, a group of academics, working primarily out of Sydney, have taken up many of the Left Realist ideas. It is interesting to note that a Left Realist perspective was taken up in New South Wales at a time when that state was experiencing a strong political emphasis on law and order by the (then) Liberal (conservative) government in the late 1980s. The government of that period promoted a law-and-order policy that purported to take crime seriously by increasing police powers and increasing the use of prison as a sentencing option, as well as increasing the time spent in detention.

A group known as the Campaign for Criminal Justice (CCJ) challenged the 'law-and-order' rhetoric of the Liberal government and proposed a new direction for crime policy. The group comprises not only academics but also youth workers, left lawyers, and those working in the criminal justice system in that state. Like Left Realists in the UK, the CCJ argued that crime was rising, and that those who were the victims were the most vulnerable—in this case old people, women, children, and the Aboriginal population. Furthermore, the group also advocated the use of the local crime victim survey, undertaking a survey in inner Sydney. This survey was concerned with the fear of crime and its connection to the local social and economic organisation of particular communities.

It is important to note that the expression of Left Realism within Australia is much broader than the predominant focus on policing that characterised Left Realism, at least in the early stages in the UK. 'Left Realism' within Australia is not seen as a radical break from critical criminology generally. However, like Left Realists in the UK, the CCJ sought to influence the political process directly. In particular it worked with the Labor opposition in the formulation of policy that could neutralise the conservative 'law-and-order' rhetoric. Both the nature of that influence, and its eventual effectiveness, deserve comment. In terms of policies, the CCJ proposed such measures as:

- all new government policy be accompanied by a crime impact statement
- crime-related social impact be a factor built into urban planning
- local safety strategies be developed
- staffing on public transport be maintained
- development of strategies be built around community participation, using local action groups such as tenants groups, refuges, and resident groups.

These measures seek to place 'crime' on the political and academic agenda in a way that recognises the social and political motives of crime and crime policy. They seek to engage government in dialogue about reforms to reduce the victimisation of vulnerable groups.

The fate of this policy was considerably undermined, if not abandoned, in the 1995 New South Wales elections. Instead of promoting a broadly Left Realist agenda, the Labor Party was in the forefront of a renewed conservative law-and-order debate, promoting tough new crime policies aimed at increasing imprisonment, especially for 'serious' offences. The trend to law-and-order policies became even more firmly entrenched in Australia as the 1990s progressed. Rather than bring criminal justice agencies under greater community control, the trend has been in the opposite direction, exemplified by the privatisation of a large proportion of the nation's prisons, replete with secrecy provisions precluding adequate public scrutiny of the financial details of contracts between prison owners and the government. Left Realists still have a way to go if they are to capture the political debate.

Interestingly, there is some question as to which political debate needs to be captured. In recent years there has been a re-evaluation of the split between 'left idealism' and 'left realism', in which some argue that the debate was from the beginning fraught with inaccuracies and misleading characterisations (Cottee 2002; for a response see Cohen & Young, 2004). Similar concerns about accuracy and representation also have been seen in discussions of law-and-order politics and policy in Australia. The political debate in this instance is within criminology itself, and those on the receiving end are the Left Realists. For example, Weatherburn (2002) has argued that researchers such as Brown and Hogg, who are closely identified with Left Realist concerns in Australia, have not taken crime seriously enough and that they do not appreciate fully the seriousness of the crime problem. The latter writers, who have been accused of lack of methodological rigour and political disinterest, have responded with a spirited defence of their empirical work. They also have distanced themselves from a purely 'evidence-driven' policy formation approach, and reaffirmed their commitment to examination of the normative and political nature of law-and-order politics (Indermaur et al. 2002). How debate is carried out is perhaps one of the more salient lessons from our review of Left Realism as a criminological development. The review also highlights the continuing commitment of those willing to translate their concerns about crime into practical forums without necessarily compromising political critique.

CRITIQUE

An adequate critique of Left Realism has to encompass both early and later versions in order to get a clear picture of the strengths and weaknesses of the theory as a whole.

It will be remembered that the criticisms of early versions of Left Realism were as follows:

- The theory treated **definitions of crime** as if they had factual, uncontested meanings.
- The **scope of victimisation covered by Left Realism was very narrow**. It omitted certain offences, most notably white-collar offences, and then presented the results as if this gave a total picture of crime.
- The **focus of response was very narrow**. The theory was almost exclusively concerned with issues of police and policing style.
- **There was a lack of any realistic penal policy**. The theory had not considered to any degree how to deal with offenders once they were apprehended.
- Finally, there were concerns, mainly expressed by radical criminologists, that **Left Realists accepted the notion that the criminal law could be liberating**. Critics argued that the problem in working-class areas was not crime, but community breakdown. This being the case, the criminal law could only exacerbate problems, not ameliorate them.

As stated, Left Realists made a concerted effort to address these problems. In particular, they broadened the scope of their analysis to include white-collar offences in their victim surveys. They also began to look at the issues surrounding an adequate penal policy. Rather than being a narrow, single-issue theory, Left Realism now attempts to look at what it calls the 'square of crime' concerned with both social control and the criminal act, as outlined above—but how successful has this been?

In broadening its focus Left Realism could be said to have lost its defining parameters, and with them any claims for being a separate theoretical entity. Many elements of Left Realism appear in similar form elsewhere: for example, elements of strain theory deal with the formation of antisocial cultures; and liberal forms of criminology also seek to redress the inequities of the system here and now. Left Realism is an eclectic mix of criminological theory of a generally liberal nature, which sees society as based on conflicting, but ultimately not irreconcilable, differences.

There is nothing wrong with an eclectic theory or one based on 'multifactorial explanations'. However, when a theoretical perspective draws together theoretical insights from diverse traditions, the question of compatibility of ideas arises. Left Realism identifies itself with a Marxist tradition; however, this tradition sees attempts to democratise sections of the state apparatus, such as the police, as being linked to wider political strategies that go directly to the heart of who controls production and government in a capitalist society. Indeed, attempts to democratise the police through local councils in the UK kindled the ire of the conservative national government; it responded by substantially reducing the power of local government in that country, effectively neutralising police reforms. The point is that eclecticism is acceptable if the theory links diverse traditions in a way that is ultimately productive and without irretrievable conflict.

Some would argue that Left Realism has failed to do this. It retains a notion of consensus concerning crime that many would argue is not sustainable. Furthermore, the aims of the theory itself may be incompatible. For example, to enlist the cooperation of police in 'fighting crime' while at the same time attempting an adequate critique of the role of the state in perpetuating crime would be seen by many as a contradiction in terms.

It is notable, therefore, that one of the leading proponents of Left Realism in the UK has in more recent years turned his attention to structural issues rather than those relating to policy implementation as such. Jock Young (1999) appears to have abandoned the quest for pragmatic criminal justice responses in favour of a more sustained analysis and critique in which the dynamics of social exclusion, antagonism, and conflict once again become central. In doing so, Young is also challenging previous approaches that fail to take into account the existential and experiential dimensions of crime. In other words, cultural criminology is accorded an important place in the new understandings of social division, and the world of crime is interpreted in the light of emotional and structural factors (Young 2003). If this is Left Realism, it is now Left Realism with 'attitude'.

Left Realism correctly identifies the central place of crime in society. People are concerned about crime. Perhaps what has been ignored by this perspective, though, is the multifaceted nature of that concern. Drawing from Durkheim, it would be possible to argue that this concern reflected, at least in part, anxiety about the state of our society as well as anxiety about the actual chances of victimisation. Further, it is this concern that is most amenable to manipulation for political ends. Fears and insecurities about jobs, education, and so on can be allayed (at least in part) by governments espousing strong law-and-order rhetoric in order to secure their political popularity. This tactic is well illustrated in Australia, as well as in the USA and the UK, in recent years.

Nonetheless, Left Realism has contributed positively to the criminological debate. It has reasserted the need to take account of those most affected by crime—the marginalised and the working class. It has sought to take the views of these people seriously and to translate their views into a workable policy agenda. This has been particularly important at a time when 'law-and-order' policies dominate the political debate.

CONCLUSION

Left Realism can be seen as a left-wing response to the law-and-order debate dominated predominantly by the Right in politics. As such, it sees itself in contrast to that criminology which sees the discipline as a value-free and neutral exercise. Left Realism identifies itself as part of a socialist strategy to democratise the state apparatus and other areas of social and economic life. Responding to crime is a political process, not a neutral research exercise. However, Left Realists argue that doing something practical in the current environment means much more than simply raising class-consciousness or working for 'the revolution' some time in the future.

Left Realism has stimulated much debate, with most of it from other radical traditions. The response to the criticisms has been for Left Realism to broaden its focus, use a wide range of empirical research, and borrow from other theoretical perspectives in order to 'fill the gaps' of its initially narrow focus. There have been some successes in this attempt, and it has spawned useful debate in the Australian context with the work of the Campaign for Criminal Justice.

In the next chapter we focus on another recent theory that is generally eclectic in nature. In this case, however, the theory starts from a very different philosophical base, that of republicanism.

FURTHER READING

Hogg, R. (1988) 'Taking Crime Seriously: Left Realism and Australian Criminology', in M. Findlay & R. Hogg (eds), *Understanding Crime and Criminal Justice*, Law Book Company, Sydney.

Lea, J. & Young, J. (1984) *What Is to Be Done about Law and Order?*, Penguin, London.

Young, J. (1986) 'The Failure of Criminology: The Need for a Radical Realism', in R. Matthews & J. Young (eds) *Confronting Crime*, Sage, London.

Young, J. (1991) 'Left Realism and the Priorities of Crime Control', in K. Stenson & D. Cowell (eds) *The Politics of Crime Control*, Sage, London.

Young, J. (1992) 'Realist Research as a Basis for Local Criminal Justice Policy', in J. Lowman & B. MacLean (eds) *Realist Criminology: Crime Control and Policing in the 1990s*, University of Toronto Press, Toronto.

Young, J. (1999) *The Exclusive Society: Social Exclusion, Crime and Difference in Late Modernity*, Sage, London.

CHAPTER 10

Republican Theory and Restorative Justice

INTRODUCTION

This chapter discusses the republican theory of criminal justice. As a relatively new theoretical perspective, republican theory draws upon a wide range of concepts and trends that we have previously examined. The hallmark of the republican approach is its stress on the need for a restorative form of justice, rather than a punitive one.

The strength of republican theory is that it provides a holistic view of crime and society. In moving towards a general theory of crime, republicanism offers a **normative** theory of crime, based on the premise of how to make a good society by outlining the values that should underpin the ideal operation of the criminal justice system. With respect to this, the theory seeks to reform or reshape our major institutions in accordance with the ideals of republican liberalism. The theory thus stands as a systematic critique of authoritarian populism, which it views as wrong and dangerous, in that it claims we can use reason and justice to inform institutional practices rather than refer to base emotions such as hatred and fear.

The theory also offers an analysis and outline of how the criminal justice system could be reorganised **in practice** to reflect restorative justice. It is here that the theory has gained much prominence, insofar as the notion of 'reintegrative shaming' has received much international attention. The theory argues that we need to emphasise positive ways in which to deal with offenders, and victims, and that a punitive response to crime will lead only to negative social consequences.

SOCIAL CONTEXT

Some criminological theories commence with a broad conception of the society we live in and what the society as a whole should be striving to achieve. Such theories usually begin with a theory of society, and a vision of 'the good'. Within the radical framework (Marxist and feminist theory), for example, society is characterised by profound inequalities, such as poverty, racism, sexism, and other exploitative situations created by imbalances of power. The solution sought is for a revolutionary change in the core structures and nature of society generally, requiring collective mobilisation for change. There is an attempt to raise the consciousness of those most affected by the discriminatory actions of the capitalist state, to expose the evils and injustices built into the system, and to expand democratic participation and economic redistribution.

Conservative theories (New Right and other populist versions of this) also start with a conception of society as a whole. Here society is charac- terised as comprising self-interested individuals, some of whom are particularly evil or bad. This perspective asserts that crime results as a consequence of the disorder in society. It therefore seeks to re-establish discipline, order, and authority. The aim is to restore society to the way things used to be; in this sense, it often appeals to a mythical 'golden age'. The theories argue that the society requires a strong state that will assert its authority in a moral way, in order to maintain the free economy. In this system, law and order must take precedence over justice. The focus is on 'street crime' and crimes committed by the less powerful; for example, social security fraud. Crime is seen to result from a breakdown in the societal moral fibre, hence the stress on morality, liberty, and authority.

As we saw, Left Realism emerged as a response to the conservative backlash of the 1980s. This perspective has tended, however, to move away from a theory of society per se (i.e., based upon socialist principles) to focus specifically on crime, which is viewed as a problem that needs to be taken seriously. There has been a consequent shift away from the big picture (that is, structural causes) to focus on specific issues, such as the victims of crime and the effects of crime on the less powerful—the working class, the poor, Blacks, females, etc. It is argued that because the community is concerned about crime, the focus should be on fighting crime at the local level, and the main concern is with developing an effective form of policing that is responsible, responsive, and democratic.

The conservative push to get tough on offenders through concerted law-and-order campaigns spurred the particular response adopted by the Left Realists. Republican theory likewise is a response to the conservative push of the last two decades (see Braithwaite & Pettit 1990). Many conservatives were critical of the crime prevention strategies of treatment and rehabilitation being pursued by the positivists in dealing with offenders. The **retributivists** claimed treatment, rehabilitation, and preventive measures had not worked, and had in some instances been grossly unjust. They pointed to cases where indeterminate sentences had been wrongly applied (e.g., in the USA, a juvenile offender making obscene phone calls was put into detention for six years). They highlighted the injustice and futility of strategies adopted by the **preventivists**, who sought to rehabilitate and deter offenders through incapacitation. The retributivists called for punishment of the offender in accordance with their 'just deserts'—that is, offenders should get what they deserve in proportion to the gravity of the offence and the culpability of the offender.

Retributivists have tended to focus on sentencing. The notion is that we must change the way in which we sentence people, because treatment is not working. Braithwaite and Pettit (1990) challenged the retributivist perspective on a variety of levels. They argued that:

- The criminal justice system should be organised so as to promote the goal of republican liberty, which is construed as personal dominion.
- A theory of criminal justice needs to cover a broad range of issues. A comprehensive theory is required to cover such things as: what should be criminalised; what guidelines should cover police surveillance; what initiatives should be possible in the pursuit of offenders; and what procedures should be followed in prosecution and adjudication, and the sentences imposed for given offences.

Braithwaite and Pettit (1990) argued that the retributivist theory does not address these questions adequately and, instead, focuses solely on subquestions. They argue that if a theory deals only with questions of sentencing, as the retributivist theory does, then any initiatives taken in respect to this area of the justice system are likely to flow on and affect other parts of the system. Hence, they argue that we cannot simply tinker with only one part of the system: we need to look at the system as a whole.

They are critical as well of other goal-oriented approaches such as **utilitarianism**—a system that suggests we should promote the greatest good for the greatest number, because injustices can lead to good for the greatest number. They are also critical of the sole goal of the criminal justice system being that of crime prevention, because this can lead to increased intrusiveness, such as holding parents totally responsible for their children's actions.

The alternative theory proposed by Pettit and Braithwaite is the **republican theory** (Braithwaite & Pettit 1990; Pettit & Braithwaite 1993). This theory seeks to link up with older republican traditions of thinking that sought to promote the notion of liberty. These theories extend from Roman times, through the philosophies of republicanism developed in the northern Italian republics, to those apparent in the course of the English Civil War and in the American Revolution in the eighteenth century. In this historical thinking about liberty, freedom was perceived as the social status enjoyed by someone other than a slave; someone so protected by the law and culture of their community that they did not have to depend upon the grace of another for the enjoyment of independent choice. Liberty was conceptualised as the negative good of not being interfered with by others.

This republican notion of negative liberty was displaced in the nineteenth century by a new, different sense of liberalism. Here the main objective was to avoid interference by the state and the law altogether, and thus, as well, to exclude the enjoyment of being protected against possible interference. This right-wing libertarian perspective promoted the notion of the free market and sought to remove government constraints on trade, the labour market, and so on. The enjoyment of non-interference in our lives was thus at the mercy of those who chose to interfere. Based upon a competitive 'law of the jungle' notion, this perspective is premised on the belief that we are all free and should be able to do what we want without any interference whatsoever.

The republican conception of liberty differs from this nineteenth-century conception. It involves the concept of personal liberty constituted by **protection of liberty by the law**. Non-interference should not be enjoyed only as a matter of contingent luck; instead, it should be extended to all by the law and its related institutions. The non-interference involved is to be of a resilient or secure nature; that is, the person who enjoys non-interference is thereby protected from the predations of the potential interferer. Should someone choose to interfere, then the law or other protective institutions would move to block that interference and provide whatever compensation is necessary in order to restore the person to their former status.

The law and its related institutions are seen to play a central role in maintaining republican liberty. There has to be equal knowledge that we collectively enjoy that status of being guarded from interference.

BASIC CONCEPTS

In the republican view, crime is seen as the denial of personal dominion—evil is always represented by this denial (see chart 10.1). Three characteristics of these denials are identified:

- The first is a negative challenge to the **dominion status** of the victim. A threat to, or disregard for, the dominion of an individual is an attack on the status of that individual as someone who holds a protected dominion status in society. If someone commits a crime against an individual then the criminal act asserts the vulnerability of the victim to the will of the criminal, nullifying the protected status of the victim.
- Second, if successful, the criminal attempt not only disregards the victim's dominion, but also undermines, **diminishes**, and perhaps even **destroys the victim's dominion**. For example, kidnapping or murdering someone will destroy their dominion, while stealing a person's property will diminish their dominion, by undermining certain exercises of dominion they might otherwise have pursued (e.g., it diminishes their liberty to use that property).
- Third, every crime also represents **communal evil**; it does an evil to the community as a whole. A crime not only affects the dominion status of the individual victim, but also endangers the community's notion of resilient status. Every act of crime represents a challenge to the dominion of people in society generally who will begin to doubt that they really do have resilient status.

If every act of crime represents damage to dominion, then the system's task is to promote dominion, by rectifying or remedying the damage caused by the crime. What should the courts do in response to the convicted offender, for example?

Theoretically, in sentencing the convicted offender the courts need to consider certain elements. First, the offender must **recognise** the personal liberty of the victim in order to restore the victim's status. In order to do this, the offender must withdraw the implicit claim that the victim did not enjoy the dominion that was challenged by the crime. Second, in order to restore the victim's former dominion—which may not only have been disregarded, but also may have been diminished or destroyed—there must be some form of **recompense** for the damage done to the individual's personal dominion. And third, there must be a general **reassurance** given to the community in general of a kind that may undo the negative impact of crime on their enjoyment of dominion.

The republican theory thus assumes an equilibrium model of criminal justice, because it seeks to **restore the dominion status of the victim** by reintegrating the victim back into society so that they can once again exercise their personal dominion. Abstractly, the recognition of dominion of the victim by the offender requires a mix of measures, both symbolic and substantive.

From a republican point of view, the causes of crime lie in a combination of social and psychological factors. Part of the problem is the lack of a **self-sanctioning conscience**. This is where an individual has not

CHART 10.1   Republican Theory

Definition of crime	▪ denial of dominion, largely reflected in legal code
Focus of analysis	▪ victim, community, and offender dominion, particularly in areas where shaming may be appropriate (drink-driving, white-collar crime, juvenile justice)
Cause of crime	▪ lack of self-sanctioning conscience and appropriate social connections (lack of interdependency) ▪ broader society characterised by mobility and a focus on individualism (lack of communitarianism)
Nature of offender	▪ partly voluntary, partly determined, responsibility and opportunity
Response to crime	▪ reintegrative shaming, least restrictive measures
Crime prevention	▪ promotion of valued norms, fostering of communitarianism
Operation of criminal justice system	▪ expansion of reintegrative shaming into social life of community through family group conferences, victim–offender meetings

learned adequately the interpretation and acceptance of societal norms as being right and just. One of the results of a punitive and stigmatising system is that it propels people into associating with other similarly ostracised individuals (for instance, in a criminal subculture) who individually and collectively do not develop this conscience.

The lack of adequate and appropriate social connections is expressed in the concept of **communitarianism**. This describes interdependency at a societal level involving relationships of loyalty, trust, and concern. Interdependency is itself reflected in a person's relationship to school, work, marriage, stable residence, and so on. The issue of social opportunity is important insofar as it affects the interdependencies and eventually the moral development of an individual.

The response to crime in a specific sense is to utilise the least restrictive measures possible, and to undo the wrong that has been committed. The republican theory of criminal justice is intended to deal with the victim so they can once again exercise public dominion and the community can be reassured. The focus is on **maximising personal dominion** for the victim. However, there is also the assumption that the offender should be reintegrated so that their dominion also can be reinstated. The theory seeks a minimalist response on the part of the state to the offender. A reintegrative equilibrium needs to be established where the victim, the community, and the offender are considered.

The republican response to crime therefore bases itself on the concept of **reintegrative shaming**. This involves a process in which the offender is shamed for their action, but is not 'cast out' as a person. It describes a process whereby the offender is publicly rebuked for the harm they have caused, but is then forgiven and reintegrated into the mainstream of society. As part of the reintegrative shaming process, the victim is directly involved in proceedings and is able to be compensated in some way for the harm done.

From a crime prevention perspective, steps should be taken to **promote valued norms** (which, in turn, become the basis for the formation of a self-sanctioning conscience) and to **foster greater communitarianism** by enhancing educational, work, and social opportunities. The criminal justice system ought to incorporate a broad range of informal and more formal institutional arrangements, such as conferences of the offender and victims, and be oriented towards the least intrusive kind of intervention possible.

HISTORICAL DEVELOPMENT

The historical development of republican theory is undoubtedly tied to the liberal tradition, outlined earlier in the chapter. It can be traced to the concern with crime and criminality as championed by Montesquieu, which aimed at 'lessening the burden of fear in the minds of ordinary citizens' (Shklar 1987, cited in Braithwaite & Pettit 1990: 61). Its roots clearly can be seen within the classical tradition.

Furthermore, however, republican theory can be seen as a liberal response to the changing shape of capitalism and the ensuing uncertainty and opportunities this engenders. Just as positivism was seen earlier in light of the challenges posed by the industrial revolution, with its emphasis on positive reform, so republican theory can be seen to have a similar emphasis on attempting constructive changes based on contemporary research and reflection about the current challenges posed by the fragmentation and fluidity of contemporary capitalism.

The advent of significant social and economic transformation, and the existence of a highly educated population as in Australia, means that current theories can, in part, be measured by their ability to provide solutions to immediate contemporary concerns. These include issues such as white-collar crime and the plight of victims of crime, particularly of family violence. In fact, republican theory has had a longstanding concern with white-collar crime. In contrast to Marxist criminology, however, with which it shares many similar concerns, republican theory is essentially optimistic about changing business practice within the current capitalist structure. Fundamentally, the principles applied to the control of 'street crime', republican theorists argue, have equal applicability in the white-collar sphere.

The concern with victims evident within republican theory can be seen as part of a much broader shift within criminology in recent years (see Mawby & Walklate 1994). Victimology, the study of victims of crime, is a recently established sub-discipline within criminology. It has gained considerable popularity at a theoretical level, and also in government policy. An example of its acceptance by governments is the introduction of victim impact statements (i.e., written statements by victims handed to the judge at sentencing) in a number of jurisdictions (White & Perrone 1997). Republican theory shares common ground with a number of perspectives that aim to integrate the needs of both victims and offenders within the same system.

Restorative justice

The overarching name usually associated with these perspectives is that of **restorative justice**. The aim of such perspectives is to develop policies whereby the offender makes reparations for wrongdoing, and in doing so restores the victim's and the general population's faith in society. Conceptually, restorative justice sees crime as fundamentally a violation of people and interpersonal relationships, and the point of action is to seek to heal and put right the wrongs (Zehr 1990). The justice process, in this framework, is seen rightly to belong to the community, rather than exclusively to the state. The emphasis is on reparation of harm to victims, addressing the offender's needs and competencies, and sending offenders a message of disapproval about the impact of the crime (Bazemore 1997).

Translated into specific assumptions and principles, the restorative justice lens can be usefully summarised as being based upon three inter-related propositions (Zehr & Mika 1998):

- **Crime is fundamentally a violation of people and interpersonal relationships**—The key issue is that victims and the community have been harmed and are in need of restoration. Importantly, victims, offenders, and the affected communities are seen as the key stakeholders in justice and, as such, ought to be directly involved in the justice process.
- **Violations create obligations and liabilities**—It is felt that the offenders' obligations are to make things right as much as possible for the harm they have caused. However, it is also argued that the community's obligations are to victims, to offenders, and for the general welfare of its members. Obligations are thus both individual and collective in nature.
- **Restorative justice seeks to heal and put right the wrong**—The starting point for justice is the need of victims for information, validation, vindication, restitution, testimony, safety, and support. The process of justice ought to maximise the opportunities for exchange of information, participation, dialogue, and mutual consent between victim and offender, and the justice process ought to belong to the community. The offenders' needs and competencies also are to be addressed. In the end, justice needs to be mindful of the outcomes, intended and unintended, of its responses to crime and victimisation.

There are various specific models of restorative justice, ranging from, for example, circle sentencing, family group conferencing, and reparative probation through to victim–offender mediation (see Bazemore 1997, 1998; Wright 1991). Each model has different key objectives—from citizen involvement to meeting victims' needs—and these shape the manner in which restorative justice is institutionalised in practice. Generally speaking, however, each programme or model tends to focus on the 'victim', the 'offender', and the 'community', and each attempts to respond to the immediate harm, and to the specific situation and individuals that are linked by a particular criminal harm. Some approaches are based upon moral categories (e.g., reintegrative shaming) where the aim is to shame the offence, while offering forgiveness to the offender (Braithwaite 1989). Others are based upon strategic assessment of offenders and events (e.g., balanced restorative approach), in which case the aim is to design interventions that best address issues of offender accountability, competency development, and community safety (Bazemore 1991; Bilchik 1998). Some approaches focus almost exclusively on meeting victim needs (usually via some method of restitution or compensation involving the offender); others placing emphasis on widespread community engagement in dealing with underlying problems and issues, of which specific offending is but one manifestation.

Under the restorative justice umbrella there are differences between those who see restorative justice as, essentially, a form of diversion from the formal criminal justice system, and those who view it as a potential **alternative** to that system and thus as something that could supplant the existing system *in toto* (see Bazemore & Walgrave 1999). Whatever the specific differences, it appears that the central thread underlying restorative justice is the spirit within which 'justice' is undertaken—the intent and outcomes of the process are meant to be primarily oriented towards repairing harm that has been caused by a crime, and this means working to heal victims, offenders and communities that have been directly injured by the crime (Bazemore & Walgrave 1999; Zehr & Mika 1998).

Republican liberty

A crucial aspect of republican theory, as a particular model of restorative justice, is that it attempts to provide a normative theory of crime and society; it comes from a particular value stance or goal of criminal justice—to maximise personal dominion, which is construed as republican liberty.

The main elements of the theory were developed in the light of differences between republican and retributivist perspectives on sentencing (Braithwaite & Pettit 1990). Retributivists argue that in sentencing an offender, the motivation of the criminal justice system is to ensure that no crime goes unpunished. The republican theorists agree that convicted offenders need to be sentenced, but this is seen as necessary because the goal of the criminal justice system should be the promotion of dominion. This view leads to different conclusions regarding the operation of the criminal justice system (see also Zehr 1990 on the difference between retributive and restorative justice).

While retributionists seek some sort of repayment for the offence and argue for penalties proportional to the crime, republican theorists argue for a **rectification of the offence**—to put the harm right. Hence, while the retributivist concentrates on the offender, the republican examines the harm done both to the victim(s) and the community. In terms of the kind and degree of penalty to be imposed, the two perspectives differ once again. The retributivists look for hard treatment as the appropriate form of response on the grounds of proportionality and a guarantee of deterrence. Thus, retributivists tend to impose upper and lower limits on sentences that are available to the courts, and generally ignore circumstantial and mitigating factors.

Republican theorists seek to impose upper limits like the retributivists; however, they disagree with the imposition of lower limits, arguing that there should be a whole range of measures available at the lower levels. Furthermore, they argue against long sentences and capital punishment.

In response to 'just deserts' retributivist perspectives, the republican theory supports four main assumptions of systems operation (see Braithwaite & Pettit 1990):

- **Parsimony**—this assumes that the onus of proof must always rest on the side of justifying criminal justice intrusions, not on the side of justifying their removal.
- **Checking of power**—controls should be established and constraints placed upon those who have the power in the system to intervene in our individual and collective lives. In this way the required accountability can be achieved.
- **Reprobation**—the criminal justice system should be designed to expose offenders in a constructive way to community disapproval.

- **Reintegration**—the system should seek to restore to the enjoyment of full dominion those who have been deprived of it by either crime or punishment.

Republican theorists argue that the practical theory can be introduced bit by bit in a strategy of incremental implementation. Some other measures that they favour include: a codification of rights; a system supporting the right to a fair trial; a system that guarantees the right to protection of the person (i.e., against capital punishment and corporal punishment); and a presumption in favour of punishments against the property rather than the province of offenders; that is, fines, restitution, and community service rather than imprisonment.

The kinds of principles that republican theorists support in practice include such things as rendering police more accountable for surveillance of suspects, and decrements to all layers of criminal justice intervention, such as less criminal law, less police surveillance, less prosecution, and less punishment. Hence, republican theorists support a system that is as unobtrusive as possible, where consideration is extended to victims, offenders, and community alike.

CONTEMPORARY EXAMPLES

The republican theory is built upon responding to crime in a manner that is unique and, theoretically, positive for all parties. As Braithwaite and Pettit (1990: 2) see it, 'we need a theory of criminal justice which allows us to respond in the best way to harmful conduct, where responding in that way sometimes will, and more often than not, entail punishment'. In broad conceptual terms, republican responses to crime entail symbolic measures plus substantive measures that involve material actions necessary to give credibility and sincerity to the symbolic measures. The measures adopted in practice depend upon the immediate circumstances of the players.

The substantive nature of recompense involves restitution, compensation, or reparation. **Restitution** means to return to the victim whatever it was that was lost in the commission of the offence. For example, it may involve giving back stolen property. **Compensation** occurs where restitution is not possible. This entails an attempt to make up for the loss the victim has experienced. **Reparation** is where neither restitution nor compensation is possible; for example, in the case of murder. This is an

offering of compensation to those close to, and dependent up
victim of the offence.

At a theoretical level, the remedies and responses put forward
republican theorists reflect their overall concerns with personal dominion
and restorative justice. The actual response to crime should reflect the
following concerns (Pettit & Braithwaite 1993):

- The offender must **recognise** the personal liberty of the victim in
  order to restore the dominion status of the victim. In order to do this,
  the offender must withdraw the implicit claim that the victim did not
  enjoy the dominion that was challenged by the crime. This can be
  achieved through some type of symbolic measure (e.g., an apology on
  the part of the offender for their behaviour, a commitment not to
  reoffend, reconciliation with the victim).
- In order to restore the victim's former dominion—which may not have
  been simply disregarded, but may have been destroyed or diminished—
  there must be some form of **recompense** for the damage done to the
  individual's personal dominion. This can be achieved through a range
  of substantive measures (e.g., restitution, compensation, or reparation).
- There must be a general **reassurance** given to the community at large
  of a kind that will undo the negative impact of the crime on their
  collective and personal enjoyment of dominion. This means that
  there has to be some guarantee that the community will be protected
  from future acts. For instance, through a process of reprobation the
  criminal justice system should be designed to expose offenders in a
  constructive way to community disapproval, and to reintegrate the
  victim and the offender back into community life.

An explanatory theory of republican justice is one that moves from a
normative view of the criminal justice system (what ought to be) to a discussion of practical intervention measures (what can be put into place).
Here the republican theory argues strongly that reintegrative shaming
is the key to crime control (Braithwaite 1989). In arguing this line,
Braithwaite looks to labelling theory in order to highlight how his
theory moves away from the undesirable effects of shaming.

In discussing labelling theory (chapter 5), we saw that when an
individual is termed 'bad', that label can stigmatise the individual. There
is a need, however, to distinguish between stigmatisation, which increases
the risks of reoffending by the shamed actor, and reintegrative shaming.
In terms of the preferred second approach, disapproval is extended while

a relationship of respect is sustained with the offender. Stigmatisation is disrespectful—it is seen as a humiliating form of shaming, where the offender is branded an evil person and is cast out permanently. Reintegrative shaming, by contrast, seeks to **shame the evil deed** but sees the offender in a respectable light. The shaming is finite and the offender is given the opportunity to re-enter society by way of recognising the wrongdoing, apologising, and being repentant. In this way, shame is seen as useful as a means of combating crime as long as it is not applied in a stigmatising fashion.

Braithwaite (1989) argues that we need a culture where we promote a self-sanctioning conscience. If we can develop in society certain norms and cultures, then individuals will not engage in certain activities because their conscience will prevent them: they will feel ashamed for doing the wrong thing. In this respect, republican theory links up with older conservative theories that look to the internalisation of controls in addition to societal imposition of controls. Thus, the theory looks to both external processes of shaming (as expressed in official institutional intervention) and also internal self-sanctioning forms of shaming (as expressed in the ideas of control theory).

The concept of reintegrative shaming has been employed in a number of different ways. The importance in the system of criminal justice of combining formal and informal processes of social control is seen to be relevant in such areas as business practices, domestic violence, and juvenile justice (see Braithwaite 1991, 1992).

The theory asserts that we need a fair degree of community shaming before the offender reaches the stage of formal institutional shaming. In this manner, we need to ensure that a 'public' conscience exists in society, along with a culture that develops this kind of conscience within each person. For example, if **domestic violence** is deemed intolerable by the community, then potential violators will stop themselves because they imagine wider community disapproval. This informal shaming process occurs outside the criminal justice system in order to prevent the crime from occurring. It is argued that formal sanctions should not be imposed until further down the track.

Peacekeeping criminology

The reluctance of republican theory to impose formal sanctions is shared by another important strand of restorative-based criminology, in this case 'peacekeeping criminology' (see Pepinsky & Quinney 1991). It is argued in this perspective that the criminal justice system fails at every level. The criminal justice system represents a state-sanctioned means of inflicting pain under the guise of reducing criminal activity and, yet, the imposition of punishment and repression never solves—and never will solve—social problems. The basic philosophy is that we cannot solve violence or human suffering with more violence and more human suffering. Instead, it is argued that humanistic and restorative principles need to be adopted at the level of dealing with the offender, and in dealing with wider social conflicts as well. The emphasis is on transformative strategies that are themselves premised upon participatory forms of conflict resolution.

Drawing upon various peacemaking traditions—such as religious, humanistic, and feminist approaches to understanding and responding to violence—peacemaking criminology criticises models of interaction based upon the idea of winners and losers. Rather, and in contrast, the approach speaks about openness, trust, and cooperation (Moyer 2001). In many cases, it is argued that, literally, peace begins at home; that is, it is important that each individual lives their everyday life based upon love, forgiveness, kindness, and hope (see, for example, Quinney 1991). These principles and concepts are also pertinent to developing a critique of a society that is class-divided, racist, and sexist, and that predominantly operates on the basis of power, domination, exploitation, and control over others.

Not surprisingly, peacemaking criminology tends to stress mediation, conflict resolution, and reconciliation as preferred methods with which to deal with human suffering and wrongdoing. Non-violent ways of thought and action are essential to the peacekeeping conception of restorative justice. The intent is to understand how and where people make peace (Pepinsky 1991) in order to supplant existing criminal justice models that are based upon the 'war' on crime.

One of the key challenges of peacemaking criminology has been to translate a philosophy of 'being nice' into the practical realities of actual conflicts and instances in which social harm is occurring. To put it differently, how does one move beyond expressing the sentiments of compassion and empathy to concretely addressing real sites of conflict? Part of the answer to this is provided in recent work by McEvoy (2003). Based upon grounded interventions with paramilitary groups in Northern Ireland, McEvoy (2003) argues that a 'new' peacemaking criminology might include:

- an explicit focus on jurisdictions where actual political or ethnic conflicts are occurring
- a recognition of the idea that political engagement is necessary and that conflict transformation be based upon the objective of trying to make a difference
- a substantive engagement with human rights discourses, particularly as a counterweight to those sorts of moral relativism that can impede practical intervention
- a reframing of the evaluation of 'what works' into a political rather than a technical exercise, thereby acknowledging the profound transformations in individuals, groups, and communities that peacemaking criminology, somewhat ambitiously, wishes to make manifest.

An important observation of peacemaking criminology generally is that very often war and the war on crime are interlinked and share many of the same attributes and institutional dynamics. Philosophically, and increasingly at a practical level of intervention, peacemaking criminologists wish to challenge violence, repression, and humiliation as preferred modes of conflict resolution—whether this be at the level of individuals, groups, families, communities, or nation-states. Conversely, drawing upon human rights discourses and restorative justice activities such as community mediation, and by stressing the positive value of non-violent alternatives and the vital need to address the material reasons for social differences, peacemaking criminology aims to transform social settings in more profound ways than traditional criminal justice approaches. Similar to republican theory, it suggests the possibilities of both a normative theory of crime, war, and violence, and the potential practices that might reflect and reinforce the restorative justice ethos.

CRITIQUE

A number of criticisms can be levelled at the republican theory. One weakness of the theory is that it does not really look at the causes of crime. What it does do is provide a whole range of variables that are associated with crime, at the level of both the individual (interdependency) and society (communitarianism). The theory thus provides a description of 'background' characteristics of the 'typical offender' (e.g., young, unemployed, male, transient) without really exploring how these factors interact with the given environment that leads to offending.

Furthermore, the societal-level variable 'communitarianism' needs greater analysis if it is to be a truly useful concept in analysing potential levels of criminality within a given society. It is one thing to link variables by way of association to an underlying construct, but it is quite another to map out, in any given society, how each is ordered, and what the 'flow' of the variables is. It is important to do this in order to explain why some parts of society are more vulnerable to crime, and in particular to locate the individual offender within society in a way that provides a meaningful explanation for the pressures to offend. Thus far, republican theory has tended to remain at the level of description when dealing with the way the world actually is, with the theory outlined in its fullest extent with respect to some notion of an ideal society.

When dealing with a less than ideal society, further problems arise. The notion of exercising self-control and the concept of the self-sanctioning conscience raise a number of questions when they are applied to a society that has a great divide between rich and poor. The theory assumes that individuals make incorrect choices that ultimately lead to their criminal behaviour. However, if the social and economic world of the individual is falling apart, the offender is obviously in a difficult situation. The theory has little to say about the structural characteristics of the young offenders being targeted. How does the family group conference or other arenas that flow from republican theory aim to take account of these issues? The policies that have been suggested thus far appear unable to deal with real clashes of interest between wealth and poverty, issues of racism, and the wider issues of class structure. The policies emanating from the theory do not address the degree to which young people may be brought into the system because of institutional biases, such as police bias, or bias in decision-making of the courts.

These problems arise partly because the theory works on the idea of a presumed consensus within society. In particular, there is a consensus concerning the nature of criminal activity: crimes are those predatory acts that are accepted by all as criminal. From previous chapters we have seen that many would argue with this. The concern is that the definition of crime itself, and the application of criminal law, are subject to political interests; as a result, both the definition and the application are biased. The theory does not take adequate account of these biases within the system itself. Rather, it relies on a policy of minimal intervention, expressed through the underlying principles of parsimony and checking of power, as a way of attempting to deal with such problems.

Interestingly, and by way of contrast, peacemaking criminology has been criticised for going too far in the other direction. That is, the problem in this perspective is that the presumed consensus is biased and socially negative: the dominant social values and ideals revolve around violence as the key means of conflict resolution. Thus, it is the systemic reliance upon violence (as manifest in institutional practices and cultural values) that is viewed as destructive, wasteful, and inhumane in contemporary societies. However, it has been argued that this particular philosophical stance provides little more than a utopian vision of society, and that, in the end, it does not provide for an adequate empirical and theoretical understanding of crime and crime control. As Akers (1997: 183 in Moyer 2001) puts it: 'This is a highly laudable philosophy of criminal justice, but it does not offer an explanation of why the system operates as it does or why offenders commit crime.' Similar types of criticism have also been noted among supporters of peacemaking criminology. For example, as discussed above, McEvoy (2003) is highly conscious of the fact that too often the tendency in peacemaking criminology is to stimulate interest in the perspective but to pay much less attention to practical application. The perspective is pitched at a level of abstraction and philosophical reflection that offers a different way of framing and thinking about crime and criminality, but as an emerging form of criminological theory it has some way to go in providing more specific, grounded analyses of relevant issues and trends. Moreover, big questions remain with respect to analysis of different types of violence, whether and under what conditions violence can be seen as liberating or repressive, the legitimacy or otherwise of violence that enables the state or community to wield authority and to enforce collective decisions, and the moral basis upon which to condemn (or support) those who utilise violence to achieve social goals. Resolution of these practical and conceptual issues is most likely through specific case studies and strategic interventions as illustrated, for example, in McEvoy (2003).

The translation of theory into practice, and of understanding into action, is more transparent and integral to republican theory than has been, to date, generally demonstrated in peacemaking criminology. However, in the case of republican theory the notion of reintegrative shaming also raises a number of issues. It is not clear from the model which comes first: effective shaming or low crime rates. It may be that low crime rates are a precondition for the success of a criminal justice process that relies on shaming a transgressor so they do not reoffend. Following on from this, it is possible to argue that it may not be possible to shame successfully in a society that is low on communitarianism. Put another way, if an offender was never integrated into society in the first place, it makes no sense to 'reintegrate' that person. Reintegrative shaming loses its meaning when faced with someone who is marginalised from society and not repentant in the least.

The difficulties of trying to 'repair the harm' in the context of social disintegration and inequality have been implicitly acknowledged in other types of restorative justice approaches. For instance, rather than being based upon a concept of 'shaming', the balanced restorative approach is based upon a 'balanced' assessment of the offender's needs and competencies (Bazemore 1991). This approach relies not so much on what is essentially a moral category (shaming), but rather on situational assessment (involving close scrutiny of offender capabilities). As such, it attempts to explore the specific requirements related to each case of offending and to variably respond to each offender in terms of their immediate situation and capacities. Such an approach appears to offer more scope in dealing with issues relating to the marginalisation and alienation experienced by young offenders in particular.

Problems also arise with the way shaming works in practice. For example how, in practice, do we distinguish between reintegrative shaming and stigmatisation? It may be that a wider form of stigmatisation occurs because so many more people are involved in situations such as the juvenile conference. There are further problems with the concept of shaming and compliance, in that there is a need to distinguish between compliance with what the group wants, which is not internalised, and conformity, which is internalised (Potter 1992). Presumably, the ideal is for shaming to lead to changes internal to the individual that will reduce the chance of future offending. Shaming, then, is ultimately a concept that is internal to the individual, and yet the theory does not detail how successful shaming is to be measured, so that we can avoid stigmatisation or mere external compliance, both of which may lead to future offending.

Furthermore, the notion of shaming is used with certain types of offenders, mainly young people. There is little discussion regarding the success or otherwise of reintegrative shaming as it might be applied to white-collar offenders. There are yet other crimes, state crimes for example, that do not lend themselves easily to the concept of reintegrative shaming, which focuses on individual transgressions.

It can also be argued that the practical examples of republican theory, such as juvenile conferencing, involve a denial of due process. If guilt is not admitted by those who are the subject of these programmes, such programmes can be seen to be attempting to shame someone before they admit to offending, which is problematic. In practice, then, those accused of offending who participate in such programmes either need to plead guilty, or to have their guilt assumed before they participate. This can be seen as a denial of due process of the law, which presumes people are innocent until proven guilty. Many pre-court processes come up against this difficulty. The problem is that, if a given body is granted the power to punish an individual, the state has to be satisfied that the individual in question really committed the offence. The traditional way for this to happen is for the case to be tried in a court. However, these programmes try to avoid the court process, because it is seen as stigmatising and also expensive, but in doing so they deny the accused the right to have their case proved in the appropriate manner in open court.

Without the mechanism of the court ensuring those who receive punishment are really guilty, it can be argued that reintegrative shaming is potentially nothing more than a net-widening process of social control, without reducing the number of people subject to punitive sanctions of the state. If the aim of the criminal justice system is to reduce the number of people being caught up in the system, programmes set up to 'reintegratively shame' people as an alternative to court may simply make the overall system larger, without any positive effect in terms of reduction of crime. It can be argued that the programme represents an extension of power into civil society in the process of shaming. Some would argue that there needs to be a clear distinction between a process that is based in the criminal justice system, and one that properly resides within the community. The concept of reintegrative shaming blurs this distinction.

Despite these problems, republican theory has some clear strengths. First, it provides a more holistic account of crime and crime prevention, as distinct from individualistic and 'bad apple' approaches. It attempts to provide an overall view of society, and then locate criminal justice policy within this broader framework. As such, it can be seen as a comprehensive theory that provides an integrated view of all parts of the criminal justice system.

The view of society posited by republican theory as a whole also has clear advantages in terms of individual liberty over those perspectives that rely heavily on punishment and deterrence, such as certain aspects of New Right criminology outlined in chapter 8. Republican theory is based on ideas of a system that respects rights and limits, and thus clearly upholds individual liberty better than more punitive systems.

Finally, republican theory is politically attractive. It provides justification for building a new type of consensus in society and has an emphasis on restorative justice that is positive. Furthermore, the method of achieving lower crime rates is relatively inexpensive in that it is based on minimal intervention. In addition, it captures many of the political concerns of the day, such as the need to take account of the victim, and the emphasis on family as the basic unit in society.

CONCLUSION

The rise in popularity of republican theory, restorative justice, and peace-keeping criminology needs to be considered. The political directions of crime in recent years have seen a concentration on individual responsibility for one's actions, with the retributivists arguing that the individual who has committed the action must be punished. Republican theory agrees that people should be responsible for their actions, but argues that our response to those actions should be constructive.

The attraction of the theory can be explained, in part, by the economic directions of criminal justice. Fiscal crises in various jurisdictions have seen governments increasingly worried about how to best constrain expenditure in order to curb state debt. In this climate, prisons are viewed as expensive, and the legal aid crisis is seen as a problem arising out of the lengthy, and hence costly, formal court process. Hence, from a strictly economic viewpoint it makes sense to look at alternative cost-effective and efficient measures of crime control.

Another attraction of the republican theory and restorative justice approaches is that they offer a perspective on conflict and conflict resolution that is intrinsically humane and socially positive. As such, they provide a refreshing change from traditional law-and-order discourses. They offer messages of hope, and redemption, in a world seemingly riven by hatred and intractable social differences. Combining powerful moral critiques and practical methods of intervention, they demonstrate that alternatives are, indeed, possible and desirable.

If conditions in the rest of society undermine the cohesiveness of that society as a whole, then this will limit and circumscribe the efficacy of the proposals put forward by republican theorists. In the next chapter we look at critical criminology, which has attempted to address some of these issues.

FURTHER READING

Bazemore, G. (1997) 'The "Community" in Community Justice: Issues, Themes, and Questions for the New Neighbourhood Sanctioning Models', *Justice System Journal*, 19(2): 193–227.

Braithwaite, J. (1989) *Crime, Shame and Reintegration*, Cambridge University Press, Cambridge.

Braithwaite, J. & Pettit, P. (1990) *Not Just Deserts: A Republican Theory of Criminal Justice*, Clarendon Press, Oxford.

McEvoy, K. (2003) 'Beyond the Metaphor: Political Violence, Human Rights and "New" Peacemaking Criminology', *Theoretical Criminology*, 7(3): 319–46.

Pepinsky, H. & Quinney, R. (eds) (1991) *Criminology as Peacemaking*, Indiana University Press, Bloomington, Indiana.

Pettit, P. & Braithwaite, J. (1993) 'Not Just Deserts, Even in Sentencing', *Current Issues in Criminal Justice*, 4(3): 225–39.

Zehr, H. (1990) *Changing Lenses: A New Focus for Crime and Justice*, Herald Press, Scotsdale.

CHAPTER 11

Critical Criminology

INTRODUCTION

The aim of this chapter is to discuss the main ideas and concepts of critical criminology. This perspective combines a wide range of concerns from across the more radical approaches, such as Marxism and feminism, and attempts to develop a type of left-wing criminology that is relevant and appropriate for contemporary society.

As with many of the perspectives in criminology, critical criminology incorporates a wide number of ideas and analytical strands. A distinguishing characteristic of critical criminology is that it is generally associated with an **oppositional** position in relation to much of the work of conventional criminology, and also to many contemporary policy developments in the field of criminal justice (see Schissel & Brooks 2002; Carrington & Hogg 2002).

Critical criminology nevertheless exhibits a number of elements that make it a natural intellectual and strategic partner of both the Left Realist and republican approaches. As will be demonstrated in this chapter, however, politically the perspective retains a strong socialist (rather than liberal-reformist) orientation. Its analytical focus emphasises the causal significance of capitalism in the generation of and responses to 'crime' (rather than relying on multifactorial descriptions).

SOCIAL CONTEXT

As much as anything, critical criminology represents a further development of the broad radical strands within criminology. In particular, it builds upon the basic concepts and strategic concerns of the Marxist and feminist perspectives. Generally speaking, it does so from the point of view of a broadly **anti-capitalist position**, which incorporates the ideas of creating a social and natural environment that is not associated with heterosexist, racist, and destructive practices of production and consumption.

There is some confusion and debate surrounding the term 'critical' criminology. It has been used by a wide range of writers to describe a wide range of theoretical and political positions. In some discussions, Left Realism is regarded as part of the critical criminology perspective; in others it is not. In some instances, any critique of the existing criminal justice system from any political position other than conservative has been associated with critical criminology. This simply equates 'critical' with specific criticisms, rather than using the term to identify a particular analytical framework.

Both liberal and radical approaches may call for change to existing criminal justice practices, and they may overlap on a range of conceptual and strategic issues (e.g., that unequal distribution of societal resources underpins much working-class crime). However, fundamental differences in ideology and ultimate goals remain, and these must be acknowledged as they have significant implications for criminological theory and practice.

The difficulties and lack of clarity in the use of the term 'critical' are due to the blurring of boundaries between liberal and radical kinds of analysis and intervention. They are also a reflection of other changes occurring in society that have had a major impact upon prevailing attitudes and ideologies. The 1980s was a period of highly volatile politics on a world scale. The demise of Stalinism in the former Soviet Union and Eastern Europe represented not only the end of the Cold War, but also part of a general rethinking of politics and ideology around the world.

The notions of *glasnost* (openness) and *perestroika* (restructuring) signalled a far-reaching process of change, reform, and transformation in the non-capitalist countries. Meanwhile, the world economy was steadily and rapidly being internationalised and globalised. Production, consumption, finance, culture, employment, debt, sport—everything was subject to processes that universalised certain ways of doing things, seeing things, and engaging in things. Simultaneously, people became aware of the increasing fragmentation of their lives, as previous loyalties, communities, and affiliations (e.g., links to a sporting club, to a neighbourhood, to a job) were no longer relevant or appreciated.

An age of profound uncertainty had been broached. By the late 1980s, it was clear that the world would never be the same again—politically, in terms of traditional capitalist versus communist ideologies; economically, in terms of employment and distribution of wealth; environmentally, in terms of ecological imbalance and degradation; or socially, in terms of how people relate to each other across many types of interactions. The hallmark of this period has been **rapid change**, often associated with technological innovation (in the form of the computer microchip) and the concentration of wealth and power into fewer and fewer hands on a global scale.

The world was not only an uncertain place, but also increasingly an unequal one. In trying to understand the nature of the processes of inequality, the concept of **difference** was highlighted in social analysis and reflected in the ongoing presence of the 'new social movements'. Gay and lesbian rights groups, environmental and conservation movements, pro-choice and broad women's rights organisations, animal rights activists, Third World solidarity action groups, human rights advocates, anti-racist groups, and so on were raising the issues, and voices, of those who had not previously been heard in mainstream political or academic circles.

The world outside criminology obviously has an impact upon what occurs within the discipline. Not surprisingly, then, a number of new strands of thought began to emerge alongside the established approaches such as those we have explored in this book so far. For example, the fascination with meaning, social difference, and discourse analysis was manifest in so-called **postmodern** analysis. This describes the use of certain analytical tools to 'deconstruct' or decode the language and meaning of law and order, and of the criminal justice system, especially 'the law'. Thus, for example, feminist jurisprudence emphasised the inbuilt biases against women in a legal system premised upon certain conceptions of the 'reasonable man' (see Naffine 1990). This type of analysis uncovers the 'hidden' text of oppression as this pertains to women, ethnic minority groups, working-class people, and so on.

In some cases, the method of the postmodern was elevated to the level of social theory. Thus, all meaning—every association between subject (you) and object (the world around you)—is entirely an artefact of language (e.g., signs and symbols), and language, in turn, is relative to and determined by your particular perspective. In other words, there is no 'objective' world that is not constructed 'subjectively' by the author of a particular 'text'. There can be no privileged interpretation of reality. For some, this also means the adoption of a new neutrality that favours no particular politics (not conservative, liberal, or radical) and that ultimately may reject the idea that there are certain dominant structures of power. Such a perspective makes it difficult to speak about and act upon oppression as a structural phenomenon (see Thompson 1992).

The term postmodernism is used in a number of different ways, some of which appear to be contradictory. Some care, therefore, has to be taken to clarify its meaning in any particular instance. For example, it has been used in reference to:

- analysis of postmodern trends (e.g., the social impact of new communication and information technology; the commodification of symbols, especially as this relates to consumption)
- the idea of a postmodern society as distinct from 'modernity' (e.g., one that exhibits high degrees of social differentiation, individuation, and diverse forms and constructions of subjectivity or personal identity)
- postmodern techniques (e.g., methods of analysis, which centre on the nature and dynamics of language)
- postmodern theory (e.g., the universalisation of its method to consider knowledge and power relations across a broad spectrum of social life)
- postmodern epistemology (e.g., a philosophical stance on the central place of language in the relationship between the 'knower' and what is 'known', which makes problematic any assigning of 'truth' to statements about the world around us).

The postmodern approaches have also gone under different names, such as 'constitutive criminology' or a 'social constructionist' paradigm (Henry & Milovanovic 1994; Arrigo & Bernard 1997).

If some of the new types of analysis stressed 'difference' and the relative rather than absolute nature of the social world, others emphasised 'commonality' and shared experience as the basis for criminological work. The idea of **peacemaking criminology** (discussed in the previous chapter) asks that we recognise our 'oneness' with the world around us. It views crime as essentially a consequence of a general violence towards and separation from people due to the ways in which society responds to offenders. Its main themes include 'connectedness', 'caring', and 'mindfulness' (Friedrichs 1991).

The relationship of increasingly fragmented societies, and pluralised modes of government, to other more homogenising social processes is also subject to criminological attention. For example, the concept of a 'risk society' (Beck 1992) has been used to describe new forms of risk related to accelerating technological change and globalisation of economic, political, and social relationships. In this framework, there are a series of threats to human life that are increasingly shared by the inhabitants of the planet, such as pollution, global warming, crime, and so on. These phenomena do not respect national borders, and nor do they necessarily privilege any particular 'victim' above another. The risks, in one sense, transcend the ordinary social differences of late modernity. Another related idea is that of 'ontological insecurity' (Giddens 1990, 1991), which describes the feeling of being physically and psychologically at risk in an unstable and rapidly changing world. The direct result of the collapse of traditional social structures, and the limitations of those that are meant to provide security and predictability (such as the family, school, work), results in a process of 'individualisation' (see Beck & Beck-Gernsheim 2002). This refers both to the process whereby individuals are institutionally made more responsible for their well-being and less reliant upon state or collective support, and to the cultural and ideological prominence given to the 'project of the self' in self-managing one's choices and action.

While not unproblematic, these conceptualisations of risk, of uncertainty, of individualisation, and of risk management have nevertheless spurred considerable interest and application in the specific area of crime and crime control. From a criminological perspective, attention has been directed at the ways in which governments have attempted to manage crime-related risk, in a context in which inequalities have increased and other social ills have grown. It is argued that many Western states have responded to this by devolving responsibility for personal security on to individuals, while simultaneously adopting more draconian methods of responding to crime (see Stenson & Sullivan 2001). The individualisation of responsibility in fact masks the social differences in capacity to deal with personal risk; it also ignores the social patterning of both victimisation and offending behaviour.

The various critical criminology perspectives reflect, in many ways, the uncertainties and the hopes of the current age. Their development has been intertwined with radically altered material circumstances, and the emergence of the new social movements as political forces in society.

The ideas of these perspectives have been drawn upon to varying degrees in contemporary criminological work.

BASIC CONCEPTS

What distinguishes critical criminology per se is its concern with **structures of power**. These are seen to be institutionalised in particular ways, and to reflect social interests that oppress specific categories of people. How power is conceptualised, however, marks out one of the main differences of approach within critical criminology.

Critical criminologists more or less agree that the present operation of the criminal justice system is unfair, biased, and operates in ways that advantage certain groups or classes above others. The primary task of the critical criminologist is to expose the nature of the underlying power relations that shape how different groups are treated in, and by, the criminal justice system. In many cases, the task is also seen as trying to initiate action and to develop strategies that will **transform** the present social order, including the criminal justice system.

The focal point of critique within this perspective is how power is mobilised within the broad sphere of criminal justice. There is a range of differing approaches within critical criminology, providing many different methods, empirical studies, and theoretical insights. For present purposes, we can identify two general trends in the critical criminological literature. The 'structuralist' approach tends to focus on power as something that is ingrained in social structures, and that manifests itself in the form of the action of institutions and the activities of sectional interest groups (see Scraton & Chadwick 1991). The 'postmodern' approach, on the other hand, sees power in terms of language, and the ways in which knowledge production shapes human experience while simultaneously engendering conflict over meaning (see Arrigo & Bernard 1997; Lea 1998). The differences between these approaches are seen by some writers to be so great as to warrant treatment as distinct models of social inquiry (Arrigo & Bernard 1997; Russell 1997). Others do not necessarily share this view or are less definitive about the 'break' between the two perspectives (Henry & Milovanovic 1994; Einstadter & Henry 1995).

Part of the complexity, and to some extent confusion, in the area of postmodern criminology arises because this form of theorising has expanded the range of disciplines from which criminology draws theoretical insight. Disciplines, each with their own separate history, may use the same term to mean very different things. There are a number of examples of this and, not surprisingly, we must clarify our meaning of one of these 'contested terms'—namely, structuralism. Within sociology, the term structuralism has meant a theoretical perspective that places an emphasis on the way economic, political, and social structures shape individual behaviour and, in the case of criminology, the definition of crime. This is this definition of the term that is used in this chapter. For some postmodernists (perhaps, more accurately, post-structuralists) the term structuralism means something quite different. In this case, structuralism generally makes some reference to the work of Ferdinand de Saussure, a French linguist. Saussure's theory (labelled 'structuralism') argued that language was a self-referential system of meaning whereby a word was given meaning not because it related to a 'thing' (such as a flower) but primarily because the giving of meaning enabled some discrimination in meaning from another word (such as 'grass') within the language system itself. Language was thus 'structured' in terms of a substantially closed, formal system of meaning. The meaning and existence of words could be explained most fully by way of understanding the structure of a particular language itself, not by reference to anything outside that language. Post-structuralism, as a theoretical perspective, draws heavily from linguistics; as such it tends to build, critically, upon the Saussurean meaning of the term structuralism, as opposed to the sociological meaning of the term.

Structuralism

While there are a number of different strands to structuralist criminology, in general it can be said that crime is defined in terms of **oppression** (see chart 11.1). Some groups are particularly vulnerable to oppression. Members of the working class (especially its more powerless sections, including the 'underclass'), women (especially those who are poor, who are sole parents, and who are socially isolated), ethnic minority groups (especially those from non-English-speaking backgrounds and refugees), and indigenous people (especially those worst-affected by long-term colonisation processes and institutional disadvantage) are those most likely to suffer from the weight of oppressive social relations based upon class division, sexism, and racism.

CHART 11.1   Structuralist Criminology

Definition of crime	■ structural forms of oppression (class, gender, 'race')
Focus of analysis	■ crimes of the powerful (the state, political economy, ideology) ■ crimes of the less powerful (specific class, gender, ethnic, 'race' groups)
Cause of crime	■ marginalisation, criminalisation (e.g., racialisation of crime)
Nature of offender	■ structurally determined context, process of homogenisation, legitimation crisis
Response to crime	■ social empowerment, redistribution of social resources, participatory democracy
Crime prevention	■ anti-racist campaigns, human rights emphasis, public ownership under community control
Operation of criminal	■ emphasis on restorative justice, self-determination at justice system community level, employment orientation, open and public accountability of state officials

The focus of analysis for structuralist criminology is both the crimes of the powerful and the crimes of the less powerful. In examining the **crimes of the powerful**, attention is directed at issues relating to ideology (e.g., the nature of 'law-and-order' politics), political economy (e.g., social impacts of privatisation), and the state (e.g., managerial rather than democratic modes of rule). The structural context of crime vis-à-vis capitalist development and institutional pressures is viewed as central to any explanation of crimes of the powerful.

The **crimes of the less powerful** are examined from the point of view of the specific experiences of particular sections of the population. Different forms of criminality are thus linked to specific layers of the working class, particular categories of women and men, certain ethnic minority groups, and indigenous people in a variety of rural and urban settings. There is a twofold emphasis: on the **specificity** of crime and criminal involvement (i.e., specific groups, specific kinds of activity); and on the **generalist** features that unite the disparate groups (i.e., shared economic, social, and political circumstances).

Crime is seen to be associated with broad processes of political economy that affect the powerful and the less powerful in quite different ways. For the powerful, there are pressures associated with the securing and maintenance of **state power** and **specific sectional interests** in the global context of international trade and transnational corporate monopolisation. For the less powerful, the cause of crime is seen to lie in the interplay between **marginalisation** (separation from mainstream institutions) and **criminalisation** (intervention by state authorities). Of particular note is the increasing **racialisation of crime**, in which certain communities are targeted for media and police attention in the 'war against crime' and 'public disorder'.

Offending behaviour is thus linked to a social context that is structurally determined by the general allocation of societal resources and by the specific nature of police intervention in people's lives. There is a **process of homogenisation**, in which the least powerful and most vulnerable in society—the poor, the less educated, the unemployed—are filtered through the system until they constitute a disproportionate number of repeat offenders and/or recidivist prisoners.

The growing disparities between rich and poor, and the expansion in the sheer number of the poor, constitute a **legitimation crisis** for the system as a whole. One response is the swing towards 'law-and-order' politics that entrenches and exacerbates the homogenising process of identifying and punishing offenders. A particular area of concern is the repressive nature of the state in relation to particular layers of the working class and in regard to particular communities.

For structuralist criminology, a response to crime must be built upon a strategy of **social empowerment**. This means involving people directly in decisions about their future through direct participatory democracy. It also requires a redistribution of social resources to communities on the basis of social need and equity.

To counter crimes committed by the powerful, there must be open and **public accountability** of all state officials. Further, as part of wealth redistribution, there has to be a transfer of wealth from private hands to public ownership under community control.

As a general crime-prevention measure, and to diminish the prevalence of certain crimes, there needs to be anti-racist and anti-sexist campaigns (including re-education and retraining of state officials such as the police). Strong emphasis is given to extending and protecting **basic human rights** (which include economic, social, cultural, and political rights), and institutionalising these by means of watchdog agencies (e.g.,

Children's Commissioner, Human Rights Commissioners) and developmental policies.

The criminal justice system should be based upon a model of **restorative justice**, rather than retribution and punishment. The state should not be repressive in orientation, but coercion may be required as part of the redistribution of community resources from the advantaged sectors of the population to the less advantaged. Moreover, the criminal justice system should operate openly, publicly, and with full community accountability. As far as possible, its functions should reflect self-determination at the community level, within the boundaries of human rights.

Postmodernism

The starting point for a postmodern (or social constructionist) approach to critical criminology is the idea that **language structures thought**. Language is seen as the crucial intervening variable between social relationships and institutions, and all methods of knowing the social world. Crime is thus defined in terms of linguistic production, and relationships of power that shape the nature of this production (see chart 11.2). The social world is effectively limited to, and constituted by, the collective reality of language. In other words, there is no necessary logical connection between the use of language and what it purports to describe—there are no 'objective truths', only different ways of speaking about and describing social reality.

Accordingly, social constructionists tend to reject the idea of any 'grand narrative' (e.g., technological revolution, enlightened social progress) as providing a foundation for understanding the world. This is because the social world is viewed as inherently chaotic and based upon contingency, rather than as a coherent system that is regulated in terms of some central steering mechanism (e.g., class struggle, social solidarity). Society is characterised as being in **constant flux and change**, and the emphasis is on fragmentation, diversity, and ambiguity. As such, reality cannot be understood, depicted, or changed as a whole; there is not one 'truth' but 'many truths', and these, in turn, are constantly changing.

The only real universal feature of social life is the way in which individuals seek power over others by gaining knowledge of them. The focus, therefore, is on power as a ubiquitous feature of social life. The point of analysis is to explore the **'micro-processes' of power**, which operate in institutions such as police, courts, and prisons, in order to reveal how power is exercised and how the exercise of power engenders resistance.

Those who **control the means of expression** are seen to hold the key to controlling and exercising power over others. Simultaneously, however, it is acknowledged that where there is power (in any social relationship), there is also **resistance** to this power. Language and meaning are contested, and there is always a dynamic tension between dominant social voices and those that are silenced or expelled by the dominant modes of expression.

The key to social transformation, therefore, lies in analysing the languages that construct social relationships in a particular way, to the advantage of some and to the disadvantage of others. Exposing the **discourses** (i.e., modes of speech, knowledge, categorisation of the social world) of everyday life opens the door to other expressions of reality that have been submerged by the dominant or hegemonic discourse. The main method of the social constructionist is that of discourse analysis, which examines how meaning and sense are constructed in everyday

CHART 11.2   Postmodernism

Definition of crime	■ not absolute ■ continuous struggle over control of linguistic production
Focus of analysis	■ human subject ■ conflicts over 'existence' or 'reality' as expressed in and through language
Cause of crime	■ hegemony of dominant discourse ■ suppression of alternatives
Nature of offender	■ discursively constituted through dominant discourses ■ relationships of resistance/power
Response to crime	■ replacement discourses ■ no action
Crime prevention	■ conflicts over discursive frames ■ new voices and listening ■ no action
Operation of criminal justice system	■ localism, plurality ■ deconstruction and critique ■ acknowledgement of diverse 'discursive subject positions'

language. This involves a process of **deconstruction of meaning** to reveal the hidden and suppressed meanings embodied in certain social relationships.

An important part of this deconstruction of meaning is to examine the **discursive subject positions** that inform the way in which people speak and think. For example, in the field of criminal justice there are a number of activities and social roles or positions. These include, for instance, offending (the offender), lawyering (the lawyer), policing (the police officer), and judging (the judge or magistrate). It is argued by postmodern writers that the people (subjects) who assume these positions speak, think, feel, and know through the language that is embodied in these structures. Thus, the person who assumes the discursive subject position of police officer, who engages thereby in 'policing', does so in a manner that reflects and embodies what it is to 'be a police officer' (rather than, say, a husband, mother, lover, or football player). Insofar as this is the case, then these subjects can be described as being decentred, in the sense of not being entirely in control of their own thoughts. They act and think like a 'police officer' from the moment that they assume or take on the policing discursive subject position.

The big question for the social constructionist is how the dominant linguistic regime (e.g., legal jargon and categories) in the criminal justice system dismisses particular languages (e.g., the emotional experiences of rape victims) that express a different view and experience of the social world. The 'languaging' of reality is demonstrated in the legitimacy found in the acceptance of certain discursive subject positions (e.g., the judge as rational), but not others (e.g., the victim as not rational). It is argued that: 'By dismissing these oppositional languages, certain versions of how to think, act, feel and be are indirectly de-valued' (Arrigo & Bernard 1997: 44). The task, therefore, is to expose the different ways in which criminal justice is languaged, and to offer a voice to those who have been silenced by the dominant discourses of the law.

Given the central importance of language, and the study of language, it is understandable that social constructionists tend to reject causal explanations of crime that portray crime as part of a 'grand narrative' (e.g., strains, biological factors). Rather, attention is drawn to how those who control the means of linguistic production also control the prevailing and official definitions of crime. The key question is 'whose "languaged" (and therefore social) interests are valued and de-valued

in the prevailing (or alternative) definitions of crime' (A.
1997: 48).

In another sense, the 'cause' of crime is seen to lie in
nation itself. That is, the linguistic domination varying
that speech, thought, and behaviour that resists, de-legiti...
opposes the potency of the discourse in effect. The solution to this
dilemma is to develop **replacement discourses** that will neutralise the
power of the dominant languages that regulate and discipline the lives of
alienated collectivities (especially ethnic minority people, indigenous
people, women, and gay men and lesbians). The emphasis, therefore, is
on social inclusiveness, diverse modes of communication, and a pluralistic
culture. To undercut the dominance of the hegemonic discourses, and
to acknowledge the specificity of different 'voices', the main focus for
action (if any) is at the local level and through decentralised means of
social control and interaction. For some writers, however, any attempt
to establish a replacement discourse is itself a form of linguistic imposition (Lea 1998; Morrison 1994). For these people, we can deconstruct
meaning, but the construction of alternative discursive frames is simply
not on the agenda (as to do so implies new conflicts revolving around
knowledge, power, and resistance).

HISTORICAL DEVELOPMENT

Critical criminology is part of an important tradition of struggle and
political conflict to win or defend social and human rights within a class–
divided, sexist, and racist social structure.

Ideologically, the perspective is most closely identified with the
socialist tradition, and its emphasis on power relations, social conflict, and
change as a result of contest over resources. The guiding rhetoric is that
of social justice and the importance of empowering the less powerful.
The critical criminology perspective is relatively new, although as a particular theoretical model within criminology it has continuity with both
the Marxist and feminist approaches.

The initial development of critical criminology as a bona fide current
within the mainstream of the discipline began with the coming to
prominence of labelling theory. Sometimes referred to as 'new deviancy
theorists', writers who spoke about crime as a social process challenged
the discipline's conventional conceptions of, and means of dealing with,

minal justice issues. As we saw in chapter 5, the combination of labelling and the power to label was seen to have a dramatic impact upon the person so labelled. Importantly, this perspective focused attention upon the institutions and forces of 'social reaction' and how through professional practices the process of crime actually occurred.

Left-wing critics of labelling theory argued that analysis of the processes and situations within which labelling took place was not enough. It was also essential to examine the structural relations of power in society, and to view crime in the context of the social relations, state institutions, and political economy of advanced capitalism (Scraton & Chadwick 1991). It was at this point that much work was done from a Marxist perspective to identify the causal basis of crime, and to make the link between dominant institutions and ruling-class interests. However, there was a tendency at times either to romanticise crime (as acts of rebellion or resistance) or to see crime solely in economic terms (as always reducible to material necessity). Later work was to explore in more detail the specific contexts and lived experiences of people involved with the criminal justice system (Hall & Scraton 1981).

The issues of racism, sexism, and heterosexism were by and large ignored or insufficiently explained in much of the Marxist writing. This was not simply an analytical problem; it was immediately relevant from a political point of view as well.

The diminished popularity of academic Marxism in the 1980s demanded a response that could speak to a wider range of people than a more restrictive, narrowly conceived approach. Furthermore, the rise of the New Right in the West, the tearing down of Stalinist institutions in the former communist nations according to capitalist free-market criteria, and the political mobilisation of the new social movements had implications for Left criminology generally.

The acknowledgement of differences (in terms of specific needs, experiences, and histories) and recognition of commonalities (in relation to marginalisation and criminalisation processes) was translated into a concern with all forms of oppression within the critical criminology framework. Issues of class, gender, and ethnicity were seen to be interrelated, and to reflect the general institutional processes of capitalism.

At the other end of the spectrum, there was a need to keep the focus on the actions of those in power, not only in relation to those marginalised in society, but also more generally in the area of what has come to be known as white-collar crime. Edwin Sutherland (1983) was the first to coin this phrase in 1939, when he led a blistering attack on the actions of the respectable in society; actions that in a different context would be labelled as criminal and dealt with accordingly. Sutherland saw a need to address the inequalities in treatment of people who engaged in harmful behaviour between those with power and those without power.

This led to a steady stream of research and writing, initially in the USA and then gradually spreading worldwide, on the topic of white-collar crime (Geis & Goff 1983). The philosophical orientation of such work was not, however, Marxist. Rather it came from Sutherland's own theorising, that of differential association (outlined in chapter 4). Critical criminology can be seen as continuing the focus on white-collar crime, with a clearer focus on the impact of contemporary capitalism in providing opportunities for corporate criminality, and providing the justification for the lack of enforcement in the area. As such, it shares a stronger legacy with Marxism than with Sutherland and his contemporaries.

The conceptual legacy of Marxism was to establish a firm interest in examining questions relating to the nature and exercise of state power. In a similar vein, and reinforced by feminist studies on the cultural and psychological basis of oppression, research was directed at the role of ideology in shaping lived experience. Racism, sexism, and individualism are all bound up with certain ways in which the world is described and categorised—the definition of who is 'dangerous' and who is not, for example. The task of critical criminology was to expose the processes whereby certain groups and categories of people are deemed to be worthy of social exclusion, and to develop strategies that could open the door to a more humane and equal society.

CONTEMPORARY EXAMPLES

One of the hallmarks of critical criminology is its association with direct interventions in various law-and-order and criminal justice debates. Indeed, more than this, one of the main contributions of this strand of criminological activity has been to raise for public discussion a series of important social issues. For example, the work of critical criminologists has been crucial to ongoing critiques of the prison system and of developments relating to the privatisation of punishment (see Moyle 1994; Mathiesen 1990; Christie 1993). Much of this type of research, scholarship, and commentary has been informed by a concern to publicise existing injustices, and potential abuses, of criminal justice institutions (Schissel & Brooks 2002; Carrington & Hogg 2002).

A key feature of critical criminology is that it is one of the few perspectives that focuses specifically on issues of racism and crime. New Right criminology tends to attribute 'blame' for crime, poverty, and unemployment to particular ethnic minority communities themselves. In the conservative framework the emphasis is on the 'bad behaviour' of community members, and the 'choices' they make to be the way they are and to do the things they do. The mainstream perspectives—such as labelling, strain, and republican theories—have a more explicit concern with issues relating to racism. Here, however, the solution is often seen simply in terms of making criminal justice processes and procedures as fair and unbiased as possible. The idea is that high rates of incarceration and contact involving certain social groups are due mainly to 'discrimination' and improper use of discretion (see Cook & Hudson 1993).

From a critical criminological perspective, the main issue is one of structural inequality. Very often this inequality has been institutionalised in a racist fashion (see Cunneen & White 2002; Schissel & Brooks 2002). In such circumstances, insensitive and coercive policing, for instance, cannot be reduced to 'bad attitudes' on the part of the police; it stems from the structural role of the police in regulating the most marginalised sectors of a class-divided society. These divisions may, in turn, be associated with particular ethnic and 'race' groupings (e.g., indigenous people, non-English-speaking immigrants from South-East Asia). Issues of under-policing and over-policing are seen as flowing from broader societal pressures and divisions that have had a particularly negative impact on indigenous people and those from ethnic minority communities.

More generally, the work of critical criminologists has been instrumental in exposing and illuminating a wide range of issues pertaining to the less powerful groups in society. The victimisation, and empowerment, of indigenous people, immigrant communities, refugees, gay men and lesbians, working-class young people, and so on have been the subject of probing analysis and insightful discussion (see Brown & Hogg 1992; Carrington & Hogg 2002). One feature of this work has been its emphasis on explaining the specific empirical aspects of a particular phenomenon, without attempting to say that 'all crime is the same' or trying to deal with 'crime in general'. Nevertheless, the discussions of specific groups (e.g., indigenous people, female prisoners) and particular institutions (e.g., special police tactical response units, private prisons) is usually framed within a general perspective that views the state and powerful social interests (e.g., corporate sector) as problematic.

In addition to the focus on the powerless, critical criminology has also been concerned with the harm directly perpetrated by those in positions of power. Studies of white-collar crime and corporate crime (crime specifically resulting from the action of organisations) have pointed to the enormity of harm perpetrated in the white-collar sphere. A consistent focus of this research has been to label such acts criminal, and to call for their inclusion as quintessentially criminal acts to be dealt with accordingly (see, for examples, Shover & Wright 2001; Friedrichs 1996; Pearce & Tombs 1990). In a similar vein, recent work has attempted to provide more precise, and from a practical point of view, operational, concepts of state crime. Thus, Green and Ward (2000) propose that the term 'state crime' be restricted to the area of overlap between violations of human rights and state organisational deviance. By using such a definition, they wish to employ a criminological understanding of those acts or omissions that contribute to, or are complicit with, breaches of human rights. Such a concept opens the door to investigation of a wide range of social harms, corruptions, and violations of rights perpetrated by agencies and officials of the state.

Researchers in the area have pointed to the way in which the structure of capitalism itself creates opportunities for crimes of the powerful. Large corporations, most notably the multinational corporations, are in a position to reap considerable gains from their activities at the expense of both the environment and the weakest in society. In addition, certain industries such as the insurance industry may actively support crimes; for instance, an insurance company may gain from the crime of car theft through the sale of wrecked cars complete with high-value identification numbers (Brill 1993). The market power of these large organisations gives them the opportunity to avoid effective enforcement of laws aimed at curbing their power (Barnett 1993). Furthermore, it has been argued that law enforcement and criminalisation of these activities may in fact have limited value, because the state has an active interest in maintaining good relations with the monopoly capitalists. Other theorists working in this area point to the nature of the dual economy, where the logic of competition pushes smaller, weaker organisations to exploit their workers and spoil the environment. While large organisations have the money to put in place extensive programmes aimed at reducing harm, smaller organisations are forced to cut corners to survive (Haines 1997). The structure of capitalism is thus directly linked to the harm that organisations perpetrate.

Yet another area of recent interest is that of green or **environmental criminology**. Much of this work has been directed at exposing different instances of substantive environmental injustice and ecological injustice. It has also involved critique of the actions of nation-states and trans-national capital for fostering particular types of harm, and for failing to adequately address or regulate harmful activity. Drawing upon a wide range of ideas and empirical materials, criminology that deals with environmental harm has ventured across a range of areas of concern. For example, it has documented the existence of law-breaking with respect to pollution, disposal of toxic waste, and misuse of environmental resources (Pearce & Tombs 1998). Other work has emphasised the dynamic links between distribution of environmental 'risk' (particularly as these affect poor and minority populations) and the claims of non-human nature to ecological justice (Bullard 1994). It has also considered the specific place of animals in relation to issues of 'rights' and human–non-human relationships on a shared planet (Benton 1998). In general, and given the pressing nature of many environmental issues, many criminologists are now seeing environmental crime and environmental victimisation as areas for concerted analytical and practical attention— as areas of work that require much more conceptual development and empirical attention (see Williams 1996; Boyd et al. 2002; Lynch & Stretsky 2003; White 2003).

There are other examples of critical criminology that illustrate the movement of the perspective beyond a Marxist base. Indeed, some theorists working from a critical standpoint actively reject Marxism as a starting point, most notably those utilising a postmodern perspective. Postmodernism stresses the plurality of knowledge, and discounts any one 'correct view'. All views, in a sense, have validity. Thus, the focus is on the subjective nature of reality, rather than on objective 'truth'.

Postmodernist writers vary considerably in their opinions regarding the importance of historical context, given their focus on the plurality of existence; this contrasts with the primacy given to history by Marxists. While some postmodern authors accord it considerable importance—for example, Foucault (1977)—others fix only on the (multiple) 'realities' of the present. As such, these approaches tend to negate the possibility of value in anything other than the present (since that is all that is 'knowable'), and it has been argued that past atrocities and social harms can thus melt into insignificance in the postmodernist agenda (Cohen 1993).

Other writers, however, point to the way postmodernism, like labelling before it, empowers those with little voice (Einstadter & Henry 1995). In this view, reality is always constituted and reconstituted in the present, but according to very specific discourses. Many postmodern authors, they argue, are concerned to give a voice to those views that are currently underplayed or ignored by those who have power—for example, the views of indigenous people, women, lesbians and gay men, and so on. Meaning is present in everything we do, but it is the task of postmodernism to unpack the complex nature of everyday 'realities', and the discourses of these realities, including those realities concerned with crime and criminality.

What unifies the many different approaches within the critical criminology perspective is a deep concern with issues of oppression and injustice. These are seen to stem from structural inequalities in resource allocation and decision-making power. Accordingly, institutional reform is not seen as an end in itself, but as part of a more profound transition towards a more equal, fairer society. To take a specific example, a call for the abolition of prisons (or at the least a radical reduction in the prison population) may reflect the position that those who end up in prison are the most vulnerable sections of the population (in terms of income, employment, and educational background) and hence are unfairly criminalised and further penalised for their predicament. But to abolish prisons is not enough. Until the conditions that give rise to the creation of 'surplus populations' and ethnic and racially based social divisions are confronted, piecemeal institutional reform will not be sufficient to forestall suffering and pain in the future.

CRITIQUE

Critical criminology, since it has much in common with Marxist criminology, shares some of the same problems. In particular, it shares the problem of the definition of crime. Structuralist criminology, like Marxist criminology, defines crime very broadly, in terms of the oppression of a particular group (e.g., indigenous people or other minority groups) or class (e.g., working people) by those with power. In this, it shares a 'human rights' definition of crime, similar to some Marxist criminologists. The problem with these definitions is how to conceive of differences in the abuse of human rights. For instance, how does one compare discrimination against a person of non-English-speaking background applying for a job to the genocide that occurred in the early 1990s in the former Yugoslavia? As previously discussed, crime/non-crime are dichotomous categories; they do not lend themselves easily to discerning different gradations of harm. Nevertheless, some writers are now systematically addressing these issues. This is particularly the case in respect to definitions of state crime, and definitions of environmental harm (see Green & Ward 2000; White 2003). It also is apparent in efforts to create more sophisticated accounts of criminal action (including acts of omission) by the state, such as in the development of a model expressing the multidimensional continuum of state crime complicity (Kauzlarich et al. 2003).

Some critical criminology, like some Marxist criminology, tends to have a simple view of the nature of power. That is, there is a notion that some people have power (the powerful) and others do not (the powerless); there is no serious attempt to analyse the nature of power. This criticism has sometimes been directed at structuralist approaches. While acknowledging the need for further analysis of, and sensitivity to, the dynamics of power at a 'micro' as well as 'macro' level, structuralist criminology nonetheless maintains that social power is best understood as being concentrated in particular directions. It is seen to have substantially different effects according to different groups' resources and capacities, and this, in turn, is related to the institutionalised nature of inequality.

Given the critique of 'capitalism' that lies at the base of structuralist criminology, it needs to be able to spell out in more precise terms the nature of this capitalism in the light of processes of internationalisation and globalisation, and how its institutions (e.g., transnational corporations, nation-states) impact on the crime debate. Again, many writers are in fact now expanding their analytical horizons with respect to issues of globalisation and social and environmental harms (see Findlay 1999; Haines 2000) and it can be expected that this will be developed further over time. Yet, it is not always clear whether critical criminology is arguing that the basis of all crime is ultimately economic, or rather that the capitalist system merely exacerbates conflict and tension that exist independently from the economic relations inherent within capitalism. In either case, there is a need to examine the precise way in which capitalism acts to exacerbate tension and both produce and define crime.

Postmodern criminologists do not conceptualise power in the same way as those who adopt a structuralist perspective. Their view tends to draw upon the work of Foucault (1980), who points to the decentralisation of power within modern society; that is, it is not held solely by the state or in one particular class or group of people. Rather, the argument is that power is dispersed throughout society. Furthermore, power is not necessarily seen as always negative but as a generalised feature of social life. Thus, power, when used to oppress, creates resistance, and this in itself is a source of power. According to Foucault, power can be associated with pleasure as well as repression. It can also flow in more than one direction simultaneously.

Foucault's ideas have been highly influential, but at times they have been over-simplified or distorted in some postmodernist work. For example, postmodern criminology emphasises that language always constitutes, and is constituted by, the relationship between knowledge, power, and resistance, and this leads to some logical dilemmas. For instance, it has been pointed out that: 'If all discourses and definitions are power effects involving repression, then power is ubiquitous. It is everywhere and therefore nowhere' (Lea 1998: 173). If power, and resistance, are always present, then by what criteria are we to discern whether or not any particular social relationship is 'oppressive' or 'liberating'? Here the notion of a power differential becomes central to conceptual analysis. Major problems arise if crucial qualitative distinctions are not made regarding the relative power differences between different individuals and groups.

Additionally, it has been argued that the rejection of 'grand narratives', including those that provide a normative basis for action (such as 'justice', 'rights', and 'equality'), makes it difficult to provide a rationale or justification for specific types of academic analyses or social action on particular criminal justice issues. Although postmodern criminology can expose the power relations exhibited through the languaging of social reality, big questions remain as to what is to be done with this knowledge, given that values themselves may be seen to be subjective and partial, and thus unsuitable as guides to action (Loader 1998).

Another difficulty with the postmodernist approach is that deconstruction as a method of analysis can lead to infinite regress (Lea 1998).
That is, if there is no 'objective' world, and there really is no reality
outside the dynamics of language, then all knowledge is indeterminate
and relative. There is no endpoint to the deconstruction process. This
can be extremely confusing as words are further defined and interrogated
in terms of other words, and the language of analysis becomes ever more
complex and obscure. It can also preclude the necessity or capability to
actually act on the understandings we currently have, since these are
always changing and are always subject to further deconstruction.
Furthermore, if there is no intrinsic foundation to 'facts' about the social
world (because these are socially constructed through language), then
what criteria can be invoked to determine whose 'voices' should be heard
and which groups to support in our work? If the key criterion is that of
looking to those voices that have been 'silenced' by the dominant languages of the law, then it raises the prospect of not only enabling oppressed
minorities (e.g., ethnic minority groups) to resist better, but also, likewise,
supporting extreme right-wing nationalist or white supremacist groups
(e.g., neo-Nazis; see Lea 1998). This can only happen, however, if there
is no normative basis to the work of the postmodern criminologist. But
implicit in a values framework is the idea of some kind of meta-narrative
regarding what is deemed to be 'good' and 'right'.

Despite these weaknesses, critical criminology (both structuralist and
postmodernist) has allowed insight into the diversity of groups that are
progressively marginalised by contemporary capitalist societies and,
further, how the activities of such groups become criminalised in a way
that leads to further marginalisation. In doing so, it allows for a number
of new voices that have not been previously heard or listened to, such as
those of gay men and lesbians, and indigenous people.

Critical criminology forces us to confront issues of the social interests
in which the state acts. It highlights the potential long-term conflict that
can be produced by a state that prioritises the interests of one group of
society over and above the interests of other groups. In doing so, it gives
advance warning of the likely social impact of the dismantling of the
welfare state, of the 'racialisation' of public order policing, and of the
social exclusion of people from basic citizenship rights. The result of such
trends may be personalised in the form of high suicide rates (affecting
the individual), and collective in the form of riots and general social
unrest (affecting whole communities).

CONCLUSION

Critical criminology reflects the concerns of many different people in contemporary societies. Generally speaking, it espouses a 'liberation' philosophy that has at its centre emancipatory concerns aimed at allowing all people to participate fully in society, regardless of 'race', ethnicity, sex, class, and sexual orientation. Furthermore, it includes among its concerns issues relating to the environment and animal rights. Ultimately, critical criminology views capitalism as essentially hostile to the promotion of human rights and personal empowerment, and seeks alternative social arrangements and philosophies that can result in a more inclusive society.

In many ways, critical criminology represents the cutting edge of socially progressive criminology in the twenty-first century. It represents an amalgamation of concerns and ideas drawn essentially from socialist and radical viewpoints, and is an attempt to analyse and develop empowering intervention strategies in a rapidly changing world. As such, it offers a critique of the dynamics of global capitalism, through a mode of investigation that holds the promise of profound social transformation across many domains of social life, including, and especially, that of criminal justice.

FURTHER READING

Arrigo, B. & Bernard, T. (1997) 'Postmodern Criminology in Relation to Radical and Conflict Criminology', *Critical Criminology*, 8(2): 39–60.

Carrington, K. & Hogg, R. (eds) (2002) *Critical Criminology: Issues, debates, challenges*, Willan Publishing, Devon.

Cook, D. & Hudson, B. (eds) (1993) *Racism and Criminology*, Sage, London.

Henry, S. & Milovanovic, D. (1994) 'The Constitution of Constitutive Criminology: A Postmodern Approach to Criminological Theory', in D. Nelken (ed.) *The Futures of Criminology*, Sage, London.

Lea, J. (1998) 'Criminology and Postmodernity', in P. Walton & J. Young (eds) *The New Criminology Revisited*, Macmillan, London.

Schissel, B. & Brooks, C. (eds) (2002) *Marginality & Condemnation: An Introduction to Critical Criminology*, Fernwood Publishing, Halifax.

Scraton, P. & Chadwick, K. (1991) 'The Theoretical and Political Priorities of Critical Criminology', in K. Stenson & D. Cowell (eds) *The Politics of Crime Control*, Sage, London.

CHAPTER 12

Conclusion

The aim of this book has been to provide an introduction to the main concepts and explanations of criminology. In particular, we have reviewed the many and varied ways in which the nature and causes of crime have been defined and analysed within the field.

As we have seen, the way in which crime is conceived, and thus prevented and controlled, is a matter of considerable dispute. Invariably, the criminological enterprise involves issues of a theoretical, empirical, and political nature. The theories and perspectives we have explored in the book focus on different and often quite specific or distinct aspects of criminal activity and behaviour. Thus, for example, some theories have concentrated attention on the individual characteristics or attributes of the offender, others on the processes whereby an action or person comes to be defined as criminal, and still others on the influence of social structure on personal and group behaviour.

The diverse explanations on offer indicate, at least in part, the inter-disciplinary nature of criminology. As a field of study, criminology incorporates ideas, methodologies, and theoretical contributions from disciplines such as psychology, sociology, political science, history, legal studies, and forensic medicine. Different starting points and different conceptual emphases stem from the diversity of academic influences in the field. However, many of the differences within criminology also reflect broader divisions with regard to the level of analysis, and the political perspective.

This is illustrated, for instance, in the debate over whether criminal behaviour is determined or voluntary. At first glance, the debate appears to be fairly straightforward. On the one hand, there are those perspectives, such as the classical, that portray human activity as entirely voluntary—as simply a matter of individual choice. On the other hand, there are those theories that present the view that behaviour is overwhelmingly determined by factors outside the individual's control, whether these are biological, psychological, or social.

Within and across this interpretive divide, however, there is considerable variation. For example, the nature, scope, and extent of determinism and voluntarism often depend upon the level of analysis. A biological approach may stress individual pathology and the fixed features of an individual's genetic make-up as the reason behind certain behaviours. A strain theorist might look at aspects of social situation, and see behaviour as a result of the combination of opportunities available and immediate learning processes. A Left Realist approach could likewise adopt a situational analysis, but with greater emphasis on social conflict and inequality, and the role of institutions of crime control, such as the police, in fostering or dampening working-class criminality. For the critical criminologist, 'choice' is circumscribed by wider structural processes of marginalisation and criminalisation, or competitive market structures, and criminal activity among both the powerful and the less powerful is seen to reflect the ways in which existing social structures ultimately narrow the scope for the full exercise of human agency.

The complex ways in which the relationship between voluntarism ('free will') and determinism ('fate') is constructed in the criminological field demonstrates the existence of a series of cross-cutting analytical and political differences that transcend strict discipline boundaries.

These differences can be further highlighted by considering the underlying assumptions of criminological theory, as indicated in broad political orientation, and 'popular' conceptions of criminality and the criminal justice system. Chart 12.1 outlines how the diverse propensities (or likelihoods), motivations (or drives), and circumstances (or opportunities) underpinning criminality might be conceived according to varying political and analytical focus. The chart provides a rough guide to the different outlooks of the conservative, liberal, and radical commentator, and also shows the possible divisions or emphases within each broad political persuasion.

Our presentation of 'needs', 'deeds', and 'greeds' merely indicates general tendencies and, as such, is intended to provide only a schematic conceptual map of the underlying assumptions. Nevertheless, it is useful as an analytical backdrop upon which can be placed most of the theories and perspectives discussed in this book. The relevance of studying criminological theory lies precisely in the way it informs and assists us in understanding the actual source of specific arguments and the ideas of contemporary debates over crime.

We began the book by stating that the relationship between crime and criminology is always reflected in, and reflective of, particular conceptions of society. Each theory or perspective embodies particular values regarding 'what is' the nature of present society, and 'what ought to be' the best way to deal with social issues such as crime.

CHART 12.1   Underlying Assumptions of Criminological Theory

Different Reform Agendas		
Needs	*Deeds*	*Greeds*
Conservative political perspective		
Focus on the individual's pathology and need to conform with socially accepted norms and mores. Emphasis on the need to counsel or treat the individual, which may require indeterminate sentencing.	Law and order. Focus on what the individual has done. The extent of harm to the status quo dictates the extent of punishment. Key issues are retribution, punishment, and deterrence.	Motivation to offend, steal, or rob is greed. Focus is on the greed of the 'street criminal' who shirks responsibility to get work and earn money respectably. A focus on 'moral training' and reaffirmation of conservative values.
Liberal political perspective		
Focus on the needs of both the victim and the offender. Needs tempered by an understanding of social conditions that influence behaviour. Emphasis on restorative justice.	Civil libertarian. Focus on individual rights, determinate sentencing, and due process. Notion of equality and proportionality. All should have access to equal justice, and like offences should be treated in like manner.	Greed is more likely to be associated with those who take 'more than their fair share' from a democratic society. Discussion of white-collar crime relevant here, with a focus on regulation and moral persuasion.
Radical political perspective		
Focus on the distortion of needs due to the capitalist system. This system places a priority on competition and the 'market'. The result is an emphasis on private profit, rather than social need, which dictates the priorities of the state.	Focus on the deeds of the system, in terms of systematic bias against certain classes or ethnic groups. The degree of harm perpetrated by white-collar crime is juxtaposed against the harm perpetrated by street crime.	Greed is associated with structural competitive pressures, and the widening gap between rich and poor within society. A focus on redistribution of societal resources and radical democracy.

In the twenty-first century, the debates over crime and criminality look set to intensify as rapid social change continues to transform traditional social, economic, and political relationships. Around the world, great upheavals are taking place, and more often than not these are associated with increasing social polarisation. As part of this change, and in this context, 'law-and-order' debates are now constantly at the centre of electoral politics and are standard fare for infotainment and 'serious media' alike.

In the light of current public perceptions about the 'crime threat'—and general unease about the future of jobs, the environment, peace, and respect for human rights—it is more essential than ever to think critically about the nature of crime, how it occurs, who it affects, and what can be done to prevent or control it.

It is our hope that this book will reinforce the fact that there are indeed alternative ways to conceptualise these issues, just as there are various options we can take to deal with them at a practical level. The doing of criminological theory, research, and practical intervention is always at one and the same time a statement about the kind of world each of us would like to see, and a response to the world of which we are an integral part.

The key questions that we feel are important for criminologists are:

- **What kind of 'work' should we be doing and why?** This refers to the means and ends of intellectual production, and raises issues concerning the social implications of our practice.
- **What kind of society do we want and why?** This implies that, in doing what we do, there is, or ought to be, a vision of an ideal world towards which we can direct our efforts.
- **How do we distinguish between 'good' and 'bad' (or 'right' and 'wrong') and why?** This is basically a question of the normative or value basis of our work.

It is our belief that attempting to answer these kinds of questions is what makes the criminological endeavour meaningful, both from a personal perspective and from a societal point of view.

The uncertainties of the world we presently inhabit are mirrored in the limitations and uncertainties of contemporary criminological theory. In the end, each theory only fully makes sense when set within an appropriate societal context and values framework. The crucial challenge for the reader, therefore, is to critically question and evaluate the ethical and explanatory basis of each theory or perspective. In so doing, it is our hope that we will be better able to clarify where we stand in relation to the great issues of the day, and to determine what our specific responsibilities and interests are in building a safer, more secure, and healthy future, one in which social harms such as crime are minimised.

References

Alder, C. (1985) 'Theories of Female Delinquency', in A. Borowski & J. Murray (eds) *Juvenile Delinquency in Australia*, Methuen, North Ryde.

Alder, C. (1991) 'Explaining Violence: Socioeconomics and Masculinity', in D. Chappell, P. Grabosky & H. Strang (eds) *Australian Violence: Contemporary Perspectives*, Australian Institute of Criminology, Canberra.

Alder, C. (1994) 'Women and the Criminal Justice System', in D. Chappell & P. Wilson (eds) *The Australian Criminal Justice System: The Mid-1990s*, Butterworths, Sydney.

Alder, C. & Wundersitz, J. (eds) (1994) *Family Conferencing and Juvenile Justice*, Australian Institute of Criminology, Canberra.

Allen, J. (1990) '"The Wild Ones": The Disavowal of Men in Criminology' in R. Graycar (ed.) *Dissenting Opinions*, Allen & Unwin, Sydney.

Arrigo, B. & Bernard, T. (1997) 'Postmodern Criminology in Relation to Radical and Conflict Criminology', *Critical Criminology*, 8(2): 39–60.

Barlow, H. (1993) *Introduction to Criminology*, Harper Collins College Publishers, New York.

Barnett, H. (1993) 'Wealth, Crime and Capital Accumulation', in D. Greenberg (ed.) *Crime and Capitalism: Readings in Marxist Criminology*, Temple University Press, Philadelphia.

Bazemore, G. (1991) 'Beyond Punishment, Surveillance and Traditional Treatment: Themes for a New Mission in U.S. Juvenile Justice', in J. Hackler (ed.) *Official Responses to Problem Juveniles: Some International Reflections*, International Institute for the Sociology of Law, Onati.

Bazemore, G. (1997) 'The "Community" in Community Justice: Issues, Themes, and Questions for the New Neighbourhood Sanctioning Models', *The Justice System Journal*, 19(2): 193–227.

Bazemore, G. (1998) 'Restorative Justice and Earned Redemption', *American Behavioral Scientist*, 41(6): 768–813.

Bazemore, G. & Walgrave, L. (eds) (1999) *Restorative Juvenile Justice: Repairing the Harm of Youth Crime*, Criminal Justice Press, Monsey, NY.

Beccaria, C. (1767) *An Essay On Crimes and Punishments*, J. Almon, London.

Beck, U. (1992) *Risk Society: Toward a New Modernity*, Sage, London.

Becker, H. (1963) *Outsiders: Studies in the Sociology of Deviance*, Free Press, New York.

Benton, T. (1998) 'Rights and Justice on a Shared Planet: More rights or new relations?', *Theoretical Criminology*, 2(2): 149–175.

Berger, P. & Luckmann, T. (1971) *The Social Construction of Reality*, Allen Lane, London.

Bilchick, S. (1998) *Guide for Implementing the Balanced and Restorative Justice Model*, Office of Juvenile Justice and Delinquency Prevention, Washington, DC.

Bottomley, S., Gunningham, N., & Parker, S. (1991) *Law in Context*, Federation Press, Sydney.

Bottoms, A. & Wiles, P. (1997) 'Environmental Criminology', in M. Maguire, R. Morgan & R. Reiner (eds) *The Oxford Handbook of Criminology* (2nd edition), Clarendon Press, Oxford.

Boyd, S., Chunn, D. & Menzies, R. (eds) (2002) *Toxic Criminology: Environment, Law and the State in Canada*, Fernwood Publishing, Halifax.

Braithwaite, J. (1989) *Crime, Shame and Reintegration*, Cambridge University Press, Cambridge.

Braithwaite, J. (1991) 'Poverty, Power, White-Collar Crime and the Paradoxes of Criminological Theory', *Australian and New Zealand Journal of Criminology*, 24(1): 40–58.

Braithwaite, J. (1992) 'Reducing the Crime Problem: A Not So Dismal Criminology—the John Barry Memorial Lecture', *Australian and New Zealand Journal of Criminology*, 25(1): 1–10.

Braithwaite, J. & Pettit, P. (1990) *Not Just Deserts: A Republican Theory of Criminal Justice*, Clarendon Press, Oxford.

Brake, M. (1985) *Comparative Youth Culture*, Routledge and Kegan Paul, London.

Brill, H. (1993) 'Auto Theft and the Role of Big Business', in D. Greenberg (ed.) *Crime and Capitalism: Readings in Marxist Criminology*, Temple University Press, Philadelphia.

Brown, C. (1979) *Understanding Society: An Introduction to Sociological Theory*, John Murray, London.

Brown, D. & Hogg, R. (1992) 'Essentialism, Radical Criminology and Left Realism', *Australian and New Zealand Journal of Criminology*, 25(3): 195–230.

Buchanan, C. & Hartley, P. (1992) *Criminal Choice: The Economic Theory of Crime and Its Implications for Crime Control*, Centre for Independent Studies, Sydney.

Bullard, R. (1994) *Unequal Protection: Environmental Justice and Communities of Color*, Sierra Club Books, San Francisco.

Carrington, K. (1993) *Offending Girls*, Allen & Unwin, Sydney.

Carrington, K. & Hogg, R. (eds) (2002) *Critical Criminology: Issues, debates, challenges*, Willan Publishing, Devon.

Catalano, R. & Hawkins, J. (1996) 'The Social Development Model: A Theory of Antisocial Behavior', in J. Hawkins (ed.) *Delinquency and Crime: Current Theories*, Cambridge University Press, Cambridge.

Chambliss, W. (1975a) 'A Sociological Analysis of the Law of Vagrancy', in W. Carson & P. Wiles (eds) *The Sociology of Crime and Delinquency in Britain, Vol. 1*, Martin Robertson, Oxford.

Chambliss, W. (1975b) 'The Political Economy of Crime: A Comparative Study of Nigeria and USA', in I. Taylor, P. Walton & J. Young (eds) *Critical Criminology*, Routledge and Kegan Paul, London.

Chambliss, W. & Mankoff, M. (1976) *Whose Law What Order? A Conflict Approach to Criminology*, John Wiley and Sons, Toronto.

Chesney-Lind, M. (1974) 'Juvenile Delinquency and the Sexualisation of Female Crime', *Psychology Today*, July: 4–7.

Chesney-Lind, M. & Shelden, R. (1992) *Girls, Delinquency and Juvenile Justice*, Brooks/Cole Publishing, California.

Christie, N. (1993) *Crime Control as Industry: Towards Gulags Western Style?*, Routledge, London.

Cicourel A. (1976) *The Social Organisation of Juvenile Justice*, Heinemann, London.

Clarke, J., Hall, S., Jefferson, T. & Roberts, B. (1976) 'Subcultures, Cultures and Class: A Theoretical Overview', in S. Hall & T. Jefferson (eds) *Resistance Through Rituals: Youth Subcultures in Post-War Britain*, Hutchinson, London.

Cloward, R. & Ohlin, L. (1960) *Delinquency and Opportunity: A Theory of Delinquent Gangs*, Free Press, Chicago.

Cohen, A. (1955) *Delinquent Boys: The Culture of the Gang*, Free Press, Chicago.

Cohen, S. (1973) *Folk Devils and Moral Panics*, Paladin, London.

Cohen, S. (1979) 'The Punitive City: Notes on the Dispersal of Social Control', *Contemporary Crises*, 3: 339–63.

Cohen, S. (1985) *Visions of Social Control*, Polity Press, Cambridge.

Cohen, S. (1988) *Against Criminology*, Transaction Books, New Brunswick.

Cohen, S. (1993) 'Human Rights and Crimes of the State: The Culture of Denial', *Australian and New Zealand Journal of Criminology*, 26(2): 97–115.

Cohen, S. & Young, J. (2004) 'Comments on Simon Cottee's "Folk devils and moral panics: 'Left Idealism' reconsidered"', in *Theoretical Criminology*, 8(1): 93–7.

Collins, J., Noble, G., Poynting, S. & Tabar, P. (2000) *Kebabs, Kids, Cops and Crime: Youth, Ethnicity and Crime*, Pluto Press, Sydney.

Connell, R. (1995) *Masculinities*, Polity, Cambridge.

Connell, R. (2000) *The Men and the Boys*, Allen & Unwin, Sydney.

Connell, R. (2002) 'On Hegemonic Masculinity and Violence: Response to Jefferson and Hall', *Theoretical Criminology*, 6(1): 89–99.

Cook, D. & Hudson, B. (eds) (1993) *Racism and Criminology*, Sage, London.

Cordella P. & Siegel L. (eds) *Readings in Contemporary Criminological Theory*, Northeastern University Press, Boston.

Cornforth, M. (1987) *Historical Materialism* (Vol. 2 of *Dialectical Materialism: An Introduction*), Lawrence and Wishart, London.

Coser, L. (1977) *Masters of Sociological Thought: Ideas in Historical and Social Context*, Harcourt Brace Jovanovich, New York.

Cottee, S. (2002) 'Folk Devils and Moral Panics: "Left Idealism" reconsidered', *Theoretical Criminology*, 6(4): 387–410.

Cunneen, C. & White, R. (2002) *Juvenile Justice: Youth and Crime in Australia*, Oxford University Press, Melbourne.

Daly, K. & Chesney-Lind, M. (1996) 'Feminism and Criminology', in P. Cordella & L. Siegal (eds) *Readings in Contemporary Criminological Theory*, Northeastern University Press, Boston.

De Haan, W. & Loader, I. (2002) 'On the emotions of crime, punishment and social control', *Theoretical Criminology*, 6(3): 243–54.

Downes, D. (1966) *The Delinquent Solution*, Routledge and Kegan Paul, London.

Durkheim, E. (1979) *Suicide: A Study in Sociology*, Routledge and Kegan Paul, London.

Edwards, S. (1990) 'Violence Against Women: Feminism and the Law', in L. Gelsthorpe & A. Morris (eds) *Feminist Perspectives in Criminology*, Open University Press, Milton Keynes.

Eisenstein, H. (1984) *Contemporary Feminist Thought*, Unwin Paperbacks, London.

Einstadter, W. & Henry, S. (1995) *Criminological Theory: An Analysis of Its Underlying Assumptions*, Harcourt Brace, New York.

Empey, L. (1982) *American Delinquency: Its Meaning and Construction*, The Dorsey Press, Chicago.

Ericson, R., Baranek, P. & Chan, J. (1991) *Representing Order: Crime, Law and Justice in the News Media*, Open University Press, Milton Keynes.

Evans, D., Fyfe, N. & Herbert, D. (eds) (1992) *Crime, Policing and Place: Essays in Environmental Criminology*, Routledge, London.

Eysenck, H. (1984) 'Crime and Personality', in D. Muller, D. Blackmann & A. Chapmann (eds) *Psychology and Law*, John Wiley and Sons, New York.

Farrington, D. (1996a) 'The Development of Offending and Antisocial Behavior from Childhood to Adulthood', in P. Cordella & L. Siegel (eds) *Readings in Contemporary Criminological Theory*, Northeastern University Press, Boston.

Farrington, D. (1996b) 'The Explanation and Prevention of Juvenile Offending', in J. Hawkins (ed.) *Delinquency and Crime: Current Theories*, Cambridge University Press, Cambridge.

Feeley, M. & Simon, J. (1994) 'Actuarial Justice: the Emerging New Criminal Law', in D. Nelken (ed.) *The Futures of Criminology*, Sage, London.

Feldman, P. (1993) *The Psychology of Crime*, Cambridge University Press, Cambridge.

Felson, M. (1994) *Crime and Everyday Life: Insights and Implications for Society*, Pine Forge Press, London.

Feminist Anthology Collective (1981) *No Turning Back: Writings from the Women's Liberation Movement 1975–80*, The Women's Press, London.

Ferrell, J. (1997) 'Youth, Crime and Cultural Space', *Social Justice*, 24(4): 21–38.

Ferrell, J. & Sanders, C. (1995) *Cultural Criminology*, Northeastern University Press, Boston.

Fine, B. (1984) *Democracy and the Rule of Law: Liberal Ideals and Marxist Critiques*, Pluto, London.

Findlay, M. (1999) *The Globalisation of Crime*, Cambridge University Press, Cambridge.

Fishbein, D. (1990) 'Biological Perspectives in Criminology', *Criminology*, 28(1): 27–72.

Fitzgerald, G. (1989) *Report of the Commission of Possible Illegal Activities and Associated Police Misconduct*, Queensland Government Printer, Brisbane.

Foucault, M. (1977) *Discipline and Punish: The Birth of the Prison*, Penguin, London.

Foucault, M. (1980) 'Truth and Power' in C. Gordon (ed.) *Power/Knowledge: Selected Interviews and Other Writings 1972–1977*, Pantheon Books, New York.

Fraser, S. (ed.) (1995) *The Bell Curve Wars: Race, Intelligence and the Future of America*, Basic Books, New York.

Freund, J. (1969) *The Sociology of Max Weber*, Vintage Books, New York.

Friedrichs, D. (1991) 'Introduction: Peacemaking Criminology in a World Filled with Conflict', in B. MacLean & D. Milovanovic (eds) *New Directions in Critical Criminology*, The Collective Press, Vancouver.

Friedrichs, D. (1996) *Trusted Criminals: White Collar Crime in Contemporary Society*, Wadsworth Publishing, Belmont, California.

Gamble, A. (1988) *The Free Economy and the Strong State: The Politics of Thatcherism*, Macmillan Education, London.

Garland, D. (1988) 'British Criminology Before 1935', *The British Journal of Criminology*, 28: 131–47.

Garland, D. (1990) *Punishment and Modern Society: A Study in Social Theory*, Clarendon Press, Oxford.

Garton, S. (1991) 'The Convict Origins Debate: Historians and the Problem of the "Criminal Class"', *Australian and New Zealand Journal of Criminology*, 24(2): 66–82.

Geis, G. & Goff, C. (1983) 'Introduction' in E. Sutherland, *White-Collar Crime: The Uncut Version*, Yale University Press, New Haven.

Gelsthorpe, L. & Morris, A. (eds) (1990) *Feminist Perspectives in Criminology*, Open University Press, Milton Keynes.

Gibbons, D. (1977) *Society, Crime and Criminal Careers*, Prentice-Hall, New Jersey.

Gibbons, D. (1979) *The Criminological Enterprise: Theories and Perspectives*, Prentice Hall, New Jersey.

Glueck, S. & Glueck, E. (1960) *Unraveling Juvenile Delinquency*, Harvard University Press, Cambridge.

Gordon, R. (1995) 'Street Gangs in Vancouver', in J. Creechan & R. Silverman (eds) *Canadian Delinquency*, Prentice Hall, Toronto.

Gordon, R. & Foley, S. (1998) *Criminal Business Organizations, Street Gangs and Related Groups in Vancouver: The Report of the Greater Vancouver Gang Study*, Ministry of Attorney-General, Vancouver.

Goring, C. (1913) *The English Convict: A Statistical Study*, His Majesty's Stationery Office, London.

Gottfredson, M. & Hirschi, T. (1990) *A General Theory of Crime*, Stanford University Press, Stanford.

Gould, S. (1981) *The Mismeasure of Man*, W.W. Norton and Co., New York.

Grabosky, P. & Wilson, P. (1989) *Journalism and Justice: How Crime Is Reported*, Pluto Press, Leichhardt.

Graycar, R. & Morgan, J. (1990) *The Hidden Gender of Law*, Federation Press, Sydney.

Green, P. & Ward, T. (2000) 'State Crime, Human Rights and the Limits of Criminology', *Social Justice*, 27(1): 101–15.

Greenberg, D. (ed.) (1993) *Crime and Capitalism: Readings in Marxist Criminology*, Temple University Press, Philadelphia.

Hagan, J. (1987) *Modern Criminology: Crime, Criminal Behavior and its Control*, McGraw-Hill, Toronto.

Haines, F. (1997) *Corporate Regulation: Beyond 'Punish or Persuade'*, Clarendon Press, Oxford.

Haines, F. (2000) 'Towards Understanding Globalisation and Control of Corporate Harm: a Preliminary Criminological Analysis', *Current Issues in Criminal Justice*, 12(2): 166–80.

Hall, S. (1980) 'Popular–Democratic vs. Authoritarian Populism: Two Ways of "Taking Democracy Seriously"', in A. Hunt (ed.) *Marxism and Democracy*, Lawrence and Wishart, London.

Hall, S. & Jefferson, T. (eds) (1976) *Resistance Through Rituals: Youth Subcultures in Post-War Britain*, Hutchinson, London.

Hall, S., Jefferson, T., Critcher, C. & Roberts, B. (1978) *Policing the Crisis: Mugging, the State, and Law and Order*, Macmillan, London.

Hall, S. & McLennan, G. (1986) 'Custom and Law: Law and Crime as Historical Processes', in *Law and Disorder: Histories of Crime and Justice*, Open University Course Material, Milton Keynes.

Hall, S. & Scraton, P. (1981) 'Law, Class and Control', in M. Fitzgerald, G. McLennan & J. Pawson (eds) *Crime and Society: Readings in History and Theory*, Routledge and Kegan Paul & Open University Press, London.

Hayward, K. (2002) 'The Vilification and Pleasures of Youthful Transgression', in J. Muncie, G. Hughes & E. McLaughlin (eds) *Youth Justice: Critical Readings*, Sage, London.

Heitmeyer, W. (2002) 'Have Cities Ceased to Function as "Integration Machines" for Young People?', in M. Tienda & W.J. Wilson (eds) *Youth in Cities: A Cross-National Perspective*, Cambridge University Press, Cambridge.

Henry, S. & Milovanovic, D. (1994) 'The Constitution of Constitutive Criminology: a Postmodern Approach to Criminological Theory', in D. Nelken (ed.) *The Futures of Criminology*, Sage, London.

Herrnstein, R. & Murray, C. (1994) *The Bell Curve*, Basic Books, New York.

Hirschi, T. (1969) *Causes of Delinquency*, University of California Press, Berkeley and Los Angeles.

Hogg, R. (1988) 'Taking Crime Seriously: Left Realism and Australian Criminology', in M. Findlay & R. Hogg (eds) *Understanding Crime and Criminal Justice*, Law Book Company, Sydney.

Hogg, R. & Brown, D. (1998) *Rethinking Law and Order*, Pluto Press, Sydney.

Howe, A. (1994) *Punish and Critique: Towards a Feminist Analysis of Penality*, Routledge, London.

Huff, R. (ed.) (1996) *Gangs in America* (2nd edition), Sage, Thousand Oaks.

Indermaur, D., Brown, D., Egger, S. & Hogg, R. (2002) 'Shadow Boxing with an Imaginary Enemy—A Response to "Law and Order Blues"', *The Australian and New Zealand Journal of Criminology*, 35(2): 145–58.

Inverarity, J., Lauderdale, P. & Feld, B. (1983) *Law and Society: Sociological Perspectives on Criminal Law*, Little, Brown and Company, Boston.

Jaggs, D. (1986) *Neglected and Criminal: Foundations of Child Welfare Legislation in Victoria*, Phillip Institute of Technology, Melbourne.

Jefferson, T. (1997) 'Masculinities and Crimes', in M. Maguire, R. Morgan & R. Reiner (eds) *The Oxford Handbook of Criminology* (2nd edition), Clarendon Press, Oxford.

Johnston, E. (1991) *National Report, 5 Vols, Royal Commission into Aboriginal Deaths in Custody*, Australian Government Publishing Service, Canberra.

Jones, T., MacLean, B. & Young, J. (1986) *The Islington Crime Survey*, Gower, Aldershot.

Jupp, V. (1989) *Methods of Criminological Research*, Routledge, London.

Katz, J. (1988) *Seductions of Crime: Moral and Sensual Attractions in Doing Evil*, Basic Books, New York.

Kauzlarich, D., Mullins, C. & Matthews, R. (2003) 'A Complicity Continuum of State Crime', *Contemporary Justice Review*, 6(3): 241–54.

Kelly, J. (1992) *A Short History of Western Legal Theory*, Clarendon Press, Oxford.

Kinsey, R., Lea, J. & Young, J. (1986) *Losing the Fight Against Crime*, Blackwell, Oxford.

Klein, M., Kerner, H-J., Maxson, C. & Weitekamp, E. (eds) (2001) *The Eurogang Paradox: Street Gangs and Youth Groups in the U.S. and Europe*, Kluwer Academic Publishers, Dordrecht.

Klein, M., Maxson, C. & Miller, J. (eds) (1995) *The Modern Gang Reader*, Roxbury Publishing, Los Angeles.

Lea, J. (1998) 'Criminology and Postmodernity', in P. Walton & J. Young (eds) *The New Criminology Revisited*, Macmillan, London.

Lea, J. & Young, J. (1982) 'The Riots in Britain 1981: Urban Violence and Political Marginalisation', in D. Cowell, T. Jones & J. Young (eds) *Policing the Riots*, Junction Books, London.

Lea, J. & Young, J. (1984) *What is to be Done about Law and Order?*, Penguin, London.

Lees, S. (1989) 'Learning to Love', in M. Cain (ed.) *Growing Up Good*, Sage, London.

Lemert, E. (1969) 'Primary and Secondary Deviation', in D. Cressy & D. Ward (eds) *Delinquency, Crime and Social Process*, Harper & Row, New York.

Lind, M. (1995) 'Brave New Right', in S. Fraser (ed.) *The Bell Curve Wars: Race, Intelligence and the Future of America*, Basic Books, New York.

Litwack, T. & Schlesinger, L. (1999) 'Dangerousness Risk Assessments: Research, Legal, and Clinical Considerations', in A. Hess & I. Weiner (eds) *The Handbook of Forensic Psychology* (2nd edition), John Wiley and Sons, New York.

Loader, I. (1998) 'Criminology and the Public Sphere: Arguments for Utopian Realism', in P. Walton & J. Young (eds) *The New Criminology Revisited*, Macmillan, London.

Loeber, R. & Farrington, D. (eds) (1998) *Serious & Violent Juvenile Offenders: Risk Factors and Successful Interventions*, Sage, Thousand Oaks.

Lombroso, C. (1911) *Crime: Its Causes and Remedies*, Little, Brown and Company, Boston.

Lowman, J. & MacLean, B. (eds) (1992) *Realist Criminology: Crime Control and Policing in the 1990s*, University of Toronto Press, Toronto.

Lukes, S. (1973) *Emile Durkheim: His Life and Work*, Penguin, London.

Lynch, M. & Stretsky, P. (2003) 'The Meaning of Green: Contrasting Criminological Perspectives', *Theoretical Criminology*, 7(2): 217–38.

MacLean, B. (1993) 'Left Realism, Local Crime Surveys and Policing of Racial Minorities: A Further Analysis of Data from the First Sweep of the Islington Crime Survey', *Crime, Law and Social Change*, 19: 51–86.

MacLean, B. & Milovanovic, D. (eds) (1991) *New Directions in Critical Criminology*, The Collective Press, Vancouver.

Males, M. (1996) *The Scapegoat Generation: America's War on Adolescents*, Common Courage Press, Maine.

Mason, G. (2002) *The Spectacle of Violence: Homophobia, Gender and Knowledge*, Routledge, London.

Mathiesen, T. (1990) *Prisons On Trial: A Critical Assessment*, Sage, London.

Matthews, R. (1989) 'Alternatives To and In Prisons: A Realist Approach', in P. Carlen & D. Cook (eds) *Paying For Crime*, Open University Press, Milton Keynes.

Matza, D. (1964) *Delinquency and Drift*, John Wiley and Sons, New York.

Mawby, R. & Walklate, S. (1994) *Critical Victimology: International Perspectives*, Sage, London.

McEvoy, K. (2003) 'Beyond the Metaphor: Political Violence, Human Rights and "New" Peacemaking Criminology', *Theoretical Criminology*, 7(3): 319–46.

Merton, R. (1957) *Social Theory and Social Structure*, Free Press, New York.

Messerschmidt, J. (1986) *Capitalism, Patriarchy and Crime*, Rowman & Littlefield, New Jersey.

Messerschmidt, J. (1997) *Crime as Structured Action: Gender, Race, Class, and Crime in the Making*, Sage, London.

Miliband, R. (1969) *The State in Capitalist Society*, Quartet Books, London.

Miller, W. (1958) 'Lower Class Culture as a Generating Milieu of Gang Delinquency', *Journal of Social Issues*, 14: 51–119.

Moffitt, T. (1996) 'The Neuropsychology of Conduct Disorder', in P. Cordella & L. Siegel (eds) *Readings in Contemporary Criminological Theory*, Northeastern University Press, Boston.

Mooney, J. (1998) 'Moral Panics and the New Right: Single Mothers and Feckless Fathers', in P. Walton & J. Young (eds) *The New Criminology Revisited*, Macmillan, London.

Morrison, W. (1994) 'Criminology, Modernity and the "Truth" of the Human Condition: Reflections on the Melancholy of Postmodernism', in D. Nelken (ed.) *The Futures of Criminology*, Sage, London.

Moyer, I. (2001) *Criminological Theories: Traditional and Nontraditional Voices and Themes*, Sage, Thousand Oaks.

Moyle, P. (ed.) (1994) *Private Prisons and Police: Recent Australian Trends*, Pluto Press, Sydney.

Muller D., Blackmann, D. & Chapmann A. (eds) *Psychology and Law*, John Wiley and Sons, New York.

Muncie, J. & Fitzgerald, M. (1981) 'Humanising the Deviant: Affinity and Affiliation Theories', in M. Fitzgerald, G. McLennan & J. Pawson (eds) *Crime and Society: Readings in History and Theory*, Routledge and Kegan Paul & Open University Press, London.

Muncie, J., McLaughlin, E. & Langan, M. (eds) (1996) *Criminological Perspectives: A Reader*, Sage, London.

Murray, C. (1990) *The Emerging Underclass*, Institute of Economic Affairs, London.

Naffine, N. (1987) *Female Crime: The Construction of Women in Criminology*, Allen & Unwin, Sydney.

Naffine, N. (1990) *Law and the Sexes: Explorations in Feminist Jurisprudence*, Allen & Unwin, Sydney.

Naffine, N. (1997) *Feminism & Criminology*, Allen & Unwin, Sydney.

Nava, M. (1984) 'Youth Service Provision, Social Order and the Question of Girls', in A. McRobbie & M. Nava (eds) *Gender and Generation*, Macmillan, London.

Nettler, G. (1984) *Explaining Crime*, McGraw-Hill, New York.

O'Leary, C. & Platt, T. (2001) 'Pledging Allegiance: The Revival of Prescriptive Patriotism', *Social Justice*, 28(3): 41–4.

O'Malley, P. (1983) *Law, Capitalism and Democracy*, George Allen & Unwin, Sydney.

Pearce, F. (1976) *Crime of the Powerful: Marxism, Crime and Deviance*, Pluto, London.

Pearce, F. & Tombs, S. (1990) 'Ideology, Hegemony and Empiricism: Compliance Theories of Regulation', *British Journal of Criminology*, 30(4): 423–43.

Pearce, F. & Tombs, S. (1998) *Toxic Capitalism: Corporate Crime and the Chemical Industry*, Dartmouth Publishing Company, Aldershot.

Pepinsky, H. (1991) 'Peacemaking in Criminology and Criminal Justice', in H. Pepinsky & R. Quinney (eds) *Criminology as Peacemaking*, Indiana University Press, Bloomington, Indiana.

Pepinsky, H. & Quinney, R. (eds) (1991) *Criminology as Peacemaking*, Indiana University Press, Bloomington, Indiana.

Pettit, P. & Braithwaite, J. (1993) 'Not Just Deserts, Even in Sentencing', *Current Issues in Criminal Justice*, 4(3): 225–39.

Pickering, S. & Lambert, C. (2001) 'Immigration Detention Centres, Human Rights and Criminology in Australia', *Current Issues in Criminal Justice*, 13(2): 219–23.

Platt, A. (1977) *The Child Savers*, University of Chicago, Chicago.

Plummer, K. (1979) 'Misunderstanding Labelling Perspectives', in D. Downes & P. Rock (eds) *Deviant Interpretations*, Martin Robertson, Oxford.

Polk, K. (1993) 'Jobs, not Gaols: A New Agenda for Youth', in L. Atkinson & S-A. Gerull (eds) *National Conference on Juvenile Justice: Conference Proceedings*, Australian Institute of Criminology, Canberra.

Polk, K. (1994a) 'Family Conferencing: Theoretical and Evaluative Questions', in C. Alder & J. Wundersitz (eds) *Family Conferencing and Juvenile Justice*, Australian Institute of Criminology, Canberra.

Polk, K. (1994b) *Why Men Kill: Scenarios of Masculine Violence*, Cambridge University Press, Melbourne.

Potter, H. (1992) 'Crime, Shame and Reintegration: Review, Questions and Comment', *Australian and New Zealand Journal of Sociology*, 28(2): 224–32.

Poulantzas, N. (1972) 'The Problem of the Capitalist State', in R. Blackburn (ed.) *Ideology and the Social Sciences*, Fontana Books, London.

Presdee, M. (2000) *Cultural Criminology and the Carnival of Crime*, Routledge, London.

Quinney, R. (1970) *The Social Reality of Crime*, Little, Brown and Company, Boston.

Quinney, R. (ed.) (1974) *Crime and Justice in America: A Critical Understanding*, Little, Brown and Company, Boston.

Quinney, R. (1977) *Class, State and Crime: On the Theory and Practice of Criminal Justice*, David McKay Company, New York.

Quinney, R. (1991) 'The Way of Peace: On Crime, Suffering and Deviance', in H. Pepinsky & R. Quinney (eds) *Criminology as Peacemaking*, Indiana University Press, Bloomington, Indiana.

Reiman, J. (1998) *The Rich Get Richer and the Poor Get Prison*, Allyn and Bacon, Boston.

Reiman, J. (1999) 'The Rich (Still) Get Richer—Understanding Ideology, Outrage and Economic Bias', *The Critical Criminologist*, 9(2):1, 4–5.

Reiss, A. (1986) 'Why Are Communities Important in Understanding Crime?', in A. Reiss & M. Tonry (eds) *Communities and Crime*, University of Chicago Press, Chicago.

Reiss, A. & Tonry, M. (eds) *Communities and Crime*, University of Chicago Press, Chicago.

Rosenthal, R. & Jacobson, L. (1968) *Pygmalion in the Classroom*, Holt, Rinehart and Winston, New York.

Ross, D. (1985) 'A Tattoo Removal Programme in Victoria', *Medical Journal of Australia*, 142: 388.

Rubington, E. & Weinberg, M. (eds) (1978) *Deviance: The Interactionist Perspective*, Macmillan, New York.

Russell, S. (1997) 'The Failure of Postmodern Criminology', *Critical Criminologist*, 8(2): 61–90.

Rutter, M., Giller, H. & Hagell, A. (1998) *Antisocial Behavior by Young People*, Cambridge University Press, Cambridge.

Sampson, R. & Wilson, W. (1993) 'Toward a Theory of Race, Crime and Urban Inequality', in J. Hagan & R. Peterson (eds) *Crime and Inequality*, Stanford University Press, Stanford.

Sarre, R. (1994) 'Violence: Patterns of Crime', in D. Chappell & P. Wilson (eds), *The Australian Criminal Justice System: The Mid-1990s*, Butterworths, Sydney.

Schissel, B. & Brooks, C. (eds) (2002) *Marginality & Condemnation: An Introduction to Critical Criminology*, Fernwood Publishing, Halifax.

Schur, E. (1973) *Radical Non-Intervention: Rethinking the Delinquency Problem*, Prentice-Hall, New Jersey.

Schwendinger, H. & Schwendinger, J. (1975) 'Defenders of Order or Guardians of Human Rights', in I. Taylor, P. Walton & J. Young (eds) *Critical Criminology*, Routledge and Kegan Paul, London.

Scraton, P. (ed.) (1987) *Law, Order and the Authoritarian State: Readings in Critical Criminology*, Open University Press, Milton Keynes.

Scraton, P. & Chadwick, K. (1991) 'The Theoretical and Political Priorities of Critical Criminology', in K. Stenson & D. Cowell (eds) *The Politics of Crime Control*, Sage, London.

Scutt, J. (1990) *Women and the Law*, Law Book Company, Sydney.

Segal, L. (1987) *Is The Future Female? Troubled Thoughts on Contemporary Feminism*, Virago Press, London.

Shaw, C. & McKay, H. (1942) *Juvenile Delinquency and Urban Areas*, Chicago University Press, Chicago.

Sheldon, W. (1940) *Varieties of Human Physique*, Harper & Row, New York.

Shoemaker, D. (1984) *Theories of Delinquency*, Oxford University Press, New York.

Shover, N. & Wright, J. (2001) *Crimes of Privilege: Readings in White-Collar Crime*, Oxford University Press, New York.

Smart, C. (1976) *Women, Crime and Criminology: A Feminist Critique*, Routledge and Kegan Paul, London.

Spitzer, S. (1975) 'Toward a Marxian Theory of Deviance', *Social Problems*, 22: 638–51.

Steadman, H. (1973) 'Follow-up on Baxtrom Patients Returned to Hospitals for the Criminally Insane', *American Journal of Psychology*, 3: 317–19.

Steinart, H. (1985) 'The Amazing New Left Law and Order Campaign', *Contemporary Crises*, 9: 327–33.

Stenson, K. & Sullivan, R. (eds) (2001) *Crime, Risk and Justice: The politics of crime control in liberal democracies*, Willan Publishing, Devon.

Sutherland, E. (1983) *White-Collar Crime: The Uncut Version*, Yale University Press, New Haven.

Sutherland, E. & Cressy, D. (1974) *Criminology*, Lippincott Company, New York.

Sykes, G. & Matza, D. (1957) 'Techniques of Neutralization: A Theory of Delinquency', *American Sociological Review*, 22: 664–70.

Tame, C. (1991) 'Freedom, Responsibility and Justice: The Criminology of the "New Right"', in K. Stenson & D. Cowell (eds) *The Politics of Crime Control*, Sage, London.

Taylor, I. (1981) *Law and Order: Arguments for Socialism*, Macmillan, London.

Taylor, I., Walton, P. & Young, J. (1973) *The New Criminology*, Routledge and Kegan Paul, London.

Thompson, A. (1992) 'Foreword: Critical Approaches to Law: Who Needs Legal Theory?', in I. Grigg-Spall & P. Ireland (eds) *The Critical Lawyers' Handbook*, Pluto Press, London.

Tomsen, S. (2002) *Hatred, Murder and Male Honour: Anti-homosexual Homicides in New South Wales, 1980–2000*, Australian Institute of Criminology Research and Public Policy Series No.43, Canberra.

Tong, R. (1989) *Feminist Thought: A Comprehensive Introduction*, Unwin Hyman, London.

Weatherburn, D. (2002) 'Law and Order Blues', *The Australian and New Zealand Journal of Criminology*, 35(2): 127–44.

Weatherburn, D. & Lind, B. (2001) *Delinquent-Prone Communities*, Cambridge University Press, Cambridge.

Weber, L. (2002) 'The Detention of Asylum Seekers: 20 Reasons Why Criminologists Should Care', *Current Issues in Criminal Justice*, 14(1): 9–30.

White, R. (2002) 'Understanding Youth Gangs', *Trends and Issues in Criminal Justice, No.237*, Australian Institute of Criminology, Canberra.

White, R. (2003) 'Environmental Issues and the Criminological Imagination', *Theoretical Criminology*, 7(4): 483–506.

White, R. & Perrone, S. (1997) *Crime and Social Control*, Oxford University Press, Melbourne.

White, R. & van der Velden, J. (1995) 'Class and Criminality', *Social Justice*, 22(1): 51–74.

White, R. & Wyn, J. (2004) *Youth and Society: Exploring the Social Dynamics of Youth Experience*, Oxford University Press, Melbourne.

Williams, C. (1996) 'An Environmental Victimology', *Social Justice*, 23(4): 16–40.

Wilson, J. (1975) *Thinking About Crime*, Vintage Books, New York.

Wilson, J. & Herrnstein, R. (1985) *Crime and Human Nature*, Simon and Schuster, New York.

Wilson, W.J. (1996) *When Work Disappears*, Knopf, New York.

Wright, M. (1991) *Justice for Victims and Offenders*, Open University Press, Milton Keynes.

Young, A. (1990) *Femininity in Dissent*, Routledge, London.

Young, J. (1971) 'The Role of the Police as Amplifiers of Deviancy, Negotiators of Reality and Translators of Fantasy: Some Consequences of Our Present System of Drug Control as Seen in Notting Hill', in S. Cohen (ed.) *Images of Deviance*, Penguin, London.

Young, J. (1981) 'Thinking Seriously About Crime: Some Models of Criminology', in M. Fitzgerald, G. McLennon & J. Pawson (eds) *Crime and Society: Readings in History and Theory*, Routledge and Kegan Paul, London.

Young, J. (1986) 'The Failure of Criminology: The Need for a Radical Realism', in R. Matthews & J. Young (eds) *Confronting Crime*, Sage, London.

Young, J. (1991) 'Left Realism and the Priorities of Crime Control', in K. Stenson & D. Cowell (eds) *The Politics of Crime Control*, Sage, London.

Young, J. (1992) 'Realist Research as a Basis for Local Criminal Justice Policy', in J. Lowman & B. MacLean (eds) *Realist Criminology: Crime Control and Policing in the 1990s*, University of Toronto Press, Toronto.

Young, J. (1999) *The Exclusive Society: Social Exclusion, Crime and Difference in Late Modernity*, Sage, London.

Young, J. (2003) 'Merton with Energy, Katz with Structure: the sociology of vindictiveness and criminology of transgression', *Theoretical Criminology*, 7(3): 389–414.

Zehr, H. (1990) *Changing Lenses: A New Focus for Crime and Justice*, Herald Press, Scotsdale.

Zehr, H. & Mika, H. (1998) 'Fundamental Concepts of Restorative Justice', *Contemporary Justice Review*, 1(1): 47–56.

Index

commitment 147
common law system of justice 23
communal evil 179
communism 97
communitarianism 181, 190–1
community-based corrections 161
compensation 186
competing interest groups in society
 98–9
competitive ethos 142
compulsory schooling 39
conditioning 48
conflict perspectives 98
conformism 67
consensus perspective 97
consensus policing 157, 158
conservative perspective
 of crime 104, 144–6, 176, 177, 222
 of society 15, 16
 see also New Right criminology
crime 3–4
 against and involving women 123
 causes of, Left Realist view 160
 causes of, republican view 181
 and culture 67–70
 defining 4–9
 as denial of personal dominion 179
 and deviancy 63, 64, 85
 emotional aspects 89
 historical constructions 6–7
 holistic view 175, 195
 labelling approach 5
 labelling perspective 81, 85
 Left Realist view 163–8, 172–3
 legal definitions 4–5
 Marxist definitions 101, 110–11
 measuring 9–11
 normative theory 175
 and opportunity 65–8, 75, 76
 and popular media 7–9
 radical definition 16, 17
 as social process 78
 sociological definitions 4–5
 structuralist view 203–6
 and victimisation 86
 as violation of general consensus 60
 as violation of the law 27
 waves 9

crime control
 Left Realist view 156, 158, 159, 161
 Marxist view 164
 media portrayal 8
 republican theory view 194–5
crime measurement
 institutional perspective 81
 see also crime statistics
crime prevention 28, 61, 102, 161, 168,
 181, 206
crime statistics 9–10, 73, 107, 163
 women 121
crime threat 223
crime victim surveys *see* local crime victim
 surveys
crime waves 9
crimes against women 127
crimes of accommodation and resistance
 105
crimes of domination 105
crimes of the less powerful 101, 106, 110,
 204, 213
 process of homogenisation 205
 public perception 109
crimes of the powerful 101, 102, 106,
 108, 158, 204, 213
 public perception 108–9
 specific laws 112
criminal activity
 definition 111
 degree of harm 111
criminal anthropology 43
criminal behaviour 29, 220–1
 biological and social environmental
 influences 48–9
 and class structure 101, 102, 105
 explanations 47–8
 inadequate opportunities 61
 learning of 68–88
 positivist criticisms 50–5
criminal justice, classical perspective
 29–32
criminal justice system
 Aboriginal women, overrepresentation
 118
 labelling process 80–1, 90, 92, 93
 Left Realist policy agenda 161
 linguistic regime 208